Mannership III

Mannership III

A Fount of Protection
and Healing

best wishes,

Mark

Mark Goodwin

PREFACE

This is the book I have wanted to write for more than fifty years. Differences between cultures in the world's nations have always fascinated me. But, my hawk-like watching of divergent traditions was destined to serve another purpose first.

As soon as I began writing, fate diverted me on a quest to understand how the human species is unique in developing self-loathing and self-destruction. Why do some societies apparently operate against their self-interest? Was this linked to the destruction of our planet Earth?

Three questions seemed critical:

I. How does an individual mind become 'poisoned' by a self-destructive tendency?

II. How is the poison hidden, and harboured, in a part of the mind which is 'out of reach' or 'unknown to us' so we cannot simply 'deal' with it?

III. How did our environment or culture develop in such a way that this 'poison' became thrust so deep into our children's minds?

My adventures among so many cultures provided important material. But, the greater urgency and necessary depth of understanding seemed to be in the first two questions.

The inquiry from the perspective of an individual mind took me ten years to fathom, and became the frame for my first book *Mannership*. After many surprises, I decided to pause and digest the implications. Clearly, differences in culture around the world could now be re-examined in the light of those first two questions.

My wish to share cultural differences could resume whilst examining the third question with a different lens in *Mannership III*; and hence the *III*. Although a sequel, this book can be read independently. Conclusions from *Mannership* are included whenever necessary.

A sudden loss of sound in my infancy spawned a hunger for other ways of connecting. During six years of silence, I honed a way of 'hearing by looking' or 'deaf-sight'. Seeking links became one of my strongest drives accompanied by an innate curiosity which led me to explore ever further and deeper. Although these two giants of curiosity and keen observation propelled my life since infancy, my wanderings through much of Africa and Asia between the age of 17 and 21 highlighted differences in the way 'intact' people communicated. The lessons were unforgettable and became the third giant in my life.

At university I seemed destined for an academic career, but my heart yearned for those times spent with nomadic peoples who 'adopted me' as if they had found their long lost son. Academia was easily and naturally swapped, without a second thought, for beginning my career with indigenous peoples in the Gilbert and Ellice Islands. They opened my eyes to another level of deliciousness and safety. This beauty and warmth of life among Pacific Islanders helped me to understand that my culture missed a *fount of protection and healing*.

After the Gilbert Islands, my career changed to working for an American management consulting company. Another opportunity led me to spend seven years as a tropical farmer in 26 countries of Africa, Asia, the Caribbean and Oceania. At the end of the '80s, civil wars in Africa became ever more challenging which coincided with a head-hunter suggesting another career with the recently merged CarnaudMetalbox, or CMB, based in Paris. The logic and attraction was that both Carnaud and Metalbox had been my clients as a consultant in the '70s; my experience of founding Booker Tate as a merger of two organisations during my farming years would be useful; and the new President of CMB did not speak French whereas I am bilingual. I accepted a position as the right-hand man of the President of CMB with a focus on changing the culture of leadership in a company with 160 factories around the world. This experience taught me a number of surprises including an unexpected paradigm shared by both Japanese production methods and indigenous societies.

In the early 1990s, after CMB, I decided to offer my experience as a freelance leadership coach. The time was just after the fall of the Berlin Wall and the demand for my support came primarily from organisations in Central Europe seeking to learn about a world outside of the Soviet Union. Thus began an opportunity to understand other aspects of the world's different cultures.

I explained that Management and Leadership are quite different. 'Management' derives from the Latin 'manus' for hand and 'agere' to act and means 'acting with the hands'. Like a farmer ploughing the land, organising the flow of water since winter, and seeking to transform nature. By contrast, 'Leadership' has roots in ancient North European languages as someone who gives confidence to follow them. The Old English lædan is more than a guide and implies 'faith to follow'. Leadership is more like a shepherd concerned for the safety of the flock whilst seeking greener pastures and co-existing with nature in the wild.

To remember the differences as well as the need for a fresh relationship between the farmer and the shepherd, I merged Management and Leadership into a new word 'Mannership'. I liked that manners were implied as well as the sense of a journey by ship.

In parallel with my leadership coaching, I delved into exploring my own mind by following the course of several therapies before training as a group psychotherapist. Friendships with Martín Prechtel, Malidoma and Subonfu Somé, shamans of indigenous cultures in Guatemala and Burkina Faso respectively, enabled me to understand aspects of 'intact' societies which otherwise would have been out of reach. My debt to them is incalculable and my interest in shamanic guidance continues to this day. There was an added bonus in learning about afflictions in my own mind while coaching leaders; the two seem to go hand in hand. Leaders who are not open to personal growth can suffocate their organisations.

Throughout the '90s, while coaching industrial leaders, I had the benefit of a mentor, Professor Yamashina, from Japan. He provided completely different paradigms which enriched my cultural understanding.

The afternoon of my career included fifteen years as President of a North American company and developing a leadership course which I taught in over 30 countries including five times in each of China and Russia. Since Britain is the land of my birth and over half of my career was spent working for a US company, these four countries are the primary focus of my observations.

Curiosity and good fortune have enabled me to meander through 169 nations while my 'deaf-sight' watched like a hawk. I have included six short stories from my collection of *Marklesparkle's Chronicles*[1] as they provide particular juice at critical times. Often, unlikely connections are provided by the smallest of nations.

I am very grateful to Meredith Belbin. Meredith's research at Henley Business School on 'team roles' identified different styles that we all bring to our meetings with others. Two million people have used his 'instrument' to determine their most effective role in a team. This research with 'management teams – why they succeed or fail' is one of my preferred instruments while coaching leaders and organisations.

Over several years, I enjoyed many sprawling conversations with Meredith sharing our experiences of different cultures. Meredith has a lovely conservatory on the sunny side of his garden with a sumptuous sofa and armchairs. We would sit there for hours, pausing for occasional teas, admiring the view of his so English garden whilst among piles of books in the warm sunshine or protected from a gentle rain. Meredith is British and has clear views of the USA. He also taught in China and Russia. The extent to which we agreed surprised both of us as we used quite different paradigms to get there. Understanding his paradigms enabled me to understand more of my own, which is a key lesson of this book. Some of our recorded conversations are included. Meredith is an avid reader with the advantage of Cambridge University Library on his doorstep. My travelling experience, or fieldwork, complemented his research.

Whereas *Mannership* focused on the individual mind, and particularly a child's mind becoming 'poisoned' by a self-destructive tendency, this book looks at the collective mind of a tribe or an agglomeration of tribes; a nation even. The exploration includes wondering how cultures may have come about; how can we attempt to understand them; and particularly how some societies could poison the next generation. There are hints of forces driving an evolution of collective minds based on similarities with individual minds. When a culture appears different from her neighbour we can ask why to see what we can learn. We can develop

---

[1] Published by Words by Design.

some ideas or templates as a fresh way of thinking about our own culture and those of others.

Cultures are influenced by so many ingredients. The geography is a major factor in terms of hospitality. The mountains, rivers and lakes, the forests or deserts will have much to say about the culture which may come. The soil has a voice. The genetics of the indigenous population must be a major influence. But, as I learned with an individual mind, the relationship between the genetics and the environment may play a bigger role than either of the parts. Our beginning, including the birth experience, matters. So the question could be more about how a culture's relationship began or evolved. The climate and her predictability have a contribution to the conversation. Other species have relationships which add to the music. Different plants turn out to exert dramatic forces on a culture, but our relationship to these plants could be even more important. There are so many ingredients and spices in the cultural cooking pot.

As Martín Prechtel reminds us, there is no such thing as a person's past as they carry it with them all the time. Tribes, nations and cultures are similar. The tribal history is hugely significant in terms of how paradigms grew – particularly the effect of giant surprises, including good or unwelcome ones. Nature may have appeared with abundance of many resources, but may later have been experienced as having turned against the tribe with drought, flood or pestilence. Many tribes were invaded and subjected or enslaved. Maybe new arrivals came with their own traumas which infected even those who had not witnessed the initial horrors. On the other hand, perhaps a few arrivals were benign or brought fresh hope. Apparently, a culture's relationship to her history is more important than the history. Does the culture remember? How were the events understood and accepted or denied?

A national mind contains the genetics of her indigenous peoples together with all those who migrated, invaded or were forcibly taken there. The national mind swallows up the relationship to geography, flora and fauna, climate and natural resources, together with all past events. Just like an individual mind, a cultural mind can choose to forget or to remember differently. If this trick in the mind affects the individual, so this must affect a culture.

Having the opportunity to spend much of my life wandering around our globe, the different paradigms encountered along the way highlight how experiences have influenced the lens through which peoples see what is around them. Once a culture sees the world in a particular way, it is less easy to change perspective without enlightened leadership, or gentle nudges from a friendly neighbour.

It seems that language shapes a culture, just as culture shapes a language. These two have a relationship but are not the same. In my reading research apparently language, culture and genetics do not always correlate. There are overlaps and correlations but just as much divergence to suggest that genetics, culture and language are quite independent forces. Sometimes a new genetic group washes away a previous language, but on other occasions the language of the land swallows the new arrivals.

Cultures sometimes suffer events which cannot be processed and are indigestible. Earthquakes, volcanic eruptions, tsunamis, devastating floods and other sudden alarms may be buried deep in a culture's mind. Again, the relationship to the disaster might be more important than the disaster himself. Other species suffered these natural disasters but often managed or adapted in some ways better than most of human-kind.

Once there is a fault line in a culture, some trauma which has been forgotten, conceivably this can make a culture vulnerable to the emotional sway of an orator who can drill into the volcano of unexpressed fury and turn that nuclear energy from the fault line towards either safety or collective devastation.

As this book began, I planned to start with the discussions which Meredith and I shared on the culture of the island of our birth, Britain. But, re-visiting the small islands of Kiribati provided such important lessons. There are a surprising number of similarities between the legends of the Pacific Ocean and the evolution of European cultures. Since we are all the same race, maybe this should not surprise us.

Looking to discover how this might have come about in small Pacific islands is easier to grasp than unpicking the spaghetti of European history. In any case, looking at another collective mind helps to understand our own. We have been thrashing about with European history for countless generations and don't yet seem to have obtained sufficient wisdom to address our ghosts. Maybe we need to learn our lessons from somewhere else. Or digest another cultural metaphor.

Almost identical Pacific islands, just 80 kilometres apart, can turn out to have dramatic divergences of culture. A group of islands with the same geography, soil, climate, plants, animals, genetics and language but with different cultures can provide extraordinary clues to an evolution of culture. Perhaps these small islands might bring forth lessons for us which could be easier to absorb as a starting point. So, *Mannership III* begins exactly on the opposite side of the globe from Britain.

INDEX

Beginning in Pacific Islands

The Greenwich Meridian won the Longitude 0° prize in 1884. Of the 25 nations meeting for this purpose in Washington DC, 22 were in favour, one was against and two abstained, including France, perhaps unsurprisingly. Spinning our globe 180° to the International Date Line, ever since 1884 the world agreed the first dawn begins each day in Kiribati. As the only country where the date line passes through, as does the equator, she boasts the cross hairs of the central Pacific Ocean in addition to each day's first rising sun.

Kiribati has 33 islands shown below with Banaba in the West, the 17 islands of Tungaru[2] from Makin to Arorae, eight islands of the Phoenix

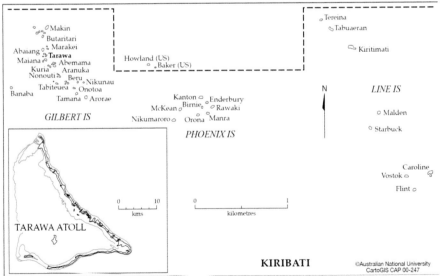

The map above comes from the Australian National University and shows the names of all the islands. Presumably the central scale is meant to be nearer to 1,000 km rather than 1 kilometre.

---

[2] Tungaru is the indigenous name for the 17 islands between Makin and Arorae. The Gilbert Islands include Tungaru, the Phoenix Islands, and the Line Islands. The abbreviated 'Gilberts' is written Kiribati in the I-Kiribati language.

Group, and eight islands of the Line Islands. Banaba is 4,500 km due north of Wellington, New Zealand. Caroline Island is 850 km north of Papeete in Tahiti. The equator floats on the south shore of Aranuka Island. The International Date Line drops 221 miles east of Arorae Island. The capital, Tarawa, is shown in more detail on the bottom left. She was my home for two years.

Maybe it is a 'Western' phenomenon to oversimplify the nature of others because Pacific Islanders are usually placed into three groupings: Melanesia, Micronesia and Polynesia (as in the map below). Kiribati can be found in the south-east corner of Micronesia. This map ignores, for simplicity, the Eastern Islands of Kiribati which run 2,350 km from south of Hawaii to north of the Society Islands. Before continuing with I-Kiribati origins, we should explore the broader picture of the earliest migrations into the Pacific Ocean.

The first people to settle in the Pacific region arrived in Papua New Guinea between 65,000 and 50,000 years ago. In those times the sea levels were about a hundred metres lower, which enabled the Australian Aborigines to cross a narrower stretch of water and settle at a similar time. The detailed migration maps in the National Museum of Honiara, Solomon Islands, show the progression of Papuan peoples into the

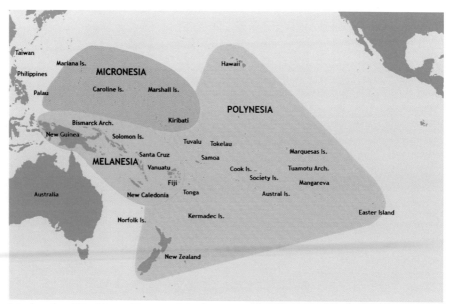

Map based on Vaka Moana: Voyages of the Ancestors - the discovery and settlement of the Pacific, K.R.Howe, 2008. The map only shows the islands of Kiribati within Micronesia and not the Phoenix or Line Islands which are further east than the Cook Islands.

Bismarck Archipelago around 40,000 years ago and into Buka Island of Bougainville about 32,000 years ago. With the lower sea level, many of the islands of the Solomon Group were connected into larger land masses or separated by short crossings. The modest Papuan sea voyages were therefore much simpler with a destination island often within sight.

As the museum in Honiara explains: *People have probably lived in all the main islands of the Solomon Islands chain, from Buka (now in Papua New Guinea) to Makira-Ulawa, for more than 10,000 years.* They would have arrived from Papua before the sea levels rose at the end of the last ice age. Further migration towards new Pacific islands to the east was impossible as the Papuans had neither the necessary vessels nor the navigational skills to proceed. For thousands of years the eastern-most Pacific advance paused in the middle of the Solomon Islands, leaving the smaller islands beyond their eastern horizon to be discovered much later.

Some caves were found to have been inhabited for over 5,000 years. The food remains at Kilu Cave on Buka Island are estimated to be 32,000 years old. Other discoveries show the foragers' diet of wild taro, coconut and ngali nuts, fish and shellfish, possums, rats, bats, birds and reptiles.[3] These large islands share topography of a very fertile mountainous jungle interior, a paradise of self-sufficiency for new arrivals.

Papua New Guinea has the greatest variety of endemic plants of any island in the world. With such natural abundance, individual tribes or clans were able to settle in the hinterland and achieve hunter gathering self-sufficiency between thirty and fifty millennia ago which explains the extraordinary language diversity. Papua New Guinea, with only 0.3% of the world's land area, retains 10% of the world's languages. However, the diversity of 'hinterland populations' is not reflected in the shoreline groups, suggesting very different movement among these two types of early populations.

In the 1980s, ten years after my stay on Kiribati, this island made a deep impression on me while managing sugar cane, cattle, crocodiles, and poultry. One of the difficulties of large scale farming of sugar on Papua was that, because sugar cane is indigenous to the island, all of the root borers and other hindrances to a higher sugar yield were also in abundance. I understood then why large plantations were often more successful in lands where the plant was not indigenous.

---

[3] National Museum, Honiara, Solomon Islands.

The paradigms of the coastal and hinterland peoples are quite different in Papua. Those on the shore are more gregarious while those further inland tend to form tighter, closed communities. There was infrequent contact between the shoreline tribes and the hinterland, but then the hinterland populations were not frequently in friendly contact with each other either, hence the many languages.

A new era in the Pacific began between 5,000 and 6,000 years ago when a people we now call the Lapita started to migrate from Southern China and Taiwan. These voyagers made major sea crossings followed by some long pauses before continuing the journey begun by their ancestors. Having moved south through the Philippines, they came to the Admiralty Islands (an extension of the Bismarck Archipelago 190 miles north of Papua) about 4,000 years ago. As well as being exceptional navigators with specially designed sailing canoes, the Lapita brought domesticated animals and plants into the Pacific region. Their cargo included chickens, pigs and different plants collected from the islands of their journey. They also brought obsidian and spoke a language which we now call 'Austronesian'.

The oldest records of these Lapita pioneers show they flourished between 1,600 BCE and 500 BCE in a wide arc of islands stretching from the northern outer islands of New Guinea to the Solomon Islands, Vanuatu, New Caledonia, Fiji, Tonga, and Samoa. Lapita pottery dated to this period is found on all these islands. The extent of 'Classic' Lapita pottery produced between 1350 and 750 BCE in the Bismarck Archipelago suggests another major pause in these islands for some.

Apart from navigating large distances, a major obstacle to settlement of the Pacific from Asia is the prevailing wind from the east. The Lapita pioneered a boat which could sail much 'closer to the wind'. Europeans were, in this respect, three millennia behind them in sailing design. Square riggers of European construction were built to 'run before the wind', with the result that a ship could be forced to wait in harbour until the wind direction changed. At least this weaker European design saved Britain from the Spanish Armada in 1588; Spanish ships could not use the adverse wind direction to reach land and disembark their vast invading force. By contrast, the Lapita boats, sailing much closer to the source of the wind, were enabled to sail a course suggested by their navigational skills.

Many birds have their initial migration imprinted on the 'hard-drive of their brain' at hatching.[4] During their first migration, birds record the sensory information to facilitate future migrations. For their first explorations into the Pacific, the Lapita may have discovered some new islands by following bird migrations. Their canoe design has a helmsman just a couple of feet above the water. Thus, they were more intimately familiar with the ocean's currents, waves and swells, smells, colour and deep phosphorescence as well as the habits of sea creatures. This proximity to the water permitted them to retain more sensory information for future navigations, just like the birds.

Birds have a number of separate navigation systems including sight, smell, infrasound, magnetics, the sun and stars. Perhaps they have other systems we do not know yet. A racing pigeon can find her way to within a mile of her home even if blindfolded. Pigeons do not take the same route over regular trips but seem to be acquiring resonance between different navigation systems to confirm their direction. Likewise, ocean creatures have a number of navigation systems including sight, smell, magnetics, electricity, low frequency calls, sonar or echolocation, ocean currents, and the sun. The early Lapita navigators may have been in touch with a number of navigation systems and an ability to connect them innately like birds or ocean creatures. Their descendants, as current Pacific navigators, teach us some of these early skills.

In I-Kiribati there is no specific word for astronomy as the stars are an integral part of navigation. Rosemary Grimble refers to her father's notes of an old man called Biria on Butaritari Island who shared some details of his training.[5] Rather than learning from looking at the sky, lines in the village *maneaba* roof delineated the stars. Grimble's notes say: *Line by line Biria was made to learn the heavens. He had to learn no fewer than 178 stars, constellations and nebulae; to indicate their relative positions in the roof and to say at what height above the eaves (the horizon) any one of them might be seen at sunrise or sunset at different seasons of the year. He learned how to navigate to and from Samoa, 1,200 miles south-east; and Truk, in the Carolines, more than 1,400 miles north-west.* If one sails more than twelve miles to one side of a coral atoll, land will not be seen directly. Navigation must be very precise. This precision comes from remembering a sequence of less than a dozen stars which are aimed for on the horizon throughout the night as they

---

[4] See chapter on Bird Navigation in *Mannership*.

[5] Rosemary Grimble, *Migrations, Myth and Magic from the Gilbert Islands*.

'rise' sequentially. This is possibly more accurate than a magnetic compass.

The Pacific contains trade winds which are so constant that an underlying undulating swell with a very long wavelength develops over vast distances. David Lewis wrote a detailed description of Pacific navigation skills in *We, the Navigators*. Lewis is no stranger to complexities of navigation as he crossed the Atlantic single-handedly three times and was the first to navigate a catamaran around the globe. Lewis writes of his journey between the Carolines and Marianas guided by a navigator Hipour, who felt and watched the shape of each swell from different angles until he could recognise them as easily as people's faces. A particular increase in accuracy comes from the interference of two different swells, especially if one of them is reflected off an island. Lewis tells us that different navigators took great patience to teach him how to detect these swells under the boat. He reports that the most sensitive balance for feeling swells is a man's testicles.

Navigators are also guided by a 'wind compass' as the winds are often predictable. Then, Arthur Grimble writes of a journey between two islands when the navigator suddenly woke from his sleep to ask the crew to tack immediately as the sea smelled differently. This navigational ability felt familiar to me because of similar experiences in 1973 while crossing the Sahara from The Nile to the West Coast of Africa with different tribes. A nomad told me he was suddenly changing direction because the sand smelled differently.[6]

The birds also help with navigation in many ways. During my time in Kiribati, in 1976, a large ocean journey canoe or *baurua* was commissioned by James Siers and built in the village of Taratai. On their first voyage to Fiji, a distance of over 2,200 km, Siers wrote of how the captain, Tenanoa, said they must have passed the latitude of Maiana Island at two in the morning as bird 'coast-watchers' had come out to see who was passing by.[7] Siers also writes of how the captain could alter his course because the wind or currents had changed, which he could tell by seeing how the 'waves were behaving differently'. Like birds, expert navigators do not rely on only one navigation system; they have an innate way of taking all signs into account in finding their safe course.

---

[6] Mark Goodwin, *Khartoum to El Aaiun*.

[7] James Siers, *Taratai*.

As well as sailing into the Pacific, some of these great Lapita navigators went west as far as Madagascar. My first visit there was bewilderingly exciting. Having landed at Antananarivo, on 2nd April 1990, my mind was capsized and confused. The connections seemed impossible. Clearly they spoke an Austronesian language and looked to me like Pacific islanders. But, the houses were often built from a yellow stone like south-west France. Many names were those of French pre-revolution aristocracy. Small monkeys or lemurs were sometimes the size of my thumb. Adoring everything about this 'outlier' island immediately, it was easy for the Minister of Agriculture to persuade me to assist them by purchasing the tea industry on behalf of Booker Tate. Since this was the first agricultural 'privatisation' following the liberation of their economy, the Minister was equally excited. He persuaded the Air Force to provide a plane, and a pilot, so that he could show me around his glorious island. Madagascar will always have a special place in my heart next to other Pacific islands.

Returning to the Pacific Ocean and the I-Kiribati, there are few, if any, records of pottery on Pacific coral atolls. This is not surprising as there is no clay to make pottery with. But, there are other ways to link I-Kiribati with the Lapita. Michael Ravell Walsh, in *A History of Kiribati*, summarises a number of different clues to help us discover more of their origins. Firstly, geological evidence suggests that the islands of Kiribati were not above sea-level until three millennia ago and not habitable until around two millennia ago. Secondly, the earliest evidence of human habitation on Kiribati comes from carbon dating of charred pandanus keys in cooking ovens on Nikunau Island which were dated about 2,000 years ago. Thirdly, the genetic evidence shows that the predominant source of I-Kiribati genes come from Taiwan with an admixture of Melanesian DNA. This suggests they migrated on the Lapita 'ocean-way' before turning northwards from a point in Melanesia, particularly starting from somewhere between Bougainville and Vanuatu. Fourthly, Walsh notes that I-Kiribati is not mutually intelligible with any other language. To help explain the language 'shift' he postulates that the ancestors of many I-Kiribati migrated southeast to the Banks Islands in Vanuatu and then either continued northwards via Kosrae or went directly north-east to Kiribati. He explains that the extent of the linguistic shift would fit with this route as well as the emergence of I-Kiribati as a separate language around 2,000 years ago. Finally, Walsh notes that coconut, breadfruit and babai plants were brought to Kiribati by early settlers. The coconut and babai are native to New Guinea, while the breadfruit grown in Kiribati is now known to be a hybrid of the Marianas and New Guinea breadfruit species.

We can compare recent scientific knowledge with Arthur Grimble's interpretation of the I-Kiribati legends a century ago. His detailed notes of the Gilbertese creation myths and legends led him to deduce that the first islanders were 'a cleaving together of two peoples and cultures': *A shorter and darker Melanesian people; the cult of Nareau, with magic which prevailed after their admixture; and a lighter skinned people with different gods; the cult of Taburimai*, who arrived to join them. In *A Pattern of Islands* he suggests they came '*by New Guinea*' up to the Caroline Islands and east to the Gilbert Islands.

With recent genetic knowledge, we can now associate the legend of the Taburimai with the Lapita and their *lighter skinned* origins. Grimble did not have the advantage of genetic analysis. But, with his language fluency, he suggested that an Indonesian would hear Gilbertese as an older slang. This was one of the factors convincing him of an Indonesian origin for the *Taburimai*. We know now that both Indonesian and I-Kiribati are Austronesian languages; they are cousins with a linguistic ancestry in Taiwan but the I-Kiribati do not have DNA from the Banda Sea in Indonesia as Grimble surmised. He was, however, not so far off in some of his assumptions since the islands of the Banda Sea are west of Papua whereas the Lapita actually travelled by the north of Papua.

Grimble did not have any evidence to know where the cult of Nareau received the sailing cult of Taburimai for their 'cleaving together'. However, the genetic data now seems to suggest this may have been in the north-eastern Melanesian islands. There is a close genetic match between I-Kiribati and Torau, a small island east of Bougainville, as well as Caroline Islanders and Malaita (illustrated in the map overleaf).[8] The data might suggest the Caroline and Gilbert Islanders are genetic cousins on both lines of their cultural parentage. They may both share an ancestry of Taburimai from China and Taiwan as well as admixture with neighbouring Melanesian islands. We do not know which route they took after significant admixture with the Melanesian cult of Nareau and the marriage of their respective traditions. However, most of the historical

---

[8] L.Luca Cavalli-Sforza, Paolo Menozzi, and Alberto Piazza, *The History and Geography of Human Genes.*

'traffic' of the Lapita at that time continued south-eastwards from the Solomon Islands to Vanuatu.

We know that groups of families with plants and domesticated animals were travelling vast ocean distances south of Kiribati three millennia ago. Samoa is 3,000 km east of the Solomon Islands whereas Kiribati is 2,000 km north-east of the Solomon Islands. The journey from Bougainville in the Solomon Islands to Kiribati is a straightforward 'beam reach' in sailing terms. No tack would have been necessary. This would have been the easiest and fastest course to sail for an expert navigator, and would have only taken between two and three weeks. Perhaps my wish that a few I-Kiribati may have come this way is influenced by memories of the ease and speed of sailing a beam reach on my racing canoe.[9] But, had they done so, they would have arrived before the islands were habitable. So, they probably continued on the main routes of the Lapita before turning north in the Banks Islands and bringing the language shift of I-Kiribati as Walsh postulates.

The map below shows the islands of the Banda Sea in the extreme west where Grimble thought the Taburimai came from, the islands of Bougainville and Malaita as well as Truk, the Caroline Islands, Kosrae, and the westernmost aspect of Kiribati. My reader can visualise the

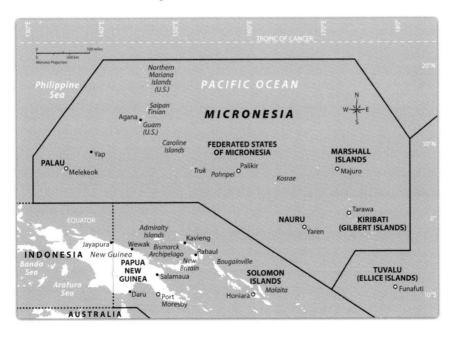

---

[9] My small racing canoe is displayed at the National Maritime Museum in Falmouth.

shortest possible north-west migration from Malaita to Truk and onward to the Caroline Islands as well as the shortest possible north-east migration from Bougainville to Nauru or Kiribati. One conclusion is that the ancient connections between peoples might be spread over even greater distances than just those between neighbouring islands. They did not simply hop over to the closest island but navigated much greater distances crossing over the migration paths of others, rather like the Pacific birds. Subsequently, some of them travelled more often among each other, as confirmed by linguistic data linking a close 'ocean-path' from the Caroline Islands through Truk, Pohnpei, Kosrae to the Marshall Islands and Kiribati.

With their extraordinary navigational abilities, there may have been much more 'toing and froing' than we imagine. In addition to seeking wives, and help after a disaster, Grimble reports they sometimes sailed 400 km, or three days, to exchange dances.

We do not know why the Lapita people, or any others, made these extraordinary ocean voyages. They may have been pulled East by a deity, such as the sun, or pushed by battles with another clan. Sudden increases in population density may have triggered a migration. Some Pacific islands have clues and legends. But, then we do not know why the builders of Stonehenge went to Britain either. Neither do we know why one of the greatest and among the oldest temples in Europe, the Ness of Brodgar, was built 5,300 years ago on the remote Orkney Islands north of Scotland. They too had to travel by sea eight centuries before Stonehenge was built.

Rapa Nui, now known as Easter Island, sits 3,500 km west of Chile. She was inhabited by genes from South East Asia fully 14,500 km further to the west of her. Genetically and linguistically, Easter Island is a 'cousin' of the Society Islands, Cook Islands and New Zealand. She is the easternmost island of the great Asian navigators. Her new name was given by the Dutch explorer Jacob Roggeveen on Easter Sunday, 5 April 1722. But, Asian navigators had arrived over a thousand years before him. The legends of Rapa Nui remember she was first settled by an expedition of two canoes led by the chief Hotu Matu'a and his captain Tu'u ko Iho.[10] Haumaka had dreamed of such a far off country and Hotu decided to flee there to escape a neighbouring chief. If they came from the Marquesas Islands, the distance of over 3,600 km by canoe is impressive. Perhaps some bird migrations may have assisted.

---

[10] Steven Fischer, *Island at the End of the World*.

Recent discoveries have concluded that the great Asian navigators went as far as the Americas and, among other interchanges, brought back the sweet potato (*Ipomoea batatas*) with her South American name *kumar*.[11]

The small atolls of the Central Pacific do not have the land mass of the major mountainous volcanic islands to the south and west. They are not even specks by comparison. The two islands, Savai'i and Upolu, in Samoa have 2,840 square kilometres (km²) of land. Fiji has over 18,000 km². A typical Kiribati atoll averages 16 km². She ranges between 4.8 km² in Tamana, 9.5 km² in Arorae and up to as much as 29.2 km² in Nonouti. For such a small island the decimal place in area matters. To help my reader visualise, Tarawa's 21 km² is arranged like a giant dinosaurian vertebra, 85 km long but on average only 250 metres wide on two of the three sides of her triangular lagoon. She is shown in the map at the beginning of this chapter, sitting up and facing west.

These tiny atoll 'specks' were found and inhabited by navigators who then travelled between them as if catching a bus. Meanwhile the Melanesian hinterland tribes found the journey to cross their mountainous jungle terrain much harder than the descendants of Lapita coastal populations to traverse half the Pacific Ocean. The two groups, with little shared DNA, were living in parallel universes.

In June 2016 a Festival of Pacific Arts was held on Guam. The Pacific Daily News of May 17, 2016 records that traditional navigators sailing to Guam from Micronesian islands were warmly greeted. As the navigator Larry Raigetal said: *These islands weren't just settled by mistake. These are islands that belong to great navigators in the past, including Guam and the whole entire Pacific. We are voyagers.* Reading the different accounts of the canoes arriving from islands in the south-east; two came 800 km from Poluwat, one came 920 km from Houk and two came 675 km from Lamotrek in the Caroline Islands. The average speed of the five canoes was about 170 km per day despite strong adverse currents. In ancient times the canoes with families and animals were larger, maybe 50 to 100 feet long,[12] and the speeds probably slower, but a 1,000 km ocean journey might have taken around a couple of weeks.

---

[11] Patrick Kirch, *Peopling of the Pacific*.

[12] A 72 foot long canoe under construction was found on Huahine Island in the Society Archipelago dated to between 600 and 1000 years ago. A canoe of 130 feet was found in New Zealand and carbon dated to 1400.

The small size of atolls emphasise the exceptional ability of the navigators to find them. By following migrations of birds, they were able to discover new islands. During the first voyages, navigators witnessed and remembered 'sea marks' provided by Mother Nature. These were shared from generation to generation as recorded in the notes made by Grimble and edited by Maude in *Tungaru Traditions*:[13]

1. *Nao aika uabwi ma itua* (the twenty-seven waves): *If the navigator, northward bound during the season of SE trade winds, overshoots Butaritari and Little Makin, he will come to a zone of ocean where a series of 27 waves arises from time to time as if from under the sea and travels past him from north to south across any prevailing swell. From this, he will know Little Makin is half a day's sail to southward.*

2. *Nei Roba* (a kind of wave): *Due south of Marakei, just out of sight of land, is encountered Nei Roba – a large periodical wave, travelling due north, across any prevailing swell, with curling crest as if ready to break.*

As the Inuit know their snow, as the Saharan camel caravans smell their sand, so the Pacific navigators know their swells, waves, currents, smells and locations of different ocean creatures. In those times the water creatures had established habits which facilitated navigation as Grimble also recorded:

3. *Between Tarawa and Maiana the voyager encounters porpoises in pairs, whose heads are always pointed in the direction of the passage into Tarawa Lagoon at the place called Bairiki.*

4. *Te baiburebure* (the mottled fin): *To NE of Little Makin, a day's sail from land, is a zone of sea teeming with the species of shark called baiburebure, the tips of whose fins are touched with ivory-white markings.*

It is probably safe to assume that the extent of commercial overfishing in the Pacific Ocean has rendered obsolete much of the navigator's ability to find his way by established behaviours of ocean creatures. That guidance from Mother Nature has been plucked out of the blue.

Another consequence of the Pacific inter-island distances is highlighted by the story of Pingelap Island. She is a very small atoll of less than 2 km² and 250 inhabitants with their own language despite being close to the Island of Pohnpei. An unusually significant proportion of the population of Pingelap has achromatopsia, a form of almost complete

---

[13] Arthur Grimble and edited by H.E.Maude, *Tungaru Traditions*.

colour blindness enabling them to see only black, white and shades of grey. It is also a condition which gives undue sensitivity to bright light. In Pingelapese it is called *maskun*, or 'not to see'. Oliver Sacks, whose books are a delight for me, wrote about them in *The Island of the Colorblind*.

This rare condition followed a population collapse in 1775 after a typhoon left barely two dozen survivors. The ruler, Nanmwarki Mwanenihsed, is assumed to have been a carrier of the genetic condition. Subsequent island inbreeding increased the incidence of the recessive affliction. The relevance to Pacific islands generally, and to their cultures, highlights the effect of natural disasters and the occasional challenge in finding sufficient genetic diversity for marriage in remote islands. Just after 1775 it would have been very hard for a few of the remaining 20 Pingelapese to travel to seek husbands or wives.

It is also possible that the tradition of a man taking the younger sisters of his wife as additional brides arose in the southern and more drought-prone islands of Kiribati during a period of a shortage of men with ancestry from outside the village. A need to leave one's village and island to find a wife could have spurred many early voyages. Natural selection favours only the best navigators.

There is something else, in addition to the navigational skills, which enabled some diverse admixtures. The Pacific Ocean is kinder than other oceans to lost navigators. The I-Kiribati boast all the records for survival when lost and *drifting* at sea. Sometimes a mast broke. They had no power to steer and could only drift. But many months later they turned up on a far flung island. According to the Guinness Book of Records, the record for drifting at sea is held by two Kiribati fishermen, from the atoll of Nikunau, who drifted for 177 days in 1992 before coming ashore on the eastern end of Samoa. However, this is common in Kiribati folklore and Guinness will only have a few of their examples. In the Central Pacific it rains throughout the year, even in the 'dry season'. On average one day in three. A drifting sailor will enjoy regularly collected rainwater in his canoe and abundant fish catches even without any bait. Just some form of hook is sufficient. If he suffers too many days without rain, drinking shark's blood will save him. Maybe this knowledge, together with the relative calmness of the weather, temperature and seas, enable him to wait patiently until an island eventually appears. During my stay on Tarawa we had a few such 'lost' fishermen returned after many months away.

Meanwhile, as the great navigators found new lands, some of the descendants of the first Melanesian Pacific settlers followed the paths of the Lapita. DNA analysis of a 3,000 year old Lapita grave in Vanuatu, and one of 2,500 years old in Tonga, found them to have genetic origins in Taiwan and the northern Philippines without any trace of Papuan DNA. However, a more recent discovery of a 2,500 year old grave in Vanuatu contains Papuan DNA. The earliest Lapita seemingly passed through the outer islands of Papua without much mixing of genes, but five centuries later there was a Melanesian admixture.

Pacific migration theories include an 'express train to Polynesia' with some groups having journeyed over 24,000 kilometres in 300 years, which is supported by the linguistic data. Other theories included a 'slow boat' of Pacific development to explain the expansion of the Melanesian population into the wider Pacific. The more recent scientific conclusion is that both theories may be correct, in part. In the case of Vanuatu, apparently the modest numbers of initial Lapita settlers were progressively replaced by genes from the Bismarck Archipelago. The original Papuan expansion towards the east, which had been 'paused' for thousands of years in the middle of the Solomon Islands, was able to continue once the Lapita taught them double hulled canoe construction and navigation.

Perhaps relatively small numbers in individual boats explains why Papuan speakers adopted a new language as they ventured. This phenomenon gave rise to a rare instance of language trumping genetics in a migration. This is most evident in Vanuatu where the language of the original Lapita settlers was absorbed and spoken by Melanesians from the Bismarck Archipelago who came along afterwards.[14] The relaxed speed of the migrations makes this possible. Had the Papuans come like a tsunami, the first Lapita language might have been washed away. Perhaps the 'slow boat' theory should be renamed 'infrequent express boats with few passengers' to account for the relatively slow introduction of Papuan and other genes east of the Solomon Islands – slow enough to allow the language of their island destination to prevail.

---

[14] Dr. Cosimo Posth et al, *Language continuity despite population replacement in Remote Oceania, Nature Ecology & Evolution* (2018).

The scale of the Pacific Ocean, representing a third of the world's surface, effectively dilutes the migration traffic to a dribble.

We can compare this to the invasions of North America. The variety of European settlers crossing the Atlantic had little choice but to adopt English as their new language. However, more recent and larger numbers arriving from Central America are able to retain Spanish at the exclusion of English.

It is not hard to get our brain around this. We are not speaking of many Pacific migrations of several hundred people all together. They would rarely have had either the size and number of boats or the coordination to stay together as they journeyed. The number of voyagers was usually much smaller. Some legends speak of a migration of 'two canoes', but we do not know the size of these canoes. It is hard to imagine more than a hundred people in such a pair of canoes and maybe much less. However, as we shall see in the next chapter, there are exceptions when events caused a sudden simultaneous migration of a homogeneous community of several hundred or even more than a thousand souls. Such was the first settlement of New Zealand.

While the Lapita culture expanded rapidly with successive canoes discovering new islands, the Melanesians who migrated often remained in the hinterlands of the few larger islands. For the most part, the Melanesian 'joiners' may have preferred the bigger islands which provided opportunities for territory resembling their ancestral origins. Perhaps this is why the larger islands in the Pacific retain more of the Melanesian populations. This may be similar to Norwegian migrations to USA preferring to settle in Minnesota and Wisconsin; perhaps the winter is familiar, which is why 60% of Norwegian settlers still choose to live in these two states.

In summary, it seems that science often confirms the legends and sacred stories. The more interesting question is why it is so hard for some of us to accept something our ancestors cherished and polished for us, and to prefer a similar conclusion obtained by our logical scientific minds. There must be an important lesson here. Can a fear of submission to ancestral wisdom hide the extent of our hunger for support from a source which is too valuable or cannot be understood?

Kiribati History, Culture and Disturbances

This chapter focuses specifically on the group of I-Kiribati islands from Makin in the north to Arorae in the south. These islands all share the same language and speak as if they are all of the same people. The atolls are quite similar. Their size does not vary so much as mentioned in the previous chapter. Most islands are clustered in the range of 10 to 18 km² each. The increase in area is mostly an increase in length, the breadth being relatively constant. They are not widely spread out in the ocean, with the longest distance between two islands being the 100 km between Butaritari and Marakei. The climate is essentially the same among them all apart from more frequent droughts in the south. Maiana Island is shown below.

The islands support similar plants: coconut, breadfruit, babai, pandanus and others which are native to East Asia. Domestic animals are the same throughout the islands: chickens, pigs and dogs. All islands share a similar diet. The meeting houses, or *maneaba*, have similar styles of construction, as do the houses and sailing canoes.

It would therefore seem reasonable to expect that, with such similarity of topography, climate, flora and fauna, genetics and language, they shared a common culture. But, as Grimble and others documented, there were surprising and major cultural differences between these small islands which are very close together. The significant divergences are in leadership, governance, personal autonomy, marriage, and funeral practices.

Before continuing, let me introduce some of my sources and caveats. My introduction to the Gilbertese culture began with Arthur Grimble's writings. It is possible that I have over romanticised some of Grimble's comments because I became District Officer, Tarawa, exactly 60 years after Grimble. However, one aspect of our beginnings is completely different. I went out to the Pacific because of my love for the indigenous people I encountered during teenage wanderings in Africa and Asia; they offered me what had been missing from the land of my infancy.[15] I already knew that the Gilbert and Ellice Islands would soon be independent, and I was due to serve as an Assistant to the Permanent Secretary for Local Government who reported to a Gilbertese Minister. Three months later, I was surprised to be promoted to the District Officer. From that moment, I learned the wishes of the elders to enact their choices since independence was imminent.

Arthur Grimble began with the vista of a long colonial career ahead of him. Independence was not on his horizon. He learned to speak fluently the everyday Gilbertese as well as the classical Gilbertese of the elders of the villages. As a Cambridge educated anthropologist, he made extraordinarily detailed notes of these conversations. Having arrived in 1914, just 22 years following the establishment of a British Protectorate in 1892, he was able to record many ancient traditions and legends. His particular interest in differences between islands made him a cultural detective. He was lucky to have such expert witnesses to interview. Since ancestry is so spiritually important, some elders could provide details of as many as thirty generations. The adventures of Robert Louis

---

[15] Mark Goodwin, *Mannership*.

Stevenson, who spent some months on Abemama and Butaritari Islands in the late 1880s, were also recalled by those who met him.

Arthur Grimble was too busy in his subsequent colonial career, in other parts of the globe, to publish all these detailed notes during his lifetime. However, as he had hoped, his daughter Rosemary incorporated many of them in her book: *Migrations, Myths and Magic from the Gilbert Islands*. Luckily Arthur's widow, Olivia, passed on the complete set of notes to Henry Maude. Henry edited and preserved them in *Tungaru Traditions*.[16] Maude and Grimble had much in common. They had both studied anthropology at Cambridge University, began their careers in the Gilbert and Ellice Islands and were fluent I-Kiribati speakers.

Just before independence, and during my stay on Tarawa, a group of thirty islanders came together to research their history and traditions culminating in a book: *Kiribati, Aspects of History*. The introduction by Ieremia Tabai, their first President, underlines the importance of this project. As he says: *almost all books about our own islands and people have been written by foreigners… Political independence needs to be associated with increased confidence and greater reliance on our own perceptions and points of view*. Their resulting book produces this gift in abundance.[17]

As referenced in the previous chapter, Michael Ravell Walsh has recently published *A History of Kiribati*. Michael has benefited from fifty years' experience of the I-Kiribati, and recently compiled an encyclopaedic book including the recent scientific data.

Arthur Grimble recorded the elders' memories of the islands before they became a British Protectorate in 1892. There were three distinguishable types of political system. Some were consensus democracies with long discussions in the village *maneaba;* they met and discussed whenever something needed the elders' attention. Some were aristocracies with chiefs, landowners and slaves. Some were feudal with a high chief and his blood relatives, subsidiary chiefs, landowners and slaves.[18] In general, slaves were either taken in war or fell into slavery as a result of a crime, particularly theft. In addition, chiefs who lost a battle could save their life by accepting servitude to the victorious chief. In this respect we can find similarities with the Norse sagas and the Arthurian legends of Europe, particularly *Parcival.*

[16] Arthur Grimble and Henry Maude, *Tungaru Traditions*.

[17] *Kiribati, Aspects of History,* 1979.

[18] *Tungaru Traditions*.

Usually a culture with a chief arose in response to war or a shortage of resources. But wars in those times often involved few combatants with basic weapons, so little loss of life. They were just a readjustment of the 'pecking order'. We can liken them to the animal fights between alpha males. As long as the defeated male accepts the new supremacy they are still a valuable part of the pack. In Kiribati, slaves could also acquire land by good cultivation, canoe building, curing the sick by magic or by fighting for a chief.

A breakdown in the 'pecking order adjustment process' occurred following the arrival of more advanced weaponry. It is not hard to imagine the effect on any species, and the traditional wrestling among males, if provided with fancy weapons. A different social order emerges because of new weaponry.

The most important possession on small atolls is land which could be received by either men or women as their inheritance. Specifically on Maiana Island, only 30 km from her nearest neighbour, the eldest daughter inherited her mother's best land.[19] In general, there was a parallel operation of both patriarchal and matriarchal traditions following the 'cleaving together' of the cults of Nareau and Taburimai, although some islands established different traditions. As Walsh writes, we have to be careful in making conclusions about gender. Before the patriarchal influence of religious Missions and the Colonial Service, women were chiefs, leaders, sorcerers, and navigators.

Customs varied in Tungaru, both between islands and between families of different social status, but most marriages were arranged. Virginity was prized, leading to strict control of young girls, and they were typically married soon after puberty. Marriages might be agreed when children were very young, and there were even speculative betrothals between families before the birth of a child. In this respect, there are early European equivalents among 'higher classes' especially to protect land or a kingdom.

Some islands practised both polygamy and polyandry, though the latter was less common and usually involved one wife married to two brothers.

When a man married the eldest daughter, some or all of her younger sisters (or close female cousins) might also become concubines and were called 'taua ni kai'. This arrangement required the supporting decision of

---

[19] *Kiribati, Aspects of History,* 1979.

the eldest sister. This custom may have arisen during times of difficulty finding potential husbands, particularly after war, fishing accidents or 'blackbirding', and was more common in the southern islands.[20]

Tungaru culture had one of the strictest anti-incest rules of any society with at least four generations of separation required. In the 'Kingly' Islands, with more rain, a chief could have many wives from different families although certainly no incest such as on Pingelap in the previous chapter.

Society recognised women called 'nikiranroro' who were sexually active outside marriage. There were also specific rules permitting adultery. For example, a husband could sleep with his wife's sisters or close cousins if given permission. Equally, a wife with her husband's brothers or close cousins, and she could be allowed by her mother-in-law to sleep with her husband's uncles. During the colonial period, the British did not usually interfere with these customs. However, since independence, Christianity was more effective in 'abolishing' such sexual freedoms, and there has been a catastrophic increase in domestic violence throughout the Pacific, not just in Kiribati.

There are some cultural aspects all the islanders shared, except with a specific exception to prove the rule. Rosemary writes: *The violation of maidenhood was everywhere looked upon as one of the most awful offences and was punished with great severity, unless of course it was part and parcel of the marriage by rape practised on Beru and Nikunau.*[21] She goes on to suggest the origin: *There are distinct indications in the traditions of many families that a small Melanesian invasion struck Beru around AD 1325 (as reckoned by the genealogies).* The link of Nikunau to the culture of Beru is explained: *It is provable that Nikunau, which lies only twenty-eight miles east of Beru, was dominated at a very early date by settlers from the latter island.* In summary, Rosemary concludes that: *It seems not unwisely venturesome to infer* that the Melanesian ancestors who came to Beru at this time were responsible for 'marriage by rape' which was unique to Beru and Nikunau. It is more surprising how many countries of the world still have such 'marriage by rape' laws or have only repealed them in the last twenty years. Back in 1914, when Beru had this tradition, much of the world would have agreed. The United Kingdom only criminalised rape within marriage in 1991.

---

[20] Blackbirding entailed kidnapping Pacific Islanders and using them as forced labour in other lands.

[21] Rosemary Grimble, *Migrations, Myth and Magic from the Gilbert Islands.*

The language also highlights that we are not speaking of small cultural variations. What is accepted on one island may be a taboo on another.

Abemama Island latterly had a chief who ruled absolutely and sometimes brutally. Walsh comments that this chiefdom only began after the invasion of Abemama from Tarawa in 1780 and was cemented following the arrival of European weapons in the 1820s. A hundred and fifty kilometres away from Abemama is an island called Tabiteuea. This name was originally '*Tabu te Uea*' meaning 'chiefs (*Uea*) are taboo'. The word *tabu* is shared by the I-Kiribati with the Fijians, Maoris, Tongans, Samoans, Hawaiians, and other Pacific cultures. *Tabu* means '*forbidden in sacred terms*'. James Cook brought the word into the English language as 'taboo' following his journey to Tonga in 1777.

Yet, the men of Tabiteuea had a reputation of being among the fiercest of Central Pacific warriors with swords of sharks' teeth and body armour. Their taboo of chiefs did not therefore imply a peaceful democracy. Every man on Tabiteuea felt himself to be a king; he was not going to be a servant or a slave to anyone.

These Tabiteueans must have experienced, or known of, chiefs and slaves to have chosen the name of their island, as well as developing armour, weaponry and determination to protect themselves. In this respect they share a tradition with countries such as Uzbekistan where the name 'Uzbek' means 'lord of oneself'.

Woodcut engraving of Tabiteuea warriors with sharks' teeth weaponry based on a drawing by Alfred Thomas Agate. Source: Charles Wilkes: Narrative of the United States Exploring Expedition of 1841

One subject on which all of the islands agreed was divorce. Rosemary writes: *Divorce was effected without formalities.* She adds: *The right to decide in such a matter was thus accorded as freely to the wife as to the husband, and this is a fair indication of a woman's general status in the Group, where mother-right and father-right seem to have impinged upon one another and eventually come to a compromise.* In this regard, the equality of women on Central Pacific Islands was many centuries ahead of the Europeans. Freedom to divorce and ease of separation may also have protected against domestic violence which was then extremely rare. The first European navigators in the Central Pacific forgot to bring this tradition of feminine freedom back with them.

Perhaps the I-Kiribati of a century ago, in the period before extensive 'Christianisation' and colonial harmonisation, might offer us a 'controlled cultural experiment'. If all other aspects of geography which might influence a culture are essentially constant, the cultural differences could be primarily due to outside influences. As found in *Mannership* for an individual mind, the relationship to events can be more important than the events themselves. For a culture, relationship to outside influences matters a great deal.

We know very little about the first few hundred years of the I-Kiribati settlers after the *Taburimai* 'cleaving together' with *Nareau* Melanesians. Perhaps, an absence of legends is good news. For the first settlers, there may have been sufficient land encouraging a peaceful coexistence. Arthur Grimble's interpretations of the legends led him to conclude that some of the Tungaru clans travelled south-east around 300 CE to Samoa. He postulated that they settled mostly on the Samoan island of Upolu beside indigenous Samoans. A period of 650 years, with not much news in legend terms, then ensued before Upolu was subjected to Tongan rule. The Tongan king, Tu'i Tonga 'Aho'eitu, begun an expansion of the Tongan Empire in 950 CE. It took a further three centuries, until 1250 CE, before the Samoan warriors were able to drive the Tongans out from the island of Upolu at the battle of Matamatame. A new dynasty of Samoan chiefs called 'Malietoa' took over. The name means 'brave warrior' and was shouted by the defeated Tongans fleeing down the beach into their canoes.

The legends don't tell us about the role of the Tungaru clans in this battle, or if they were even participants. However, the first Samoan Malietoa was not magnanimous in victory. As Grimble writes: *After the better part of a millennium of settlement on Savai'I and Upolu,* (they) *were driven forth by the indigenous people from whom their forefathers had won a foothold.*[22] We can only imagine possible reasons. Were the Tungaru clans felt to have been unreliable in supporting the first Lapita or indigenous Samoans? Had they sided with the Tongan rulers on occasion during the previous three centuries? Were the indigenous Samoans so glad to be rid of the Tongans that they wanted insurance against another foreign ruler by ejecting everyone except their own Lapita clan? We don't know. But the reality was more like a total purge. A mass of expulsions caused waves of migrations in all directions: to the Cook Islands and Marquesas Islands in the east, to Niue in the south, to the islands of Tokelau and Tuvalu in the north.

The oral traditions in these islands contain the surges of ancestral voyages from Samoa. Many new islands were suddenly 'discovered' by these surges and waves. It is more than possible that the most significant Māori migration to New Zealand, which began between 1250 and 1280 CE with a flotilla of canoes from the Cook and Society Islands, was also spawned as a result of the Samoan expulsions. In particular this could explain the suddenness and the size of the first Māori settlement of New Zealand which may have exceeded a thousand ocean voyagers. Perhaps they fled first from Samoa to the Cook and Society Islands and, finding insufficient land, continued onwards.

In the case of the Tungaru clans, the legends say they went back to the islands which their ancestors had left. Arthur Grimble writes: *It is significant that the flooding of the Gilbert Group by swarms of warriors from Samoa took place, according to our genealogies, within a very short time of the expulsion of the Tonga-fiti from the coasts of Savai'I and Upolu.*[23] The list of ancestral names and the assumed 25 years per generation gives the same dates for the legends in both Samoa and Kiribati. These returning clans were not all 'warmly greeted' like the canoes for the 2016 Festival of Pacific Arts on Guam. Their reception was rather mixed depending on the island they returned to and their clan. Only seven of the islands of Kiribati bore the brunt of the tsunami of warriors. This may have generated significant divergences of culture among the islands.

Grimble's interviews and notes include very detailed knowledge of the Tungaru clans. Recording their individual legends, traditions and totems

---

[22] Arthur Grimble, *A Pattern of Islands.*

[23] Arthur Grimble and Henry Maude, *Tungaru Traditions.*

or symbols, enabled him to detect whether each clan was reunited with a former friend or foe upon their return from Samoa. The warmest greeting was on Tarawa where Grimble's words sound more like a herald's trumpet: *Around about the time Edward III became king of England, Tarawan and Samoan branches of that far-voyaging race, after a thousand years of separation by a thousand miles of ocean, were reunited.*[24] From this reunion ensued a line of hero-kings named Kirata on Tarawa. On other islands we can assume it was rather less friendly as it took a full *ten generations for this Samoan invasion and their children to 'settle down' during a long period of unrest with squabbling over land, or of who owned what.*[25]

After the ten generations, or 250 years of *The Age of Unrest*, there was a quieter period of almost two centuries. Peace was destroyed in 1680 by *the war of Kaitu* of Beru and *Uakeia* of Nikunau. The island of Beru had *so many people that there was no land left.* A war was launched by warriors from Beru, supported by their allies from Nikunau, and *swept forth to conquer the whole group from south to north.*[26]

The warrior leadership of Kaitu and Uakeia conquered the nearest islands, Onotoa, Tabiteuea, and Nonouti and established chiefdoms as far north as Marakei. But the war did not go further as a delegation from the island of Butaritari sought a truce which was granted. *On the islands of Abaiang and Abemama the war wrecked the ancient democratic scheme of the islanders and erected in its ruins a dynastic system of kings.* Land ownership changed throughout the Tungaru group. The effects rumbled on in many islands long after this war.[27]

To a European this might sound all too familiar. But the parallels build up even more.

Some islands managed to find their way back to a more democratic structure. Meanwhile, civil wars continued on others with chiefs. These were usually caused by local chiefs attempting to strong-arm another, or get back a title which had belonged to a relative. This usually concerned a small band attacking another village with simple weapons and little loss of life, just like the Nordic sagas of a king with a dozen berserkers going after a rival king or impostor. It seems the I-Kiribati had their Viking equivalents.

---

[24] Arthur Grimble, *A Pattern of Islands*.

[25] Arthur Grimble and Henry Maude, *Tungaru Traditions*.

[26] idem.

[27] idem.

During the 19th century a number of other tragic 'disturbances' affected islands quite differently. There was more diversity of disturbance, with different 'fuses' or 'triggers' among the island histories. Some islands suffered unique experiences.

The first was the arrival of whaling ships from the 1820s onwards. Whalers hunted primarily in the South, around the islands of Tamana and Nikunau. After their hunts they sought women for comfort from these islands. Some women spent time on board ship and were then returned with a payment in tobacco. Others were promised to return but were 'retained' as the whaling ship set sail. Kuria Island was also impacted in this way. The whaling trade also affected the two islands of Makin and Butaritari in the north, but differently as a processor of the whale fat. Perhaps other islands did not experience the same exposure.

From 1857 onwards some islands saw the arrival of missionaries. One of the first was Reverend Hiram Bingham and his wife who built a Protestant church on Abaiang Island. Other islands received missionaries from the Roman Catholic Church followed later by other denominations. Some of the followers of these churches encouraged hatred of others with different Christian faiths, just as they did in Europe and elsewhere, although Walsh comments that these religious disputes often reflected earlier unresolved issues.

Religious quarrels ensued. The most tragic took place on the island of Tabiteuea. Two Hawaiian pastors, Kapu and Nalimu, had landed in 1868. Having converted the villages in the north of Tabiteuea to Christianity, they decided to go on a 'crusade' against the pagans in the south of the island in the religious war of 1881. No mercy was given, even towards relatives. All the northern men joined in with the last ones out of fear of being killed or stripped of their land for desertion of the cause. A few of the southern islanders were saved by taking refuge in the house of Aberaam, who had already accepted Christianity. Without him, probably the entire population of South Tabiteuea would have been massacred. This is unparalleled in the history of the other islands.[28]

My reactions to this story are two-fold. Firstly, there is a knee-jerk reaction to put all the blame on the Pastor Kapu. But, secondly, there must have been a traumatic fault line in the psyche of the North Tabiteuean warriors which had been awakened by Kapu's oratory. What aspect of Tabiteuea's history had traumatised them to this excess? What

[28] *Kiribati Aspects of History*, 1979.

had they forgotten that an orator could lead them so easily astray? Why was there no one who could have sent Kapu away? It seems that Kapu had lit a fuse reaching into a tragically disturbing aspect of the warrior nature of the North Tabiteueans and their taboo against chiefs. Kapu may have 'liberated' an energy which his congregation were relieved to be able to express. In this respect there are many European equivalents. Not just the crusades to Jerusalem but also the ease with which some orators in Europe's history were able to 'mine' the energy of a volcanic fault line in the psyche of their national subjects.

In addition to the whalers and missionaries, European and Asian traders on a few islands brought a different 'disturbance' by offering to trade firearms to encourage more coconut production, or copra. The effect is predictable with former quarrels becoming deadly. Although, it would have been hard to predict that the High Chief of Abemama Island, Tem Baiteke, and his successor Tem Binoka, could become so monstrous once they had a gun in hand. Tem Binoka was described as *a ruthless island potentate, who held the lives of his own subjects so cheap that he would shoot them down from tree tops for the pleasure of seeing them fall sprawling.*[29]

The Abemama islanders lived in terror as did those of the two neighbouring islands. In 1872 the population of Kuria was about 1,500 and Aranuka about 1,000. Tem Baiteke reduced their population to between 100 and 150 each by 1881. Most fled as refugees on canoes to other islands although many perished at sea.[30] By the time Kiribati became a British Protectorate in 1892 there were only 30 souls left on Kuria Island, a loss of 98% of her population twenty years previously.[31] The terror was such that fertility collapsed and very few children were born on Abemama at this time. H.E. Maude identified that *for some unknown reason many women did not have children* and the absence of children was noted by other visitors. Of the 1,416 from Abemama whose deaths were registered between 1898 and 1948 the Lands Commission found that almost 70 percent (973) had died childless.[32] This trauma is unparalleled in the Tungaru group. Reading the numbers now it is

---

[29] Arthur Grimble, *A Pattern of Islands*.

[30] Only two canoes from Kuria are reported to have reached the neighbouring island of Maiana suggesting that most drowned. Aranuka was luckier as many of them reached three other islands according to the population estimates.

[31] In the 2010 census the population of Kuria was 980.

[32] Richard Bedford University of Canterbury, Barrie Macdonald Massey University and Doug Munro University of the South Pacific, *Population Estimates for Kiribati and Tuvalu, 1850–1900: Review and Speculation*.

perhaps not so difficult to explain the absence of fertility. Who would have a child in this time of terror, apart from those who could escape to other islands? It seems more like living in a time of Herod the King of Israel. Tem Mwea, a fierce warrior from the 1680 war of *Kaitu and Uakeia* had thus spawned in his descendants a pair of monsters two centuries later once a steel gun was placed in their hands.

Abemama means 'land of moonlight'. Fond memories of the beauty of this island remain with me. Tony English, District Officer Central Gilberts, had warned me to bring sunglasses for a walk along the reef at night. The reflection of the moon on the white coral is dazzlingly bright. But the stories that the coral witnessed sent shudders up my spine. What can be more terrible than a mixture of extreme beauty and terror, with a vicious betrayal by a chief killing, laughing, and trashing ancestral traditions?

There is another unique aspect of Abemama. The island was said to have a 'university of cunnilingus'. To borrow Rosemary Grimble's very British stiff upper lip phrase, *it seems not unwisely venturesome to infer* that the distinctive emphasis of the Abemama interest in cunnilingus might have begun during the reign of terror as a form of birth control. This thought reminds me of my girlfriend during the latter part of my stay on Tarawa. She was from Abemama. So beautiful, delicate and tender but she eventually decided that I was 'not marriage material'. She never explained why and we drifted apart. Perhaps my Oxford education was insufficient and had been the 'wrong' university. I have to admit though, that knowing myself better now, she is right. I was far too immature for marriage back then, but I loved her. I could not be the man she wanted as my upbringing was too reserved.

From the 1860s the Gilbert and Ellice islands suffered from what was loosely called 'labour recruiting'. In reality, this consisted mostly of 'blackbirding' and kidnapping together with some desperate volunteers. A story from the 1870s tells of Uaititi, a twelve-year-old boy from Makin Island. He, with many others, was invited on board ship and asked to dance. Having been plied with '*te kiraoki*' (grog), they all slept and woke to find themselves taken to Hawaii to work on plantations.[33] Uaititi returned home after several years to tell the tale. Other ships took 'recruits' to work on plantations in Hawaii, Samoa, Fiji, Tahiti and even mines in Peru.[34] The effect of 'blackbirding' expeditions varied

---

[33] *Kiribati Aspects of History.*

enormously from one island to another. Because some of the Kiribati 'recruits' returned home after a number of years, the full extent of this 'disturbance' is easier to deny. Although the recruiting took place long after the abolition of slavery, it was only 'regulated' by Britain and Australia.

Detailed figures have been researched in a paper on the population estimates for Kiribati and Tuvalu between 1850 and 1900 as referred to in the footnote. The records identify that *the net loss of population between 1860 and 1900 was between 5,650 and 9,250* primarily due to 'labour recruiting'. This represents between 15% and 20% of the I-Kiribati.

I am staggered by some of the records of the 'labour recruiting' period, particularly the euphemistic language. Such as: *Recruiting was not always popular in the island communities.* What kind of stiff upper lip can write such words when sat alongside the comments: *The Micronesians quickly learned to fear the 'mensteating ships' from Tahiti which began seeking recruits in Kiribati in 1867. Between 1867 and 1872 a total of 687, mostly from the southern islands, were taken by men who had great sport in the bush catching them and making them fast.*[35] The records also say: *Neither the Tahitian Government nor the planters adhered to repatriation undertakings, mainly because of the cost involved in charters to an area not served by regular shipping.*

The number of souls lost per island varied enormously. Kiribati's neighbours to the south, the nine islands of Tuvalu, highlight two specific island effects of raids by Peruvian recruiters. *In 1863 several ships called seeking labour but only Nukulaelae and Funafuti lost significant proportions of their residents through kidnapping. At Nukulaelae about 250 from an estimated population of 300 were enticed on board two Peruvian vessels with the promise of being taken to a nearby island for six months where they could make coconut oil and learn Christianity, before being returned home with good payment and mission teachers. At Funafuti 171 from a total of about 300 were similarly inveigled aboard.*[36]

The ship *Ellen Elizabeth*, with 161 I-Kiribati aboard, arrived in Peru in 1863 after licences to recruit and employ Pacific Islanders had been

---

[34] Between 1862 and 1864, Peru seized 3,500 islanders from as far west as the Gilbert Islands to mine the guano deposits on the Chincha Islands. They also captured a third of the population of Easter Island.

[35] *Population Estimates for Kiribati and Tuvalu, 1850–1900: Review and Speculation*, page 11 Oates 1871, quoted in Maude and Leeson 1968.

[36] idem.

withdrawn. Unable to disembark passengers, 110 were 'off-loaded' on Penrhyn Island in the northern Cooks while 41 of them perished at sea. From Penryyn, many were 'recruited' a second time by Tahitian ships.

Another account records: *The Micronesians did not remain entirely passive when subjected to this kind of treatment. In 1869, 80 men from Kiribati, who had been transferred from the Anna (out of Fiji) to the barque Moaroa (destined for Tahiti), broke clear of the hold, killed the captain and some members of his crew, and then escaped over the side. Most reached shore safely at Nikunau.*[37]

In addition to Tem Binoka's wickedness on Abemama, he was involved in selling other islanders. Apparently: *There was no further recruiting from Kiribati for Tahiti until 1885 when the Forçade de la Roquette obtained 165 labourers (90 men, 75 women) and 46 children. About half were conscripts from Nonouti 'sold' to the recruiters by Tem Binoka.*[38]

Some of the 'recruits' were lucky. Eventually, after several years, they came home from a few destinations. David Lewis, while researching Pacific navigational skills, found a story: *In the second part of the 19th century, the Reef Islander Backapu and a companion, having been kidnapped by 'blackbirders' and taken to Fiji, stole a small craft and returned home across nearly 1,000 miles of open sea directly to their own island.*

I feel a need to apologise to my reader for all the stories in this chapter. But, sadly they are the 'disturbances' which have troubled these I-Kiribati and it is a credit to the beauty of their indigenous nature that they have not only survived but continue to shine forth through their wholesome smiles. Perhaps the greatest lesson for us is the importance of remembering what our ancestors suffered. That we might metabolise old memories rather than trying to run away from them and thereby afflict others with our forgotten past. In addition, like other indigenous people, the I-Kiribati believe in total freedom from revengeful motives: *The sun and the ancestors will do what they will to your ill-wishers.*[39]

In conversations with Michael Ravell Walsh, he highlighted a few other aspects of I-Kiribati culture and the framework of *aia mwaan ikawai* or 'the customs and values of the ancients':

- A widespread tolerance of individualism.

---

[37] idem.

[38] idem.

[39] *Kiribati Aspects of History..*

- A tradition of taking decisions by consensus, however long this took.
- A culture that never needed a concept of money unlike most other Pacific societies. The I-Kiribati were archetypal satisficers and ensured everyone had the minimum required.
- A belief that it is reprehensible either not to provide adequately for your family or to indulge in conspicuous consumption and display greater wealth than your neighbour. This is different from suggesting that everyone should be equal and is rooted in displaying respect for others which is at the heart of *aia mwaan ikawai.*

In *Mannership*, I wrote that the Gilbertese 'family unit' was the *kaainga* or village with up to a hundred related islanders. Much was done communally which enabled the most effective distribution of roles among the members. Children were sometimes more collectively brought up by the generation of grandparents, together with uncles and aunts. This left the middle generation free to build houses out of pandanus beams and thatch, and to fish. There were no orphans as the village would take care of all the children. Our Western society has broken when we have strayed so far from communities that could satisfactorily and simultaneously look after the very young and very old for their mutual benefit.

Perhaps we can conclude this chapter with a wonderful lesson from the I-Kiribati. It is the gift inside their words *aomata* which implies 'a real person' and *Katei ni Kiribati* or 'the Gilbertese identity'. By this they mean that: *Children should be taught to know themselves; they should learn their genealogies, skills and knowledge. A person who has pride in himself, and what he is, would be less likely to get into trouble. He would be hard working and able to face hardship in times of drought and at sea. He or she is emotional, friendly to strangers, and can be the best of friends and the worst of enemies. A man is a real person when he practises and believes te katei ni Kiribati.*[40]

If only our culture was travelling in this direction.

---

[40] *Kiribati Aspects of History.*

Intermission

Before considering other parts of the world, there are a number of aspects in the history of Kiribati which I feel need more digestion. During my time with these wonderful islanders, I enjoyed their freedom of spirit, sexuality, and spontaneity but did not appreciate the extent of the lessons until much later in my career and following exposure to many cultures. After writing of these Pacific stories, new connections appeared to me.

I was struck by a surprising number of resemblances with Europe. Has the madness of a crusade without mercy for other souls, including relatives, suggested a deeper 'fault line' in the national psyche? Or, has the Church much to answer for with their orators fanning the flames? The naked greed of kidnapping and brutalising others for personal financial gain always shocks me. The development of 'fancier' weapons has had negative results everywhere in the world, sadly. These, and other similarities in respect of violence and slavery, will be explored while looking at other nations.

In the '70s, I do not remember sensing any repression of women in the Gilbert Islands. Both men and women were freely in charge of their bodies and sexuality. If two people of any gender were attracted they could just follow their feelings immediately, and then resume whatever they were doing afterwards. There was negligible domestic violence. Perhaps Arthur Grimble's daughter Rosemary put her finger on this when she says that *divorce was effected without formalities and with the right to decide accorded as freely to the wife as to the husband.* To put this liberty in perspective, the 'No-fault Divorce Bill' was first introduced in the British Parliament in June 2019 and might become law by 2022. California introduced 'no fault divorce' in 1970. The UK and USA are both way behind the cultures of little islands in this respect. In the early '70s divorce was still banned in a number of European countries.

There is another jarring lesson in Rosemary's observations on 'marriage by rape' which only became part of the culture on two islands. The extent to which many of the world's cultures took so long to criminalise rape within marriage suggests the depth and spread of this sickness within a great many nations. Some countries still allow a man to escape justice if he marries his victim. Does this tell us something about the local history?

There are many other points which the I-Kiribati history brings forth. But, the greatest lesson for me, and one which took a very long time to digest, is fundamental and quite different. The islanders had something, in the way they all reacted together, which was fabulous to be with and was infectious. The joy was so deep, the laughter so consuming, and the spontaneity so delicious.

Aomata and Katei ni Kiribati, real persons with Gilbertese Identity, 1975

When the children smiled, all of their body smiled. The French would say 'they were in their skin'. They were whole. Just watching the children filled me with warmth and admiration. My childhood culture was not like that.

Fifteen years and two different careers later, I attended a gathering of the American Men's movement, led by Robert Bly. One of the teachers, Michael Meade, said: *If the First Layer of human interaction is the common ground of manners, kind speech, polite greeting, and working agreements; if the Third Layer is the area of deeply shared humanity, the universal brotherhood and sisterhood of all people, of the underlying, fundamental oneness of human love, justice, and peaceful coexistence; then the Second Layer is the territory of anger, hatred, wrath, rage, outrage, jealousy, envy, contempt, disgust, and acrimony. And, the Second Layer always exists between the First Layer and the Third.*

I sat up and understood immediately that the I-Kiribati mesmerised me with the delicious way in which they communicated in *the Third Layer*. Michael had put his finger on what I had seen. Suddenly I remembered my travels differently; which cultures operated in the Third Layer and which in the First. A few were stuck in the Second Layer.

My thoughts were racing. There was no doubt that Britain was a culture of the First Layer. Could the British have learned to avoid some of their 'middle layer' with a 'stiff upper lip' or 'aloofness' which leads to expressions like 'how do you do'. This is neither a question, nor permits an answer apart from the repetition 'how do you do'. No question mark is necessary at the end of the phrase. This is a safe statement from the 'First Layer of politeness'. Of course, my great aunt Maud would have been certain that her politeness came from the Third Layer. How could a Victorian lady have known otherwise?

The USA modified the British greeting to 'have a nice day' as a similar first layer comment. We both avoid risks in polite society by apologising quickly when we bump into someone on the street, even when clearly their fault. We take the blame quickly, even when plainly the other's fault, as a simple way to reduce the risk of conflict.

We will return to this fundamental subject, but must say a little more before moving onwards. The silence of my childhood and my hunger to understand connections by looking had enabled me to discern easily the cultures in the third layer. Sometimes just reading about them is enough. For example, in Okla Hannali, Lafferty writes: …*a thing which distinguishes the Choctaws from other people, that they will sit silent for a long time, and will then begin to chuckle as though they would rupture themselves.* They are unable to hold in their glee, but a first layer holding of the glee misses the experience. This delight is found scattered all over the world but only in some places.

In some cultures of the first layer, there are lucky families who can reach the third layer despite the general cultural repression.

In *Mannership,* looking into the question of how an individual mind can become whole, or cured of self-destruction, I found that a great many philosophers and prophets agreed on two conditions, understanding and spontaneity. After my adventures around the world, apparently the same conditions apply to cultures.

The understanding part is easier to grasp. Some cultures know themselves. They have legends, stories, oral traditions, theatre or rhymes which enable them to continually metabolise their history. Martín Prechtel, a shaman from the Tzutujil Mayan culture of Guatemala, often told to me how cultures that forget their past are at risk of 'running away' from their traumas and thereby doing to others what was done to them. Ouch.

Perhaps a culture that does not 'know themselves' also hinders their young children from knowing themselves. Could this be the significance of *aomata* and *Katei ni Kiribati* or 'a real person with Gilbertese identity'? Particularly their emphasis, *Children should be taught to know themselves; their genealogies, skills and knowledge. A person who has pride in himself would be less likely to get into trouble. He would be hard working and able to face hardship in times of drought and at sea. He or she is emotional, friendly to strangers, and can be the best of friends and the worst of enemies.* Or, in my language, they would be a 'whole' person which seems to be the meaning behind *aomata* as a 'real person'.

Spontaneity is harder to grasp as, by definition, the subject cannot be grasped. We know whether someone is 'bubbly' or wooden, but cannot explain how to get there. It is harder for children to remain spontaneous if their culture is violent or reserved. Quietly or brutally some cultures strangle the aliveness. The I-Kiribati are fully spontaneous, enjoying the sprit and sexuality. This beauty and aliveness among children is much harder to find in our Western culture. Perhaps this explains our children's hunger to be associated with a Facebook profile. They are not themselves anymore but an extension of the profile. Out of their skins.

There is a critical consequence of a culture having both understanding and spontaneity; these attributes seem to be potential antidotes to revenge. This lesson took me so long to learn. Later in my career, after many global wanderings, one of the most important discoveries was how 'intact' societies would agree with the I-Kiribati avoidance of vengeful motives by trusting that *The sun and the ancestors will do what they will to your ill-wishers*. There was no doubt for me that these were cultures of the *third layer*. They were too busy enjoying themselves chuckling to have any inclination to plot vengeful activity. Being infected by spontaneity is their victory.

This also just happens to be something which Christ taught, incidentally. Many Christian churches somehow forgot about that. But, as Leo Tolstoy wrote; *In Christianity there was only ever one Christian.*[41] Confucius says simply: *Before you embark on a journey of revenge, dig two graves.*

Confucius taught a similar principle in the need for both awareness and spontaneity: *At fifteen I set my mind upon learning; at thirty I took my place in society; at forty I became free of doubts; at fifty I understood Heaven's Mandate; at sixty my ear was attuned; and at seventy I could follow my heart's desire without overstepping the bounds of propriety.*

Socrates felt similarly: *when we know fully and completely, suitable actions follow automatically and reflectively.* Choices are made without conflict and with full spontaneity.

In indigenous society, a key role of shamans is attending to leaks or blocks in the 'spirit plumbing' by assuring the 'living water' of the 'third layer' flows or spouts like a fountain. I wondered if the cultural loss of this 'living water' may be described by Jeremiah as: *For my people have committed two evils; they have forsaken me the fountain of living waters, and hewed them out cisterns, broken cisterns, that can hold no water.*[42]

Before embarking on the historic traumas of Britain, and perhaps because of my reluctance to leave the delightful I-Kiribati, a short story might serve as a 'sorbet' between meaty courses.

---

[41] Leo Tolstoy, *The Kingdom of God is within you*.

[42] Jeremiah ii, 13.

Looking for water, Egypt 1973

PAUL AND THE BABAI BEETLE

In Kiribati there is only one vegetable and she is a large corm called 'Babai'. Babai is well known to Pacific peoples. She is called 'pulaka' in Niue and in Tokelau, 'puraka' in the Cook Islands, 'pula'a' in Samoa, 'simiden' in Chuuk, and 'navia' in Vanuatu. But, this knowledge will not make us much wiser apart from noting that she has travelled for many centuries. She has been growing in Papua New Guinea for over ten thousand years and has many names. But, that's because ten per cent of the world's languages live on Papua. More commonly, she is known as 'swamp taro'. Her fancy name is Cyrtosperma merkusii. The Pacific myths say she was first born in Indonesia and science has finally caught up in confirming that this is right. The myth turns her nose up as if to fret that nothing is right until science says so. But it has been like that for a long time now.

Babai cannot tolerate salt water, though, so she must have been brought to Kiribati on the early canoe migrations, and very carefully packed in some soil. There is insufficient rain on most Central Pacific atolls to irrigate her, but the ancestors of the I-Kiribati discovered how to overcome this. If one digs down into the limestone of the coral sands, in the centre of an atoll, until about a foot above the seawater level, there is sometimes a freshwater 'pond'. And magically this water is always fresh because salts don't travel in through a limestone filter. Freshwater is lighter than salty water and just floats on the top in the same way that cream sits or floats on milk. By digging a pit for her to just the right depth, our well-travelled babai is very cosily nestled in a deep sided pool. She looks like she is in a nursery there. Since she doesn't like wind, the depth of her pit serves a double purpose. Her giant leaves have thick rich veins which seem to pulse as we watch her moving gently in a reduced breeze like sails of a canoe. Suitable locations for babai pits are treasured, and often far from a family's house. The babai nurseries are handed down from generation to generation together with all the knowledge of seeding and husbanding the babai plant.

The particular babai pit we are talking about now is in the village of Banreaba, on the island of Tarawa in the Gilbert and Ellice Islands as she was then known. This family pit belonged to Reuben Uatioa who was no ordinary farmer. Reuben was one of the founders of the Gilbertese National Party in 1965. Once the House of Representatives was formed in 1971, he was elected as the first 'Chief Member'. He was very wise as well as quietly progressive. Reuben had tempered his impatience for rapid political progress so as to ensure the best form of Government post-independence. Clearly a wise man who knows that nature cannot be rushed when we hope for a healthy harvest. Reuben was a lovely man. Gentle, kind, and interested in everything, especially the grandchildren of his village.

Reuben was also my mentor and a special guide. At the age of just twenty-one when appointed as the last English District Officer on Tarawa before Independence, a great deal of guidance on local matters was necessary. I could not have hoped for a better teacher. Reuben encouraged me carefully towards decisions that were gentle and helpful on Tarawa, helping me to serve as a bridge from the colonial past to a fully Gilbertese future. Knowing myself to be the last in a line which went back to Arthur Grimble, I was anxious not to upset my hosts nor do anything toxic.

Speaking of toxic, the babai plant is very toxic. Babai is a rich source of carbohydrate and calcium. But, if not properly prepared, the sensation can be shocking. The mouth reels as if needles have been inserted right through the cheeks and tongue, or so Reuben told me. Luckily, Pacific Islanders know how to neutralise any toxicity of this giant corm by slow cooking in an earth oven with coconut cream. She is then delicious and tastes more like a nutty sweet potato with an occasional whiff of vanilla bean. I cannot resist adding that, apparently, the swamp taro is the largest plant in the world which produces an edible corm and, in the centre of the Pacific; she is growing on one of the narrowest islands on earth.

I enjoyed my regular visits to Reuben and his family for advice. I sometimes felt like pinching myself with my good fortune to have such a friend and guide who was so wise, an elder among elders with his experience as the first leader of the House of Assembly. The evening of his life coincided with the beginning of my career. We had the same objectives. He enjoyed my practicality. With his support, there was no need for me to doubt my energy or enthusiasm to 'get things done'. The journey up the coral reef mud road to his village was by motorcycle, a mere fifteen minutes from my house overlooking the ocean in Bairiki village. To say 'motorcycle' is a little strong really. This was a 50 cc light green Honda ladies' model and rather sedate but the perfect transport for all eleven miles of Tarawa's main road. With anything faster the island would have been too short. I am not sure why I say 'main road'. Perhaps this is a habit, because there was no other road on Tarawa.

Reuben's babai pit was directly on the narrow path from the 'main road' to his house. I had to pay particular attention to drive carefully around the edge before riding up to his porch. We spoke about many things of great importance to the local elders but not about the babai plant except in passing. She was there, carefully tended by Reuben's family and carefully navigated by my motorcycle, and so this pit might always have been but for the visit of Paul.

As a child, my mother used to sing in a choir and she had a close friend, Erica, who sang with her. One of Erica's sons was called Paul. We knew each other from the few occasions that our mothers took tea together in the garden and dragged their children along. We were not in the same school so we did not meet often, perhaps once or twice a year. But Paul was my age and a nice boy. Geography can change relationships overnight, though. Paul had finished his degree in agriculture and was travelling around. He found himself in New Zealand and a letter from his mother suggested that he visit me as I was in the same neck of the woods, or whichever expression Erica had favoured. It is true that the Pacific Ocean is a body of water that New Zealand and the Gilbert Islands share, but we are not exactly in the same neck of the woods. Four thousand kilometres by sea would be a better description. Never mind; when Paul wrote to me and asked if he could 'pop by', I said "of course, I would be delighted, and there is a spare room in my house."

In the coming days, I began to look forward to Paul's visit. The idea of a family friend from Cambridge would be most interesting and pleasant. I wondered how Paul would get to Tarawa, but of course he would figure that out. It was a lovely surprise when he arrived a few weeks later. And such a pleasure to be able to talk about our Cambridge homes and families over dinner each evening.

Paul's stay got longer. This is easy to understand if one knows the Gilbert Islands. They are one of the few paradises left on earth. Or, 'left on water' might be a better description. After a few weeks, Paul decided to do something useful, but what? Having a degree in agriculture, I suggested he contact the Ministry of Agriculture and ask how he could help. Now, unbeknownst to me, one of the most pressing agricultural issues at the time was the babai beetle. How had I missed this information? A good District Officer should know of the troubles of the local population. They had only the one vegetable, babai, and there was a beetle which could ravage her roots. Clearly this was an urgent matter. The next day, after my motorcycle ride to Reuben's house and refreshed by one of his king coconut juices, I introduced the idea to our former Chief Member. "Wonderful," he said and then quickly added, "and Paul could use my babai pit for his research. Then we can both follow the matter with interest."

Thus was set the next two months' research in Reuben's babai pit. How to conquer the babai beetle? I had never met this beetle, so the mite was a mystery to me. But, during our dinners of fish and rice, and of course babai, Paul introduced me to the specifics of the babai beetle. He was about nine millimetres long apparently. After further explanation, an image of a vine weevil came to mind. The challenge was how to catch him.

Being fresh from his degree, Paul thought quickly and knew he had not much time. Only about eight weeks of his planned stay in Tarawa remained before returning to Cambridge. Somehow, in just eight weeks, he had to trap the beetle which was causing the babai so much grief. Paul decided that it was too dangerous to use a chemical from the Ministry of Agriculture to try and kill the beetle owing to possible harmful effects on the natural environment. With this, I agreed whole-heartedly.

Paul had already thought further. He decided to make a babai beetle trap.

"How will you do that, Paul?"

"I can make a trap by cutting a Coke can in half and then the babai beetle, once in, will not be able to climb out."

"But why would the beetle be there in the first place?"

"I shall put a concoction in the bottom of the can which attracts the babai beetle."

"What attracts the babai beetle?"

"I don't know, but I have eight weeks to find out. I can vary the mixture at the bottom of the can every few days and record when there are more or less beetles to guide us to the perfect concoction."

I liked his idea and saw the brilliance of his plan. "So you are going to make a sort of moth trap for the babai beetle; he will be attracted to something and then get stuck. Are you going to start tomorrow?" Paul smiled.

The idea of successful research into the liquids which would entice a babai beetle to a Coke trap was exciting if Paul could pull it off. No doubt the Atoll Pioneer had a few column inches on this important development with anticipated results, although I cannot recall the details.

At the time, there were many other matters which preoccupied me. The days went by quickly. Eight weeks is more than fifty of them. Every evening over dinner I received an update of the beetles. Paul's records were meticulous. The exact ingredients of his various concoctions, the proportion of the mix, and the number of beetles who had found their way in was recorded carefully as every researcher must. The results were sporadic. A few beetles here and there but never enough to give a clue as to the direction of the trial. Sometimes there was a sudden increase in trapped beetles but a repeat with the same concoction a few days later produced quite different results. Perhaps the babai beetle knew something which Paul didn't.

More days went by. Paul worked ever more frantically and borrowed my sedate Honda every day to visit Reuben's babai pit at dawn and at dusk.

I had almost given up, or forgotten, as Paul's last week approached. But, in his last week, I found him in my house with tears in his eyes. "What happened?"

"The tins were full of beetles this morning!" he said, with a grin through the tears.

Being very British and knowing a thing or two about 'reserve', I encouraged him to write everything up meticulously and thoroughly. He nodded sagely. He knew he needed a few more days to complete his research report. A couple of days later, the writing still unfinished, Paul left Tarawa on the weekly flight to Fiji. I saw him off with a firm handshake and further encouragement to write up his research speedily.

The next few days were quieter. I had forgotten how quiet my evenings had been before Paul had come to stay for three months. Our evening dinners together had been such a delight.

A further week passed before my next visit to Reuben. I mentioned how happy Paul was when he left. Reuben smiled warmly as he told me the village elders often discussed Paul's work as the babai beetle was such a problem for them. They also had another long discussion in the maneaba a few nights before Paul left. I wondered what they had talked about.

Reuben replied, "They wanted to give him a reward for all his efforts and dedication. He really had tried so hard."

"So, what did they decide to give him?" I asked.

"Well, knowing how hard he tried to fill his tins with beetles, we asked all the children of the village to catch some beetles and to put them in his tins."

A short pause followed. My emotions were rather mixed while realising my need to write a letter to Paul, and quickly. I was wondering how he would take the news when Reuben drew my attention to the meatier subjects before us - a complete overhaul of the local tax system.

Britain's Culture and Disturbances

There were several lessons from the dawn in Kiribati to help me think differently about culture. In particular: Does the culture remember, through legends or oral traditions, what she had suffered so that the experience could be metabolised? Or has the culture forgotten and continually runs away from the experiences thus risking doing the same to others? Does the culture foster a child's growth so they can know and be known? Is revenge constantly on the dinner menu?

Applying this new yardstick to the land of my infancy left me feeling rather small. The lesson was, on the contrary, rather larger. I had to research, learn and think differently about the disturbances which my small island had suffered. Not the small island of Tarawa, but the small island of Britain. If, during this chapter, my reader feels thrown overboard or misguided, then my advice would be to skip ahead to the short chapter on 'Ancestral lessons' before coming back. Maybe some ancestral support and nudging will help wading through a history not entirely dissimilar from some of the little Pacific Islands.

My first discovery was that Britain has been uninhabitable during most of her history. Everyone either perished or escaped at the beginning of each ice age. The first hominoids lived around 950,000 years ago as hunter-gatherers of 'Homo antecessor' using stone tools. Traces of their presence are found at Happisburgh in Norfolk. An ice age took them all away. As a family we often went to the Happisburgh beach during my silent years; rather windy and chilly it was.

'Homo heidelbergensis' lived in Britain around 500,000 years ago, with fossil evidence found in Sussex. They were frozen out too.

In the next 100,000 years, Britain became an island with a Neanderthal population. During colder periods the population also left, and new immigrants appeared as we 'warmed up'.

The earliest record of modern humans is a 44,000 year old jaw-bone. These were mammoth hunters. Their presence was intermittent too; there were at least three periods when it was much too cold for their survival. Britain was covered by a mile of ice in the Younger Dryas, which lasted around 1,500 years until 11,500 years ago. Our next visitors were a hunter-gatherer group in the Mesolithic Stone Age. They were in turn replaced by Neolithic farmers arriving from West Europe 6,000 years ago.

Whilst fascinating, at least for me trying to imagine these folk, my curiosity spiked while learning of a settlement in the Orkney Islands which had early traditions of the culture of Stonehenge. Especially interesting was a realisation that the construction of the Ness of Brodgar, a huge temple on a tiny island north of Britain, had begun around 3,300 BCE, at the same time the ancestors of the Lapita left China and Taiwan bound for the Pacific. Two different peoples, who followed the movement of the sun and knew the rising of the stars in her different seasons, inhabited opposite sides of the globe more than 5,000 years ago. Our British forebears share something with the first Pacific Island migrations. Some were perhaps pulled by their respect for beauty and wholeness, guided by their deity the sun. Others were possibly running away from violence, oppression, or a shortage of resources. Perhaps both forces came together at different times. Both these peoples shared that they were running to, or away from something; they breached completely new frontiers. The Lapita trusted the birds to guide them thousands of miles. The builders of Brodgar had found the limit of their navigational skills at the farthest north-western point of Europe which they could reach; serious faith, or determination, in both cases.

With so many periods without habitation, Britain has no indigenous population and we are all descendants of immigrants. We often forget that. Sadly, the builders of the Ness of Brodgar or Stonehenge are unlikely to have been my ancestors. The culture which built Stonehenge was fading, and the forests were already taking over again, several hundred years before the lighter skinned and blue-eyed 'Beaker folk' arrived from the north of the Black Sea and Central Asian Steppe. It is wonderful what science can find in a little DNA and a few teeth in graves. At the beginning of the Bronze Age in Britain, 4,000 years ago, over 90% of our population consisted of families of Beaker folk. As Britain has been continuously inhabited ever since, the Beaker folk represent most of the British 'genetic foundation'. We do not know if the Beaker folk who came to Britain were fore-runners of the early Indo-Europeans or a pastoral people escaping from them. But, to our island, the difference does not matter. Both waves were fleeing the terror of slavery with one wave overtaking another, whether they knew the trauma or not. Our earliest ancestors on this island have this poison in a memory which can no longer be reached.

Over the following two thousand years many other clans arrived in Britain, including many Celtic tribes who, when they were not fighting among themselves, made large thatched communal buildings rather like the Gilbertese *maneaba*. During the Iron Age, our ancestors lived in tribal groups and were ruled by chiefs, a similar structure to many islands of Kiribati. There were apparently 27 tribes in Britain. Relations between them cannot have been entirely peaceful as over 2,000 hill forts were built long before the Romans arrived. And being on the tops of hills they cannot have had wells, so were clearly for defence and not for picnics. Written records of our land, observed by the Greek geographer Pytheus in the 4th century BCE, saw our ancestors as wheat farmers. But, later Roman sources say that our main exports were hunting dogs, animal skins and slaves.

By 2,500 years ago, some of our island ancestors had 'graduated' from slavery escapees to slave traders. Some with power were no better than the rogue chief Tem Binoka of Abemama Island who sold slaves to a Tahitian ship. We had a culture of terror with many suffering worse atrocities than their ancestors had escaped from many centuries or millennia previously.

The Romans brought their own version of brutality. Flogging and raping Queen Boudicca's two daughters to try and make their mother subservient to the Roman rule, which only inspired her to lead our ancestors to a victory in revenge. As soon as the Romans abandoned Britain at the beginning of the 5th century, we suffered invasions by Angles, Jutes and Saxons. The Beaker folk ancestry thus acquired a Germanic influence in addition to the Roman genetics; more violence in both cases. Simon Jenkins writes of *the obliteration of the culture of the Iceni and Trinovantes*.[43] Jenkins also highlights the Saxon loyalty to family,

---

[43] Simon Jenkins *A Short History of England.*

settlement and clan in 'kith and kin' which is similar to the principles of early Kiribati clans. The Saxon hierarchy of chiefs and aldermen with subordinate thegns (servants or attendants) is surprisingly similar to some of the early Kiribati islands. Some Saxon chiefs had a more consultative discussion around important decisions which became a council, the 'Witan'. The history of regular invasions did not permit a consensus democracy such as chosen by the more peaceful Pacific islands.

The ancestors of the I-Kiribati were luckier. Firstly, the distances in the Pacific are so great that invasions by foreigners were rare. Apart from a possible Melanesian invasion of Beru, most of the troubles in Kiribati prior to the 19th century were internally caused by different clans. Such as the return of warriors from Samoa to islands where they were not welcomed, or the war spawned by the lack of land on Beru. Could there be a coincidence that Beru was involved in most of the cases? Did their Melanesian invasion spark the idea for a similar invasion of other islands?

After regular invasions including Jutes, Angles and Saxons, Britain had invasions of Danish and Scandinavian Vikings from the end of the 8th century, prior to the arrival of the Norman Vikings in the 11th century which added fuel to the fire.

Perhaps the traumatic fault lines in the British psyche were imported by the Beaker folk in 2,400 BCE. Why else did they come? But the development of traders who exported slaves before the Romans arrived and many waves of vicious invasions by Romans, Jutes, Angles, Saxons, Danes and Vikings might have scrambled the minds of the earlier immigrants to Britain. There were far too many traumas. A faith shared by the I-Kiribati that *the sun and the ancestors will do what they will to your ill-wishers* could not be sustained by traumatised Britons. Perhaps, since Stonehenge, we have not had an 'inner place of safety'. This small island had truly forsaken the fountain *of living waters*. Many institutions set up 'for the protection of children' did everything but look after them.

There has been no sacred *maneaba* system, or safe temple of the sun and stars. The British history is also affected significantly by the power and riches given to the early Christian Church. The behaviour of the Church often bore so little resemblance to many of the fundamental teachings of Christ that really they should not have used his name. But, as Leo Tolstoy explains, there is a fundamental fault line in the Church foundations. One cannot believe in both the Sermon on the Mount and the Nicene Creed.[44] The church has often failed children, as have most of the secular organisations and orphanages in particular. It is no surprise that revenge was the main item on the menu when there was no lightning conductor to safety for children or adults.

The Kiribati *maneaba* is crucial to the protection of their culture. The thatched *maneaba* was a sacred house and temple to the sun, serving as a sanctuary for everyone. Even in ancient times, with wars between chiefs, once someone reached a *maneaba* they could not be harmed. Grimble wrote how a young girl could run to the *maneaba* to protest a marriage suggested by her parents. Or a wife could protest some behaviour of her husband. The elders in the *maneaba* took care of everyone. If only my culture had such a safe place for young children to run to and be protected.

My ancestors were well primed British warriors; rather like Tabiteueans who went on their own crusade. The Britons were as ready for religious wars as the North Tabiteueans had been in 1881 and English knights were significant participants throughout the Crusades despite being the farthest European nation from the Holy Land.

We have to thank William the Conqueror for abolishing the export of slaves from Britain. However our ancestors had jumped out of the frying pan into the fire. The Normans introduced the most vicious version of serfdom in Europe. Serfs were still slaves in all but name; and many of them were branded like cattle. The British psyche remembers the Vikings, sometimes with misplaced pride, but we forget easily the victims in our ancestors; those who came for a place of safety and were brutally branded as serfs.

When Martín Prechtel first came to London and stayed at my house, he spent only a couple of minutes dropping his bags in the bedroom before we went out for lunch. Waiting for our food, he told me that he sensed lion cubs and other exotic animals had been looked after in the house. Wondering about this, I checked with my neighbours. They confirmed that, forty years previously, my house was owned by two retired lady veterinarians who regularly took in exotic animals. They remembered the sound of the lion cubs particularly. Martín had sensed something about my home which I had not known about. I was not at all surprised when

---

[44] Leo Tolstoy, *The Kingdom of God is within you*.

he told me later that "I came from a people who struggled with escapes from slavery on the one hand and enslaving behaviour on the other." I turned his comment into a shorthand of the 'Viking and victim' to name this forgotten memory. The discovery of this internal trauma in my mind is described in *Mannership*.

Although both Netflix and Amazon Prime have played rather fast and loose with some historical dates or the possible relations of some British and Viking characters, there is sufficient accuracy to make their retelling of the Viking period compelling. That *The Last Kingdom* and *The Vikings* are of such fascination to their audiences confirms how many of us harbour this history in a part of our minds we cannot reach. Both television series offer a very vivid picture of the extent of the suffering. We make a huge mistake if we believe that this trauma has been cleansed from the British psyche.

We suffered a civil war from 1120 with a period known as 'the Anarchy'. This was one of England's darkest ages when supposed nobles and other marauders raped and pillaged their neighbours' villages. This period of our history is movingly described by Ken Follett's tome: *The Pillars of the Earth*. Sometimes it seems that the Magna Carta could be seen less as an act of brilliance but more as a desperate solution to the mess into which our ancestors had degenerated during the 12th century. Was the Magna Carta an antidote to a psychically violent poison which had to be overcome? We had to 'put a lid on it somehow'. Since that time our island has never been long between wars; often going to look for one when our own shores were not threatened. So perhaps it is not a surprise that the warrior genotype is strongly ingrained in the British Isles. Our small island psyche contains those who were the most determined to escape violence, and thus went to the farthest north-west of Europe to flee; together with the extreme brutality they suffered in their new island home from a mix of many other tribes or invaders who were likewise fleeing and forgetting.

A little later, the British also experienced 'blackbirding' three centuries before the I-Kiribati. Turkish and Moorish pirates raided the English coast to seize natives for sale as slaves in Algiers during the 1500s.

We should not forget the many internal wars against the Welsh and the Scots. There were times when either had the upper hand and could have, perhaps temporarily, colonised all of England. But they got bored and went home. This fury is just under the surface in all sports between

England and the neighbouring Celtic peoples.

One of our mathematicians, Lewis Richardson, made a detailed analysis of the causes of war. Being rather British, he called his work *Statistics of Deadly Quarrels*.

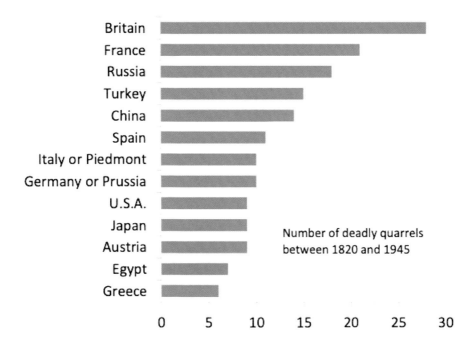

Number of deadly quarrels between 1820 and 1945

His analysis is surprising. This table shows wars between 1820 and 1945, and who was involved among the top 13 participants. Britain was involved in more wars by quite a margin. My knee-jerk reaction was that the number of wars must be skewed by the chosen period coinciding with the height of the British Empire. But analysis of the last five hundred years shows that it is even worse from a British point of view.

Between 1480 and 1945 there were 278 wars around the world. Britain was involved in 78 of them. Again our country is top of the list by quite a distance.

No other nation can compete with Stuart Laycock's analysis; "During its history, British forces or forces with a British mandate have invaded, had some control over or fought conflicts in 171 of the world's 193 countries that are currently UN member states, or nine out of ten of all countries."[45] Some of us are proud. I am deeply shocked.

We can recognise this tribal and warrior behaviour in the way our football clubs are supported. As Neil Jones wrote in 2009, *"the game brings to the surface emotions that don't usually appear in everyday life, the anger, the venom, the vitriol, the bitterness, the greed, the elation, the relief. They are all extremities too. If a ref disallows a perfectly good goal, it's as if he has burgled your shed. If your side secures a late winner, you act like it's the birth of your first child. All conventional logic goes out the window when football is involved."*

The English fans were the worst culprits in terms of what became called 'football hooliganism'. Special trains were made for away supporters without amenities which could be easily destroyed. English fans revelled in their media attention, particularly when it came to looting abroad. As a result English clubs were banned from Europe for five years. It seems that the combination of the warrior and tribal history in our psyche found the ideal outlet in supporting a football club.

Over a few days, after discovering Richardson's table, I asked people on the street at random which country they thought had been involved in more war than any other over the last 2,500 years. Nobody suggested the correct answer - Britain. Clearly we have not been explaining our island history in school. Having mentioned this to Meredith Belbin during one of our delightful chats, he replied, "To gain a more objective view of one's country it is often better to take an outsider's assessment. For committed patriots this can be an agonising activity." I could only smile.

In every century in the last two and a half thousand years, the British have apparently either suffered or sought a hefty dose of warfare. In my early work with Martín Prechtel, one of my tasks was to research my ancestors and collect soil from different ancestral sources. Having my DNA analysed showed my father's side has an 18,000 year old strain from Denmark, whereas my mother's side has an even more ancient strain from Jordan. The feminine line would therefore have struggled through the traumas of tribes like the Hebrews. This realisation was just at the time Martín was teaching me about slavery.

Wrapping my brain around this gave me a picture of a masculine Viking and a feminine Victim. Quite independently, and in a discussion with Martín, my preoccupation had been why feelings of fear sometimes

---

[45] Stuart Laycock *All the Countries We've Ever Invaded: And the Few We Never Got Round To.*

arose when standing on a subway station or on the balcony of a tall building. My fear was 'what might stop me falling or jumping'? He told me, "you come from a people that wrestles with that." I wondered whether this was rare or common. Asking at British psychological conferences how common this was, about 70% of the audience put up their hands. The majority of us may have, in the deep recesses of our minds, both the Viking and the Victim. We 'wrestle with that'. My first therapist Robin Skynner sometimes referred to how the British are drawn to reading stories of rape in the newspapers and then are shocked that the story had been printed. Does this also alert us to the Viking / Victim trauma dynamic in the depths of our mind? Certainly the subject is fuel for many of our film makers, which would not be the case in societies without this aspect in their history.

No wonder it is so hard for the British to metabolise shame. There is too much, and it is too deep. The Confucian teaching to look for our energy next to shame is too hard; too much pain must be navigated.

From my consultancy work in all European countries, there is no doubt that the British public is more 'up for war' than any other in the region. That so many falsified their birth certificates so they could sign up for the First World War at the age of 14 or 15 is an indication. We will revisit this when we come to the chapter on Russia. Nothing can rouse the British psyche towards war more easily than the idea of saving a victim. At the beginning of the Falklands war, it was touch and go whether we should go to war with Argentina or negotiate. But once a few of the English warrior newspapers suggested the faintest possibility that a Falkland's island lady might have been molested, the die was cast. The British public and press would have accepted nothing less than outright war against Argentina. Margaret Thatcher was able to ride this wave, as if she was the lady on the bowsprit of the British fleet. A few months after 'her' victory, she secured a landslide in the June 1983 election. In the autumn of 1981, just a few months before the Argentine invasion, riots in Brixton and Toxteth had made her the least popular Prime Minister in British polling history. She had been facing the greatest loss of support for the conservative party in over a century with a popularity rating of just 23%. Her popularity soared to 59% in less than six months as a result of the Falklands War. Can there be a clearer barometric indicator for the importance of the warrior in the British psyche?

We can acknowledge that this war also became a tipping point for the collapse of a number of South American dictatorships. President Leopoldo Galtieri of Argentina was overthrown within four days of the British victory in the islands. Galtieri's quick departure may have encouraged those who subsequently overthrew the dictators of four Argentine neighbours; Bolivia, Brazil, Paraguay and Uruguay during the following few months and years. This is another aspect of the 'deadly quarrel' we are proud to remember.

Perhaps we can also reflect how we have diverted or sublimated this warrior energy into inventing sports. It is remarkable how many sports the British invented: Badminton, base-ball, cricket, rugby, billiards, snooker, tennis, croquet, darts, modern football, table tennis, golf, bowls, curling, field hockey, squash, and rounders to start with. Although proud of this diversity, the connection to our need to provide an outlet for the warrior energy had not previously been obvious to me. Maybe this is why we have spread our democratic tradition with such fervour. It is a sublimated warrior behaviour turned into a philosophy. However, just like our American cousins, we have preserved the duels in the regular conflict between the Government and the Opposition. Heaven forbid that we should have a coalition like our more evolved European neighbours! But, coalitions have often been successful parts of our history.

There is another aspect we might consider, connected with shame. Imperialism is not just warrior behaviour. There is another aspect which may arise from an inability to metabolise shame, and therefore to look for techniques to avoid shame. One way is superiority or aloofness. Another is to export the shame by humiliating others. Imperialism is an outlet for warrior and tribal behaviour as well as a way to 'export shame'. In their different ways, all European nations who had empires or colonies are guilty of this. By forgetting our past we were doing to others what was done to us. The mantra; 'to do unto others that which you would wish them to do to you', recommended by Christ and Confucius in almost identical words, was trampled underfoot and inverted.

Much of the shame rooted deeply in the British psyche comes from the millennia of slavery and the centuries of serfdom from the arrival of the Normans until abolished in the reign of Elizabeth I in 1574. Is it a coincidence that John Hawkins, the first English slave trader, started our island history of slave ships in 1562 just as British serfdom was coming to an end? Is it possible that warriors and greedy buccaneers who could no longer control slaves or serfs within Britain simply continued their trade abroad?

Not so long ago, at a London event on group psychology, a Chinese presenter mentioned their shame over the opium wars. It was extraordinarily difficult to find any British person attending who could admit our shame about the opium wars. Why is it so hard for us to feel shame for these aspects of our history? Maybe we could help our children by sharing more of the balance of virtue and misdeeds in our history, explaining that shame is normal for a pure heart and should be felt, as Confucius and Gawain in Parzival recommend. Some may feel that we should not - we must keep our pride. But then we have to pay the price of not reaching the *Third Layer*.

Perhaps, this could explain our fascination with the nursery rhyme:

Humpty Dumpty sat on a wall,

Humpty Dumpty had a great fall.

All the king's horses and all the king's men

Couldn't put Humpty together again.

Many historians have suggested this popular rhyme relates to King Richard III who was defeated at Bosworth Field in 1485 or to a siege in the Civil War.[46] But such an interpretation would not cause the rhyme to be so avidly and enduringly absorbed by the British psyche. Why would we care anymore about Bosworth Field or a siege? Nor would such a reference explain the popularity of this rhyme in USA culture. Rather like the nursery rhyme 'Jack and Jill went up the hill', it seems more likely that there is a theme resonating with a deep aspect of British culture.[47] My instincts link the rhyme to a splitting or disassociation in the psyche in order to forget trauma that we do not want to remember. The stiff upper lip could be a consequence, enabling us to dissociate and step back from feelings which might remind us of something... This could be why we struggle to put ourselves together again. Most rhymes and metaphors, as well as some sacred stories, may have begun in history as

---

[46] Some suggest the siege of Gloucester in 1643, others suggest the siege of Colchester in 1648.

[47] The rhyme of Jack and Jill went up the hill to fetch a pail of water is analysed in Mannership. My suggestion is that to fetch a pail of water is a pun for 'arouse a small amount of love'. Just like wells are never found on the top of a hill, the rhyme reminds our culture that we look for love in the wrong places and fall down in despair.

events but endure because of their unconscious connection to forgotten traumas in culture. They hold value as ancestral lessons for us.

As a teenager, meandering over Africa and Asia, I took pride in the realisation that apparently 90% of democratic countries outside Western Europe were former British colonies. I was amused by noting that all countries which had 'democratic' in their name were undemocratic, like the German Democratic Republic or the Democratic Republic of Korea. But, my true education and understanding had not begun. When discussing this subject with Meredith, he suggested, "Imperialism is essentially a raiding and looting society dressed up in noble and patriotic clothing."

Now that we are hopefully going to be involved in less war, the feelings which can be displaced by war will come home to roost. We need to focus instead on the traumas in our own minds and help others struggling with mental illness. This book will consider this in a later chapter, but a major advance would be achieved just by becoming fully aware of the truth. The Brexit saga, in which the island is almost divided down the middle, also reflects our split cultural mind between those who seek safety and a joining with Europe and those with more Viking instincts feeling sure we will manage in our small boats.

There are many aspects of my island culture which are so precious to me that it is necessary to conclude with just a few of them. This small island has produced such creativity and innovation for the benefit of so many, in fields of literature, poetry, theatre, cinema, music, humour, architecture, art, mathematics, science, surgery, medicine and vaccination, nursing, astronomy, philosophy, democracy, economics, finance, insurance and individual freedom to name but a few. We can add our British breakfast, the double decker bus, the London black taxi, a wonderful Queen, great universities, and so much more. None of these are in doubt, nor ever forgotten.

Since 1970 those represented on our banknotes include only one soldier, the Duke of Wellington. Others represented include: Sir Isaac Newton, George Stephenson, Elizabeth Fry, Sir Winston Churchill, Florence Nightingale, Charles Dickens, Charles Darwin, William Shakespeare, Michael Faraday, Sir Edward Elgar, Adam Smith, Sir Christopher Wren, Sir John Houblon, Matthew Boulton, James Watt, Jane Austen and from 2020 the arts will be represented on the £20 note by JMW Turner who was selected from a shortlist also including Barbara Hepworth, Charlie Chaplin, Josiah Wedgewood and William Hogarth.

Perhaps, sometimes we take for granted the precious virtues we share in our legal system, jury system, and our respect for individual freedom. We are also lucky to have a professional and committed army without conscripts, although they are sent to war by our Government rather 'too often'.

Before moving onwards, I wonder if the fact that our island has never had an indigenous population living in harmony with their natural habitat for millennia, while establishing a peaceful understanding with nature, is one of our major disadvantages. The Americas, Asia, Europe and other parts of the world had millennia of settled populations before most of the trouble and strife came.

GENOTYPES

Before discussing the USA, one of Meredith Belbin's paradigms provided me with short-hand to compare genetic aspects of cultures. During Meredith's research at Henley Business School on 'team roles' he discovered five main clusters or types of behaviour. He explained this thinking originated in his teenage years.

Meredith was at school in Sevenoaks, Kent, when the Second World War began. As soon as the Luftwaffe flew overhead on their way to bomb London, his father evacuated the family to the west of London. Meredith continued his education at the Royal Grammar School in High Wycombe where the Headmaster, E.R. Tucker, was a jolly Welshman and taught Latin. Tucker had ambitions for his pupils to win Classical scholarships at Oxford or Cambridge.

Meredith continued the story of his last school year. *There were three of us studying Classics; Roy Fredericks or 'Freddie', handsome, ginger, musical, highly talented, and lazy. Freddie had a way of always landing on his feet. With a loving mother, and later a loving wife, he was called up for military service and gained an immediate commission in the army. Classics and music must have done the trick for him to be seen as a potential Chinese interpreter. The other was Patrick Scally, son of a railway worker; he proved an amazingly brilliant scholar in all subjects.*

Tucker arranged for us three to go to Oxford for coaching from his old academic tutor, Pop Seymour. Seymour was an Australian with evident mixed race aboriginal features. This Oxford tuition set us on a road for life. Seymour would talk about issues in Ancient Greece, forbade us to take notes and then set us a demanding essay title. Back at school we rushed to find answers by looking up the authoritative volumes of Cambridge Ancient History. Finding little to help us, we had to develop our own intellect. This investment in our future produced an early reward when Patrick Scally won the top prize which Tucker had set his mind on, a Classical scholarship at Balliol College Oxford.

I think this showed how diverse we humans are. From our early years, whatever our upbringing, it would seem we are destined to move in our own unique directions. It is a lesson frequently borne out in large families, and a generator of surprises. Reflecting on Seymour's amazing combination of characteristics and on what I later learned in my favourite pastime as a gardener in hybridising plants, I began to realise humans too are hybrids. The mixing of different ethnic groups increases the range of outcomes in their progeny. We humans, it would seem, are all subject to the inexorable laws of nature.

Our genes interact with other genes from our forebears and with the culture in which we are raised. Yet there is a pattern that emerges. Appropriate behaviour is the key to human success and survival. In the case of animals, particular body forms evolved to facilitate given types of survival behaviour – fur, feathers, claws and so on. In the case of modern humans, there is nothing comparable; body forms are unrelated to behaviour. That is why particular behavioural genotypes are so important for us to recognise.

The first genotype which Meredith suggested was '**primordial**'. My early teenage wanderings, and my time in the Pacific Ocean, had introduced me to the behaviour of those who carry our foundation, our relationship to nature and the environment. We agreed some other characteristics; nomadic and peaceful, spiritual continuity with the deceased, the extended family at the centre of social organisation, equality of gender, feelings and thoughts interlocked and inseparable, belief and respect for the forces of nature, and people seen as belonging to the land rather than owning the land.

Meredith suggested that the second genotype was '**tribal**' with institutional practices, dances, and chanting creating a sense of togetherness. The development of religion contributed to a fixed belief about the world while serving to bond the community through language and thought. A tribe might become dedicated to a territory and a fuller development of the resources. Typically, a tribe would have a chief with elders in decision-making roles.

His third genotype was '**warrior**'. This did not need much explanation. Meredith volunteered some particular characteristics: addiction to war, plunder and rape, a society valuing glory and heroes, kings becoming supreme rulers in alliance with a priestly hierarchy, dominance over marriage and procreation, goddesses replaced by gods, personal greed and ambition, women reduced to subordinates and mistresses, punishment meted out on the basis of power.

The fourth genotype was '**service**' and included acceptance of the status quo, respect for a key religious figure or doctrine, loyalty to those in more senior ranks, help and sympathy towards those in need.

Finally, the fifth genotype which Meredith called '**civic**' included a democratic elite leading to civic government, philosophy restricting any single religious monopoly, values including ethics and education, debating of issues, writing for spreading ideas and facilitating learning, a cosmopolitan and tolerant culture, and wealth from trade or entrepreneurial class.

Meredith explained how the civic genotype manifested in some of the earliest cities which were spin-offs from larger tribal groups. These early pioneers were inventive, had a wider philosophic outlook, and a capacity for civic administration. Becoming merchants was a short transition from these strengths. As a result, small cities became significant players in the known world. The spread of their fame attracted like-minded settlers.

We both recognised our preferences for the civic genotype, but Meredith surprised me as he had also developed a test or a questionnaire which enabled him to understand an individual's 'constructs' or behavioural thinking. I took the test immediately and was not surprised by the result. He found I was an absolute zero on the tribal genotype, with strong preferences for primordial and civic. He mused that, as a result, indigenous societies would have trusted me.

I liked the simplicity of Meredith's paradigm and immediately saw how these ideas could connect with Michael Meade's three layers. Meredith asked me to explain more, so I organised five 'stones' in the form of a Roman classical three. I suggested that the primordial was the foundation and base, the 'third layer'. The top was like a lid with the civic

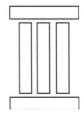 genotype and the 'first layer'. Between these two horizontals were tribal, warrior and service behaviours. I have to confess to my reader that the choice of title for this book includes the Roman writing for 'three' to recognise and combine Meredith's contribution to my thinking, the third question on the subject of self-destruction, as well as Meade's three layers.

As a test, we chose a dozen major countries of the world and agreed, before we met next, that we would write down the percentage mix for each of these five behaviours in a sample of twelve countries. While 'doing my homework', I thought about my feelings and instincts on my travels to these nations. I weighed them up using my 'deaf-sight' observations. When we met again and compared notes, our scores for each country were almost identical. The simplicity of Meredith's idea thus appealed to me. But, I was curious about how he had come up with his scores and asked him to explain his percentages for Britain, the shared island of our birth. Meredith's reply and our discussion follows:

Meredith: *As a rough guess my percentage would be perhaps 20% for primordial, 30% for warrior, and 30% for tribal. Then I put service probably about 15%. Finally for civic, I think we're talking about 8% or something like that. I tell you what gives me a numerical feeling regarding this – when I go to a newsagent, I look at the height of stacks of newspapers they've got, and you can see the percentages there.*

Mark: *Which newspapers do you associate with which genotype?*

Meredith: *Well I associate the Times, the Independent and the Guardian with the civic.*

Mark: *What about the Sun?*

Meredith: *Well, it's definitely not civic. I think it's a combination of primordial and tribal. They try to make everybody, even a celebrity, seem a member of your family. It reads as though discussing a member of your family. The whole front page is taken over with an association of somebody you've never heard of.*

Mark: *Which is the biggest warrior newspaper?*

Meredith: *I think the Telegraph has been traditionally on the warrior side.*

Mark: *I agree. They often refer to 'Great British wars' as if they are magnificent in the eyes of the Telegraph. I remember a picture of the Crimean War of the 1850s with a headline saying something like: "The War that made Britain Great." It is hard to think of anything which was 'great' about the Crimean war apart from the invention of the sandwich and the balaclava... and Florence Nightingale of course. This is the only major land war in which Russians and British fought against each other directly. We suffered enormous losses such as in the charge of the Light Brigade. I was going to say, for me, a newspaper which is both warrior and primordial could be the Communist Morning Star.*

Meredith: *Yes, you have a point there. Bear in mind, when you look for the warrior genotype, a point is to see who your enemies are. A lot of the newspapers try to pillory a certain group. That's the real warrior stuff.*

Mark: *The Daily Express?*

Meredith: *You could say that. It has exhibited its warrior genotype in a big way with the crusader shield that has long been its emblem. With a xenophobic touch it can pick on some groups of people, like immigrants and sometimes foreigners. The emblem is a reminder of the Crusade directed against the Islamic inhabitants of Palestine and remarkable for the brutality and 'un-Christian' treatment of opponents. Of course the image of the paper does not detract from some of the worthwhile articles and treatment of news.*

Mark: *The image of an Express is very warrior like. It reminds me of fast trains or fast horses. I can see how the genotypes are written in the symbols and names of newspapers. This evidence is right under our noses every day. I realise that we walk alongside without noticing until you mentioned this. What would you choose as a service newspaper?*

Meredith: *I think the service newspapers are the ones tagging on to celebrity. I know what used to be a service newspaper, it's no longer there now, and it used to be the Daily Sketch. A service paper usually follows Royalty.*

Mark: *I was thinking of Hello magazine.*

Meredith: *Yes, adulation of royalty and a focus on the very personal issues of celebrities brings them into the family, so to speak. And of course that magazine has a massive circulation. If we examine the big circulation publications the one thing they have little room for are the interests of the civic genotype.*

Mark: *My favourite newspaper is The Economist which is almost pure civic.*

Our meandering conversation, after a short pause for another Lapsang souchong tea, reminded Meredith of his time at Clare College, Cambridge. He continued: *The crest of my College is testimony to the founder, Lady Clare, the beneficiary of a large fortune bequeathed by two successive husbands who had embarked on the crusades: hence the cross on the right. The surrounding tears represent grief at her losses. Rather than backing another expedition, Lady Clare used the proceeds of her legacy to fund education for poor scholars. I can well imagine Lady Clare's husbands were fired by the warrior genotype whereas she was actuated by the civic genotype.*

The split of Meredith's genotypes for Britain served as a very useful paradigm which helped me to explain differences in the settlers who went west over the Atlantic.

European Settlers in America

Meredith was very keen to learn, since my deafness made me such a sharp observer, what stood out for me in the United States of America. Having reminded him that over half of my career included working for an American company, he cautioned me *not to present the USA through rose tinted spectacles. After all, you lived in New York, you married an American and your daughter Alika has maintained strong links there. Should I feel the need to restore the balance I will say so bearing in mind there is so much on which we agree.* I concurred and valued his shared insights.

Unlike Britain, the USA does have indigenous populations.

The first peoples came from West Asia, skipping over the northern edge of the Pacific Ocean at the time of a wide bridge between Siberia and Alaska, called Beringia, maybe as long ago as 40,000 years. There is evidence of people living in the 'bluefish caves', northern Yukon Territory of Canada, from 24,000 years ago. The Central Asians may have spent 8,000 years in Beringia until the North American ice melted. They continued south into a habitat of bison with tallgrass prairies and forests many millennia old. Quite quickly these peoples spread throughout the Americas. Some new theories are emerging that the habitation of America may have been even earlier.

Reading such ancient histories remind me of the first Pacific migrations, with peoples who had spent a few thousand years on Buka Island, about 32,000 years ago. My heart opens towards them just like my first adventure into the Gilbert Islands. But a chill and a shudder shakes me while remembering what both peoples suffered from European interference. In the last five hundred years, waves of Indo-Europeans swarmed to invade or colonise American lands until over three quarters of the population were of European descent at the time when my course first took me 'over there'.

During a variety of careers in different parts of the globe, more of my life has been spent in North America than anywhere else. My knowledge of the American Indian cultures is sadly far too limited to be able to contribute to this chapter. However, I cannot continue without acknowledging my greatest debt to some of those who migrated from Asia, over the bridge of Beringia, to the Americas. The American Indian traditions have been crucial to enliven my existence. At the age of forty, a Native American initiation opened my eyes to dimensions and aspects of myself I had not seen before. The elders guided me towards an understanding of how my mind was obstructing me from feeling or seeing clearly, teaching the origins of some of my fears. Without this experience I might never have been interested in shamanic traditions nor discovered sufficient depths in my mind to make the journey described in *Mannership*.

This chapter primarily concerns my observation of descendants of Indo-European settlers and invaders who overran much of the indigenous population just as they had done throughout Europe. In particular, the differences between Europeans who chose to settle in America and those they left behind are easier to understand.

After my return from the Gilbert Islands, I attended a London interview with an American management consulting company. They were tickled by the idea of recruiting a former British colonial officer and offered me a position to start the following Monday. My work was initially in Europe. However, a few years later, I was directed to analyse a beef abattoir in Fort Morgan, an hour's drive east of Denver. My task was to look carefully to see what could be 'improved'. I imagined that 'looking carefully' should be easy enough and my curiosity was excited. Never having seen an abattoir before, there was much to learn. This first real experience of America was fascinating. My eyes lit up with the space they had, and the width of the roads.

One of my first discoveries was that they had over 100% staff turnover. I wondered how they managed. Apparently many employees worked for nine months or so and then left for a few weeks before coming back. The turnover was therefore perhaps not as dramatic as I had imagined, but the idea intrigued me. Most of the 'new staff' was former employees. This seemed odd, and was rather different from any experience in Europe.

I wondered what they were all 'up to' during their periods away. Were they harvesting a crop? But the times of year didn't correlate. Having bumped into a few former employees in a bar one evening, I asked them with my typical open curiosity and eagerness to understand. They expressed their views in different ways, but overall the main reason was that they did not want to feel as if they were owned by a company. A break from employment affirmed their independence even if financially disadvantageous. After a few weeks or months off they went back. Immediately a link with the first European settlers came to mind. A different way of thinking, among those who had migrated, had persisted. They had strong drives to be seen to be free. While discussing more, there were similarities in how much more easily they accepted being 'fired', or having their employment terminated. They did not take this as personally as a European would. Instead, they moved on more easily and didn't seem to suffer the same 'stigma'. Digesting these early discoveries led me to conclude they were less 'attached' to their employer. Just like the settlers who had abandoned their life in Europe and set off to start afresh without knowing where this might lead. They trusted their own energy and were less attached to their tribe. That adventurousness is thus part of their psyche and not entirely unknown to me either. Was that why, during my interview, the American consultancy company had stressed I could leave whenever I wanted? An employer in Europe would not think to remind someone of this freedom while hiring them.

I did not have the benefit of Meredith's paradigm of five genotypes at the time. But, looking back, I can now see that the mainstream of settlers going west over the Atlantic would have been lower on the 'tribal' category; less attached to a group. Except, of course, the small groups of settlers who migrated together specifically to enable them to maintain their own religious beliefs separately from others.

My consultancy employer had a strict formula for the two week analysis period. The first week consisted of analysing the factory for opportunities. These were to be presented to the factory manager on the Friday to see if he was interested in the early findings. If so, we could prepare a plan of engagement during the second week of findings. In Fort Morgan, many possible improvements were soon found in productivity, organisation and in the yield of meat. On the Wednesday, according to my checklist, I met the factory manager briefly to advise how the work was proceeding and to reconfirm the Friday presentation, but he told me he had decided to go fishing and would not be available.

At first I was shocked, having had a clear commitment to present everything to him on the Friday. Not easily deterred, I asked him where he was going fishing. It turned out to be roughly a five hour drive north into Wyoming. So I said, *"Ok. Then I will drive over there and present my findings to you while you are fishing."* It was his turn to be surprised. He agreed and we arranged to meet in his fishing cabin on the Friday morning. I remember thinking this would not happen in Europe.

I spent all of the Thursday night making my charts. This was long before Microsoft and Excel so thin strips of colour had to be cut with a knife and glued to cardboard to make my graphs. Once complete, the visual presentation was dramatic and showed clearly the improvements which could be made, together with my estimate of financial gains. In the morning over coffee the factory manager listened attentively. He was excited by the potential and delayed his fishing. He said the results were so unexpected that we should present them to all of the shareholders on the following Tuesday; they would be impressed.

There were not many shareholders, less than half a dozen, and they all lived locally so came readily. During the shareholders' meeting, the same charts were presented. From the interest and questions, I was certain to obtain my first assignment, or so I thought. Then, they asked me to excuse myself while they discussed among themselves. But a shocking and complete surprise came next. After half an hour, one of the shareholders came out to thank me for my presentation. He said that they were very shocked by the amount of improvements and even more shocked that the factory manager had not known. If there was that much which could be improved, he should have known. So they had fired him on the spot.

I was transfixed. This was completely out of the blue. The shareholders decided to find a better manager and my first American assignment would have to be somewhere else. While driving to Denver airport, I reflected that this would not have happened in Europe. The speed of the decision was a surprise, and the immediacy, for something which wasn't exactly a felony. This was my first exposure to something else very American; complete and instant ownership of decisions with the action that follows. They say that the worst decision you can make is not to make one. Americans are quicker than Europeans to make decisions.

Perhaps early European settlers self-selected as the more decisive and entrepreneurial ones, as well as fast thinkers. Rather like how the Pacific Ocean favoured good navigators.

The following week, my second analysis in a bank taught me something different. Their head office was in Chicago and while meeting with the Chairman on a Monday morning we agreed to choose a pilot area to explore in more detail. He selected a branch in Phoenix and gave me the address. At this time I was busier and managing two 'analysis' assignments in parallel. A colleague went to Phoenix for the ground work. We made a plan, deciding exactly what we should look at and what we needed to accomplish before meeting the Chairman again on Friday morning to present our findings.

Everything started well. My colleague flew to Phoenix and began the detailed analysis. He set about the task very diligently, telephoning me each lunch-time and in the evening to report back or for advice. Listening to his discoveries, everything seemed to be going very smoothly. I was excited to share my first impressions of the opportunities at a brief meeting with the Chairman on the Wednesday afternoon.

The Chairman was very polite and sharp. The meeting began with my excitement of my colleagues' discoveries. At first, the Chairman seemed very interested in my detailed explanations of what we had found. I told him how helpful his staff had been. But then he interrupted me quite politely to say that we had a problem. He had telephoned the branch manager just before he came in to have some feedback of his own. The branch manager said nobody had been to visit his branch. I couldn't believe it. I worried that my colleague might have made everything up, but the findings were all so clear and well presented.

The Chairman was very kind, and as surprised as I was. He knew we hadn't made it all up. We investigated together by calling my colleague in Phoenix. We learned he had walked into a branch of a bank across the street, a branch that belonged to a competitor. I was astounded. Naturally I could not present any more of the findings and that prospect collapsed at once. This was very embarrassing.

Just like after Denver, this taught me another interesting aspect of the American culture. How trusting they are of a stranger. At the time I remember thinking to myself this could not have happened outside America. The error was my colleague's but his error was compounded by the openness and willingness of the competitor's branch manager to share his information with a consultant who came in with confidence, even without clearance from head office. I learned that an American is much more trusting of a stranger than the European, especially one with an air of self-confidence. Of course this could not happen now in the current climate of internet and email, but the difference with Europe is still there.

My learning curve in American business was rather steep. Perhaps, not being tribal, I share a few of the settler American traits which helped me to understand the culture quickly. I also have an above average interest in adventures together with a trust of strangers which might be why I felt at home with an American executive.

As the weeks went by, and while working for many global companies, I noticed that factory managers in America had a lower limit of financial authority than their European counterparts which seemed a paradox. I wondered if the American factory manager was, by nature, so much more independent that stricter controls were felt to be needed by corporate bosses. Maybe the European factory managers would be less likely to do something entrepreneurial as they were more tribal. There was less need to have a European manager on a leash.

The 1980 American census highlighted that almost half of American ancestry came from England, Ireland, Scotland and Wales. Having observed both sides of the Atlantic closely led me to re-examine why the settlers had left Europe in the hope that this might explain the clear differences between Europe and those settlers who had travelled to North America.

Some have suggested that many of the first settlers were driven by a desire to escape religious persecution. However, this may be an over-simplification. Many were Protestant Puritans from a Protestant United Kingdom. Perhaps they were not seriously persecuted but just wanted more. Their beliefs were more demanding than the Government. At the time, England was publishing the King James Bible and Protestantism was the religion of the majority. The British Parliament was liberated by the Puritan army of Oliver Cromwell. The Puritans could have strengthened the English 'revolution'. But they didn't. It was not moving far enough or fast enough for them. Many set off with a drive to create their own 'Kingdom of Heaven' on earth, something 'purer' than the country they left behind. Irrespective of their reasons, the only certainty is that most of the first settlers *chose* to go to America. They 'self-selected'. They felt able to empower themselves to create a 'better world'. Their faith was very strong, in every sense. They thought differently from those they left behind and were able to abandon their roots easily. They were not high on the 'tribal index'. Their own convictions were much stronger than their faith in the Government of their day. This aspect of relationship to Government persists in modern America and may explain a part of the gun ownership culture, as if they want to be their own Government. My observation was how Americans had a much greater dislike of Government than other advanced economies. When their Government is grid-locked, many are delighted. Some feel this gives them the freedom to get on with their lives, that part of their origins is still with them.

Like cream floating on milk, there are discernible differences between the psyche of those who sailed across the Atlantic and those they left behind. They were less tribal and initially less 'warrior like' except with warrior fervour for their faith. They had greater faith and self-belief. This difference is still visible in war and football. In terms of war, the American public are not 'up for the fight' in the way the British are. Often, in British history, the people pushed the Government towards war. In the USA, the public has less appetite for foreign wars. Americans attending a British football match are surprised by the extent to which rival fans need to be separated. For them the supporters can be all jumbled up while enjoying a more social outing.

The statistics for American 'faith' were extraordinary. Almost 90% professed affiliation to a faith. But the surprise is that more than a quarter of adults in the USA have changed the faith in which they were raised for another. If we include the different branches of Christianity, then over 40% of adults have switched religious affiliation. This is not just freedom, but also a very competitive religious marketplace; a free market in religion. Four out of every ten Americans have married someone of a different faith. These statistics are unique for a nation, suggesting both their strength of faith as well as the sense of individual empowerment in choice of faith. Americans have greater ease to choose their faith which may have underpinned why many settlers risked their lives to travel there.

The freedom Americans feel to travel across state boundaries to look for work mirrors their self-selection. Their ancestors had been able to 'up sticks' and move across the Atlantic. In the creation of the European Union, the assumption was that Europeans would do the same, at least partly. But the average European psyche is much more attached to their physical and tribal roots. It is harder to leave countries with high unemployment like Spain or Greece to seek work in Germany or the Netherlands. That aspect of the European project could not overcome the headwinds of minds.

Those with self-belief, faith and a sense of empowerment in America grew in wealth rapidly. They were free of the constraints in the more tribal and traditional European society that their ancestors emerged from. It is completely beyond me to address the different attitudes of the new settlers to the indigenous Indian populations. Some settlers initially developed excellent relationships with local Indian tribes. But, books like *Bury My Heart at Wounded Knee* remind me of the atrocities. Meredith's view was that, whilst lower on the 'tribal' genotype, the 'warrior' element was strong and this underscores the continuing gun culture. Perhaps some settlers were taking their 'running away from ancient traumas' to greater extremes; they were guilty of humiliating more indigenous people just as their ancestors had done centuries before in Europe. Their faith was no obstacle to enslaving or benefitting from slavery. Those settlers had no interest in benefitting from Native Indian knowledge and cooperation in a territory which had enough land for both; they simply wanted to take everything the Indians had. Just like some of the early Viking invaders arriving in Britain.

As I learned in the chapter on Britain, my island caught, in a giant north-west European fishing net, those who were the most determined to escape the ancient traumas of slavery. Ireland was similar in this respect, even if less imperial as a consequence. Those who continued west by sea to the Americas seem like a self-selected group of Indo-European carriers *'forgetting what they were running away from'*.

Two centuries after the first settlers, many others arrived fleeing more immediate struggles. Some were escaping either religious or other Governmental persecution. Others were seeking a better life for economic reasons or, more recently, Central Americans escaping violence. They all severed their links and abandoned their country to seek a better world for themselves. This 'self-selection' in the gene pool is an unique aspect of the USA as no other major country in modern world history has been created in the same way.

Charles Darwin reminded us that selection is much faster than evolution. My observations were that the settler genotype pool was different than the land of their origins because of their self-selection. Whereas Britain was primarily 'warrior tribal', the USA settlers were more 'warrior civic'. They were much lower in the tribal and primordial categories.

Remembering my consultancy work since the late '70s, there were other differences in the USA which were obvious to me. Perhaps the European history of nobility had left us with a greater acceptance of 'power distance' in organisations. By contrast, the most successful early settlements of immigrants, like the Massachusetts Bay Company, were led by the best organiser irrespective of rank.[48] The idea of meritocracy has been established in the American culture since four hundred years. Americans have a more natural tendency to ask the craftsmen rather than assuming that, as managers, they should know. A European manager feels he should know more and is less open to the views of the craftsmen. I was often struck, when visiting an American factory, how the factory manager was not only in jeans like everyone else but also how it was not immediately obvious who was in charge. The American manager has less need to set himself apart. At the other extreme, in France for example, there would never be any doubt who was the boss even before anybody spoke.

It was not uncommon for a potential American client to try some aspect of my suggestions after just a first meeting of discussion. Many would try something in one area of their factory to experiment whereas their European counterpart wanted to know much more before trying anything. To give an analogy, if an American manager met someone in a bar who said he was a decorator, he would be more likely to size up the decorator and invite him to paint one room of the house to see how it looked before deciding to do more. Thus, they take more immediate risks but the risk is measured instinctively.

The relationship to envy is almost opposite between Europe and America. In Europe envy tends to be destructive, whereas in America it leads more often to admiration and emulation. I remember fondly a teaching of my group therapist, Lionel Kreeger. Lionel was a truly wonderful man, very warm and kind. He wrote a paper called "envy pre-emption" in which he illustrated how cultures with destructive envy found ways to pre-empt the feeling. In early history they might wear

[48] This is very well described in *The Puritan Gift* by Kenneth and William Hopper.

something to protect against the '*evil eye*', or in our British culture we would be sure to be self-deprecatory before saying something which might appear grand. But the American can be the opposite. They have no difficulty in being proud of their achievements in public because the relationship to envy in their culture is different to ours.

Another aspect, which is unique to the USA, is their religious tolerance. It is hard to recall a religious fight in North America like the many we have suffered throughout much of European history. The early settlers fanned out with many different religions, or variants, and were able to establish their own traditions. If we take the example of Pennsylvania and the Amish; the roads are widened with a lane marked for the horse drawn buggies. It is hard to think of another country which has gone out of their way to make as much room for religious diversity.

However, this tolerance of religious diversity did not, for some reason, apply to Native Indian traditions and boundaries. The relationship between settlers and Indians was initially very good in many cases. They traded, shared and helped each other. Indian tribes taught some settlers how to survive. Many more would have perished without Indian help. In some areas, like the Quakers in Pennsylvania, they had excellent relations with the Indian tribes initially. I am unable to explain the trigger for everything falling apart; this is beyond my imagination. Was it provoked by settlers who felt they had a 'God given right' to the land instead of cooperating? Is there a possibility that the Indo-European unconscious hunger for the 'third layer' was too great for them to examine within themselves when meeting a truly indigenous population? That it was easier for many to murder and destroy than to acknowledge the hunger for what they had lost? If so, we will have to conclude that their spiritual jealousy had overtaken them. Was this a repeat of the Indo-European destruction of all indigenous society in Europe? Were the Indo-European settlers unable to handle their shame and thus turned to violence?

Lastly, in this chapter, the relationship to foreign wars has a different evolution in America. Although many of the first settlers came from the most warrior Indo-European group, there has generally been much less public appetite for foreign wars. Between American Independence and 1945 they were not very aggressive outside their own borders, and certainly much less than any British ancestry. During my work in North America it was very clear how the US population is much less supportive of wars than the British public. The US did not join the first or second World Wars initially and came in much later. Without the Japanese attack at Pearl Harbor, it is not certain that they would have joined at all. Once victorious they were more magnanimous in victory than any nation in history has ever been. Look at how much they gave to enable Germany and Japan to rebuild. This 'civic' aspect of their culture is unparalleled in history.

When we look at what has happened since 1945 it is a different story as if the attack at Pearl Harbor changed the American psyche. The end of the Second World War seems to have spooked paranoia about communism. This brought their warrior genotypes to the fore in Government. With the benefit of hindsight, we can see now that they had little need to be paranoid about communism but it did not look that way to them throughout the Cold War. Between 1945 and 9/11, roughly half of American conflicts overseas can be attributed to a fear of communism.

We could reflect that, without the paranoia of communism, the Americans would never have armed the Afghans against Russia. In so doing they poured petrol on the fire of Kandahar and inadvertently helped a group that later became so wickedly distorted against them in Al Qaeda. Americans are tired of the re-enactment of the expeditions of Alexander the Great. After all, the wars they have fought since 1945 have not been so successful. One of the few successes is Grenada where American intervention restored democratic government.

The real challenge for America is her relationship to China. My experiences of China taught me that the American fear is misplaced.

CHINA

When Lewis Richardson first made his detailed analysis of *Deadly Quarrels*, he was very surprised. The statistics showed how much China stood out by her relative absence from war. Particularly when he realised that China was bigger than Europe and had been involved in less war than most minor European states. He spent a lot of time researching the matter before arriving at a number of conclusions.

Richardson identified three factors. Firstly, he put his finger on the *vigorous original thought of Lao Tzu, Confucius, Mozi, Mencius* and other Chinese philosophers concerned with how to arrange society for a successful life.

Secondly, he suggests their philosophical thought was made into a system. *Confucianism believed that human society could prosper only as men preserved right relations to each other and to the universe. Ethics was stressed.* He observed that their philosophy involved *leading by the example of the ruling classes rather than by force.* He concluded that, in China, the integrity of the culture persisted *even if the structure of the state was disrupted.*

Thirdly, he stressed the very competitive examinations on the Confucian classics which were a requirement for a bureaucrat. Thus, Richardson found strong reasons for a conscious adoption of culture. Perhaps the British might feel they have done something similar with democracy and the civil service. Maybe, but we cannot ignore our history of warfare. Nor can we ignore how many Indo-European nationals followed their rulers out of an expectation of personal gain, like a dukedom, following success in battle. Winning in Britain is associated with battles.

Since 2004, having had the honour to deliver five leadership courses in each of China and Russia, a number of other forces encouraging cultural difference came to my attention. On my first trip to Russia, just like many other countries, there was a little white disembarkation form to be filled in. There were the usual questions: name and date of birth; passport number; the fact that you're a tourist; where you're going to stay and so on. It's basically the same information the world over. But this form was only in Russian. Each time the stewardess passed me, I asked her what each section was and she'd reply 'first name' and so on. It took almost all the flight to fill the form with a little help each time she passed my seat. On arrival in Moscow, at the immigration desk and having handed over the form to a lady immigration officer who spoke English, I said quite innocently: "I hope I've filled it in correctly because it's only in Russian." Without a missing a beat, she said, "If you go to the United States it's only in English." Her response surprised me and I wanted to laugh but thought that unwise; she clearly had not meant her response to be a joke.

On my first visit to China, a factory manager said to me, "One of the difficulties we have is that not many of our operators speak English, so it's not easy for them to benchmark with some of the creative things that are being done by operators elsewhere in the world. We've decided to teach all the operators English, then they can better learn from what's going on outside." In the West, we have issues with 'theft of intellectual property'. However, the world benefits from sharing our discoveries. There is a balance which lies somewhere between Chinese and Western aspirations, a balance between benefits for the world or benefits for a few.

My first impression of China was how they are such avid absorbers. With more than eight million university graduates a year, this can only increase. A visit to a modern factory in Inner Mongolia surprised me. Almost every shop-floor employee seemed to have a university degree; just imagine that. They are hardly going to forget all they learned about the world at large while producing products. The factory looked more like a James Bond film set. I remember explaining my error in having imagined the source of strength of China was in the size of their population and their great history, but now they had taught me how advanced they were in some managerial respects. But a new challenge for China is labour mobility; now the young are changing careers much faster; just like the West.

There are many other independent factors which have influenced the Chinese culture over millennia. Richardson's list is useful but quite incomplete. China has been better protected geographically since ancient times. She has a desert border to the north and to the west; a Himalayan 'fence' to the south and a sea moat to the East. There is no surprise that her name means the 'Middle Kingdom'. Her ability to retreat, into the centre of the Middle Kingdom, when threatened has given her a place of safety against many aggressors over the millennia. Unlike Britain, she has not suffered as many incursions with new warrior genes. Also, with a much greater population, any warrior invasions have had a more diluted 'pollution effect' on the genetics. Meredith also taught in China. We both agreed that the Han Chinese are very low on the scale of 'warrior genotypes'. They are not an aggressive people.

Chinese history of slavery has very important differences from the Indo-European traumas. The Shang Dynasty in the second millennium BCE raided surrounding states for slaves. A few dynasties allowed slavery on a small scale, or as punishment for a crime, but were followed by a dynasty which abolished the practice. Slavery does not appear to have been widespread and generally affected a small percentage of the population. That the records show regular pronouncements against slavery or oppressive serfdom, for which many European populations would have been grateful, highlight the frequent distaste for this subject among Chinese Emperors. Some laws forbade enslaving free people, but allowed enslavement of criminals and foreigners.

A significant difference in Chinese history is found in the relationship of her people to Government. Four thousand years ago, following the great flood of the Yellow and Yangtze Rivers, a recovery required major works which may be the basis for their first traditional dynasty, the Xia dynasty, with Emperor Yu. Like in Kiribati, a chief is sometimes needed, in times of disaster or war, whether the challenge comes from other people or Mother Nature. Whereas an individual can hunt and attack, major flood works require teamwork and an organiser. Yu the Great was famous for organising the digging of canals and teaching others how to manage the flood waters. Some have suggested that his success was a basis for Confucius' leadership system. There seems little doubt that confidence in great works undertaken by Government is another hallmark of the Chinese psyche.

Confucius was born, around 550 BCE, in an era when private ownership of land had already begun. Traces of slavery were on the decline together with a limit of Government taxation to one ninth of the crop yield, which is manageable. There is another force influencing the cultural trends in China; the power of the rice plant.

During my experience of tropical farming with Booker Tate, we grew many crops in twenty-six countries. But the plant which stands out is rice. To put her in perspective, one could say all other plants are like grazing herds, but rice is like a child. Knowing that the rice plant would have her place in the journey of this book, I took the opportunity for a 'refresher course' on rice culture during my last visit to my oldest friend, Bahu in Sri Lanka. We walked together into the paddy fields in Mangalagame district to speak with two farmers, Premaratne and Gunadasa. With Bahu interpreting, I asked the farmers to pretend they were teaching me to grow rice from no knowledge.

They began; "First of all, the earth must be very moist but with no standing water when the seeds are planted. The preparation is critical. The mud must stay like this for the first seven days. The seeds need to germinate in moist mud but standing water drowns them. This is why you have to start with a nursery as you cannot maintain the conditions over all your land area. The nursery ground is like a safe and soft place for the infant's arrival. Then, on the 7th day, once the first shoots have sprouted, you must add an inch of water until the 9th day when the water level must be reduced to half an inch."

I asked them to remind me the reason for this ritual, the lowering of the water level. They continued; "initially you need the water depth because the young plant needs a lot to drink. But more than half an inch encourages water borne insects and crabs that attack the young plants. So, for the next 25 days the water must be raised to 2 inches and then lowered to help the plant drink but avoid attacks. We cannot have standing water. The water must be almost completely drained out before refilling the paddy."

 Since this book is not a treatise on rice growing, we should skip the detailed checklist and jump to the effects of rice on a culture. There is a Japanese proverb saying there are 88 steps to grow a rice crop. In the proverb, the Chinese character for rice (米 kome) is composed by two eights (八 hachi) and ten (十 jū) which makes eighty-eight (八十八 hachi-jū-hachi), eight – ten – eight, 88.

'Aththam': Planting out the young rice plants throughout the paddy fields, Sri Lanka

Returning to the farmers' interview, I asked if they agreed that there is no other plant that needs as much continuous care. Immediately they agreed joyously. They said, "planting rice is like raising a child." We invited them up to Bahu's house for tea while continuing the conversation and my recollections of the effect of rice on a culture. They added, "you cannot grow rice without an interchange of labour with your neighbours." Bahu volunteered how rice had given rise to a concept called *aththam* in Sri Lanka which translates literally as *holding each other's hand*. The rice plant obliges everyone to ask for help on the days when there is much to do, and then to offer the assistance to your neighbour during his challenges when the month old plants are transferred from the dense nursery to be spread across the paddy field.

A memory of a conversation with Sobonfu Somé came to me. She had described her village in Burkina Faso, with the Dagara tribe, and told me how a parent would not worry if their two-year-old infant went missing for a couple of days. They knew that someone else in the village would be looking after them. Just contrast that with our society. These early farming cultures had such strong mutual support of watching each other's children and each other's rice. Thousands of years of the rice plant domesticating the culture has influenced the evolution of their psyche, leading to ethics and family support. One needs neighbours to warn when a paddy field must be drained or watered. Everybody watches over the paddy of everyone else. There is a manual on rice growing in China that is over 3,000 years old, if my memory is not playing tricks on me. Perhaps this is one of the reasons why, in China, the unit is the family rather than the individual. Property belongs to a family and not to an individual in Chinese law.

During the many conversations in Meredith's warm conservatory overlooking his garden, there were few subjects on which we agreed more than the future of China. Having both lectured and taught leadership there, we had noticed two trends; a move towards a more consensual society and a return of Confucian Institutes. We also agreed, because China has so few periods of external aggression in the last four millennia, that neither of us felt threatened by a more powerful China. On the contrary, we welcomed this development.

My observations suggested that the Chinese would eventually look back on the communist period as an experiment. Like an American President glossing over his experimentation with cannabis as a student. Perhaps they will be thankful that communism was just a chapter and in 50 years' time think about this phase as one of their life experiences. But they will not adopt a Western economic model; they will develop their own, uniquely Chinese, solution. They have seen the faults in the Western model of too many Vikings. The future of our planet requires that we recognise major faults with both communist and capitalist models. A meeting of open minds should be able to find something better than either.

The domestication of plants and animals in China was completely independent of the Fertile Crescent. They domesticated pigs around 7,600 BCE, followed by millet in the north and rice further south shortly thereafter. With rice, I would say this the other way around; the rice plant domesticated farmers. Dogs and cows were domesticated next, a thousand years later. By around 3,600 BCE they were producing silk in the Yangshao culture on the Yellow river. But, unlike the Fertile Crescent, they did not enslave the population. Although a few dynasties had some similarities with European serfdom, they had a philosophical tradition of teaching leaders and rulers which led to a different relationship between the ruled and the rulers.

China has different genotypes with a low warrior index, different geography, different animals and plants from the early Civilisations of the Middle East, different beginnings with Government together with different experiences. They have been xenophobic as a result of many bad experiences with the West, such as the 'opium wars', and have negligible appetite for conflict far from their borders. We should not be surprised that a different culture and philosophy of leadership evolved. What is more surprising is how Confucius and early Greek philosophers came up with so many similar ideas. Perhaps this tells us something about our fundamental human existence, that we share a common human condition. Much of Confucian teaching focuses on the way that the Emperors should conduct themselves for long term success in society, unlike warrior leaders who are short term thinkers.

Our error is to continually 'measure up' China using our Indo-European 'yardstick'. The Indo-European and Chinese cultures have much to learn from each other; nearly all of us would benefit from meeting China half way. Those who might suffer most will only be the corrupt in either culture, the pirates and the greedy.

Russian Music and Discord

My grandmother Eva, with her extended family stories, opened my boyhood eyes to ideas of globetrotting. She often told me how much she regretted the invention of the passport in 1916. Before then, "One could just take the train to Moscow," she would say. Eva's grandmother, Henrietta, had run away from her husband to be with Karl Klindworth. In 1868 they travelled together to Moscow when Karl accepted the position as 'professor of the pianoforte' at the Conservatorium.

For much of the 19th century Eva's family, spread across Europe to Moscow, was lit by the spirit of musicians. Perhaps my reader could forgive an inability to imagine a family life filled with music. Instead, an image of a web of delicious friendly connections with a spirit which took no notice of nationality or religion captures my mind. Peoples from Russia, Hungary, Poland, Czechoslovakia, Austria, Germany, Denmark, Netherlands and Britain moved as freely as people now move in the USA without state borders or religion having any consequence at all.

Karl Klindworth was born at Hanover in 1830 and was quite a violinist as a boy. In those days the Kingdom of Hanover was ruled in union with the United Kingdom of Great Britain. The personal union between the British and Hanoverian crowns, which had existed since 1714, came to an end when Queen Victoria succeeded her uncle William IV in 1837. Whilst Britain could have a Queen, the Kingdom of Hanover could not if any male of the dynasty was alive. For them, a Queen was clearly a last resort. Luckily for the British, Queens were often more successful than the males of the line.

Instead, The Kingdom of Hanover was ruled by Victoria's uncle, the fifth son of King George III. Having unsuccessfully attempted to remain neutral in the Austro-Prussian War of 1866, Hanover was annexed as a Prussian Province until becoming part of the German Empire in 1871.

Klindworth had taught himself to play the piano. He spent two years with Franz Liszt in Weimar and became one of his closest friends. After moving to London in 1854 as a pianist and conductor, he met Richard Wagner and another long friendship began. He made many piano arrangements for Wagner's works. In Moscow he continued to prosper, achieving fame for his skilful arrangements of great orchestral works for the piano including Chopin and Liszt. He completed the piano arrangements for Wagner's *'Ring'*. Tchaikovsky became a close friend, corresponding in French, and dedicated two piano works to him: *Capriccio in G-flat major* in 1870 and *Grand Sonata in G major* in 1878.

Meanwhile, two years after Karl's birth, George Karop arrived in London from Denmark seeking work as a tailor in 1832. His youngest daughter, Henrietta, played the piano most beautifully.

Eva's Dutch grandfather, Wilhelm de Witt, was born in Hamburg in 1826 and was a child prodigy with the violin. Wilhelm and the Hungarian Jewish violinist József Joachim, who was five years younger, were jointly tutored by Spohr. Wilhelm's daughter Lulu later recounted the stories of these two as boys and young men. They spent much time together throughout their lives.

József Joachim made his London debut in 1844 as a 12-year-old, playing the solo in Beethoven's violin concerto with Mendelssohn conducting at the Philharmonic. An exception had been made to the rules concerning young performers. Despite Beethoven's recognition, many say that his violin concerto did not become famous until József Joachim's performance set the music alight. József had written some of his own cadenzas and memorized the whole piece. Despite audience anticipation from the rumours, they were overwhelmed. *Frenetic applause began* as soon as Joachim stepped onto the stage. The reviewers were ecstatic and described József's performance as beyond praise or description.

Wilhelm De Witt moved with his violin, a Stradivarius, to London and married Henrietta Karop. They had a daughter, Gertrude, my great-grandmother. When Karl Klindworth arrived in London during 1854 they often performed together; Wilhelm on the violin and Karl on the piano. But, one afternoon when Gertrude was eighteen months old, Henrietta retired to bed at midday with a headache. She felt unable to go to a party that evening where Wilhelm had promised to play. Returning home early from the party, Wilhelm found his wife had gone. She had run away to be with Karl Klindworth, her husband's best friend.

In the family stories, there is not much said about Gertrude's early childhood. Trying to imagine her distress, as an eighteen month old infant, unable to process the 'sonic boom carpet' of her mother's sudden disappearance reminded me of the loss of my hearing at the same age. Victorian society was not the most sympathetic to a small child wondering where her mother was. Perhaps, with other difficulties around the 'elopement', the subject was never discussed.

My grandmother Eva only met Henrietta once. In May, 1898, Karl was in London to conduct the Philharmonic Orchestra. He came with Henrietta to visit Gertrude and her five children. Eva's brother, Arthur, wrote that Henrietta *was gracious, charming and, in the best sense of the word, elegant; we all took to her and I think that it was a pity that my mother did not tell us that she was our grandmother. But it still had to be Aunt Henrietta. I am convinced that my mother felt a far deeper affection for her mother…, but her strong sense of right and wrong dominated and for some years the pain of an ancient story was allowed to hurt.* Perhaps my reading of Arthur's words is inaccurate. Was he referring to the hurt of Henrietta leaving Wilhelm, or the much *deeper hurt* of his mother Gertrude having been abandoned at the age of 18 months? Perhaps, to Gertrude, these feelings made the pain too deep for her to be able to introduce Henrietta as 'her mother'. A well might have opened up in the floor. Or, was there an unconscious desire to hurt her mother by referring to her as an 'aunt', denying her the title of mother?

In *Mannership*, I recount the story in an airport of watching an infant, Anna, having a tantrum. Her parents threatened her with being left behind if she didn't stop crying and then they followed through with the threat and hid behind some pillars. I was only a few feet from Anna and watched her intently. Re-reading my own words: *Realising she was alone, the terror soared diagonally across Anna's chest as if she had been struck by lightning. The lightning strike took her breath away. No air remained to continue her temper. No air was left to cry. It was as if the deluge had disappeared into a drop, vaporised by the lightning. Everything dried up. Then, just as suddenly, a different soul emerged. She took 'charge of herself'. As if this was another sister.*

The lightning strike had taken Anna's tears and petrified her. Not having heard words the way a hearing person does, but instead looking at the polishing of ancestral waves makes me smile. Suddenly the ancestral wisdom seems to say they all knew that when they polished particular words for us. Can this be why, in English, 'petrify' means both to *make someone so frightened that they are unable to move* as well as *to change something alive into a mineral or fossil*? Watching Anna, and re-reading my words to refresh the memory, she experienced both meanings of the word. An infant's brain is not able to comprehend that she has just become her 'own sister'. Instead the relationship becomes 'flipped' and mother becomes 'mother's sister' or aunt. Is this a variation of the 'step-mother' of the *Grimms' Fairy Tales*? That the 'step-mother' is the aunt because our own 'sisterhood' cannot be grasped?

Life, or something resembling her, goes on somehow despite these chasms of hurt.

József Joachim became Master of Royal Music at the court of King George of Hanover. The King, being blind, wanted to listen to song and József was commissioned to find the finest voice. He chose Maria Meyerstein, a beautiful 23-year-old Jewish singer. While Maria was at the Royal Court, József asked for her hand in marriage but she declined. With Maria's voice becoming well known, she travelled to London where she met Wilhelm de Witt, alone after the elopement of Henrietta. They fell in love and were married the following year. Wilhelm returned to Germany, living in Hamburg with Maria. They had a son and five daughters, but the youngest two were consumed by cholera and the family once again returned to London. They had three more daughters of whom Lulu was the eldest.[49] Lulu, writing to my great uncle Arthur, remembers that music played the greatest part of her family life with singing, piano and violin every day.

Wilhelm had become the owner of a music publishing company Ewer & Co in 1859. His daughter, Lulu, wrote *his knowledge of music was so outstanding that all the artists showed him their works. Pa had to visit Queen Victoria quite often to show her new publications. Pa would drive in his coach and four to Buckingham Palace to take tea with the Queen. Many big frontispieces were designed for Schumann, Schubert, Brahms… and the Queen was most interested in choosing these designs herself.* In 1867 Wilhelm sold his musical publishing

---

[49] Wilhelm and Maria had a son Arnold in London in May 1886 before moving to Graumannweg in Hamburg where daughters Lily, Adele, Frieda, Clara and Helene were born. Clara and Helene died of cholera within 2 days of each other, aged 2 and 3. This was such a blow for Wilhelm and Maria that they moved the family back to London where the last three daughters were born, Lulu, Anna and Emmy.

enterprise to Novello and was able, with the monies released, to support other musicians.

Lulu continues: *Antonín Dvořák played often at our house. Unfortunately Dvořák had taken to drink and made an exhibition of himself in society more than once. Pa suggested he should leave London for a while and paid his passage to Australia. He returned and behaved himself for almost a year until he started drinking again. In 1888, Pa once more gave him money to make a journey abroad. He went to America where he lived a decent life and was soon recognised for his great work 'From the New World'.*[50]

Perhaps Eva's family history, and the great number of musicians with whom they mingled, influences my views of Russia. Sadly, I would not have been able to listen to them as a boy, even if we had lived in the same time. For my eldest sister Ann's 60th birthday, the four of us including my three sisters went to St Petersburg for a long weekend. On the first evening we walked to the Literary café, a favoured haunt of Aleksandr Pushkin. There was a lady playing the grand piano. She was playing Eva's favourite piece, which my sisters had frequently heard as children but had been missed by me.

We all remembered the aspect of our grandmother Eva we admired the most. She had been a widow since 1927 and struggled to bring up her two children on her meagre earnings as a piano teacher. But, on the evening of 25th November 1938, she was listening to Viscount Samuel make an appeal on the BBC Home Service radio for a home for Jewish children. She noted the details and wrote to Viscount Samuel at once. Shortly thereafter two children came, Frances and Freddy. Frances lived with Eva while her brother lived with another family close by. They both went to the same school in Norwich as my mother and her brother had. My mother will never forget, after the war, the day when Frances' mother arrived. She had miraculously survived the camps and came to find her children. My mother remembers leaving the two mothers to weep together all afternoon.

Whilst the 19th century was glorious for the violin, this was a time of uncertain relations with Russia. The Kingdom of England and the Tsar of Russia had established relations in 1553. Our first connections developed during the long reign and 'golden period' of Queen Elizabeth I. In the ensuing five centuries Russia and England have mostly been on

---

[50] Correspondence in German from Lulu to my great uncle Arthur.

the same side in wars. We have relied on Russia at critical times. Without the huge losses suffered by Russia in the two World Wars, perhaps our own safety would not have been secured.

Although Russia was technically on the same side as France in the Seven Years' War from 1756, which began with Britain and France fighting over settlements in North America, Russia and Britain continued to trade. When Russia was defeated by France at the Battle of Friedland in June 1807, she was forced by Napoleon to break off friendly trading relations with Britain. The consequential Anglo-Russian skirmishes in the Baltic and Barents Seas were not caused by Russian design; they were half-hearted with few casualties.

Britain and Russia were realigned together by the defeat of Napoleon in 1815. But, they were at odds during the 'Great Game' for control of central Asia soon afterwards. On this occasion they were again anxious about the encroachment of the other into 'their colonies'. Britain was anxious about potential, although unfounded, Russian designs on India. Russia was concerned by genuine British designs through Afghanistan to further north. This was more of a 'cold war' and, although containing much mistrust, did not lead to direct conflict between them. Some might reasonably argue that the British started this 'Game' by seeking, in 1830, to build a trade route from India through to Bukhara with the added aim of making Afghanistan a protectorate as a 'buffer' north of India. The 'Game' was instead won by Afghan tribesmen who prevented the British advance. The end result was for the lands north of Afghanistan to become annexed by Russia.

There was only one war between Britain and Russia which was direct and very bloody; the war in the Crimea from 1853 – 1856. This was rather more complicated in origin.

In 1844 Tsar Nicholas, while attending a ball at St Petersburg's Winter Palace, mentioned that he would like to visit England again since he had not been there since 1817. This was the result of several months' negotiations between Russian diplomats and Queen Victoria's Ministers. Both sides were seeking warmer relations. The British Prime Minister, Lord Aberdeen, also hoped Russia's Emperor would soon visit England.

The visit went very well. Queen Victoria, writing at length to her uncle following the visit, refers to Tsar Nicholas with many superlatives. *The people here are extremely flattered. He is certainly a very striking man; still very handsome; his profile is beautiful, and his manners most dignified and graceful; extremely civil... He is very easy to get on with. Really, it seems like a dream when I think that we breakfast and walk out with this greatest of all earthly Potentates.* It is not surprising that Nicolas misunderstood the complicated British relations in Europe.

The Turkish Ottoman Empire had become more fragile and seemed on the verge of a breakup. The usual suspects, Russia, England, France and Austria were all anxious about the possible denouement. They were perhaps less interested in territorial gain but more concerned that one of the others might gain a territorial advantage. Hence the constant meddling, muddling, stirring up and frequent changes of alliance as the balances shifted.

Tsar Nicolas genuinely felt he had support from Queen Victoria. But, Wilhelm de Witt thought he had a happy marriage with Henrietta. In these Victorian times one did not always reveal feelings and intentions, and the alliances changed quickly anyway as we have seen. After the defeat of Napoleon at Waterloo in 1815 enabling a resumption of Anglo-Russian trade, and following a 'wonderful' visit to Queen Victoria in June 1844, it was not so obvious to Tsar Nicolas that the British would reunite with France against Russia less than ten years later.

As Orlando Figes writes in his detailed book, *Crimea*, this was the first war launched as a result of media frenzy. Russia had sunk some Turkish ships in the Black Sea. *The British Press immediately declared it a 'violent outrage' and a 'massacre', and made wildly exaggerated claims of 4,000 civilians killed by the Russians.*[51] Queen Victoria did not want to go to war, nor did the Prime Minister Lord Aberdeen. Both the Queen and the Government were still willing to trust Tsar Nicolas.

Figes tells us *the Queen noted in her journal* how the Government had become more warlike from fear of the newspapers. Figes suggests this frenzy was a by-product of our new railways that could distribute papers all over the island with speed. With the daily arrival of more 'news', public meetings sprung up to discuss the 'outrage'. Stirred by railways and the media, the British Government lost the plot to the baying public who were exhibiting football hooliganism on a national scale. The extent of the warrior and tribal genotypes in the British psyche must however be the deeper root behind this frenzy. The warrior newspapers only write

---

[51] Orlando Figes, *Crimea.*

what their readers are hungry for. The resulting loss of life in the Crimean War is quite staggering. Over 900,000 soldiers died.

The truth, as Orlando Figes explains exceptionally well, is that Britain was influenced at different times by a diverse series of anxieties. Overall, the British were not going to let the Russians get the upper hand anywhere. The real danger for us right now is that we are not learning the lessons of the mid-19th century. Our current relations with Russia are uncannily similar to the time before the Crimean War. In *Crimea*, Figes explains the Russian frustration with British double standards in the following passage written by Mikhail Pogodin, a professor at Moscow University and founding editor of Muscovite.

France takes Algeria from Turkey, and almost every year England annexes another Indian principality: none of this disturbs the balance of power; but when Russia occupies Moldavia and Wallachia, albeit only temporarily, that disturbs the balance of power. France occupies Rome and stays there several years in peacetime: that is nothing; but Russia only thinks of occupying Constantinople, and the peace of Europe is threatened. The English declare war on the Chinese, who have, it seems, offended them: no one has a right to intervene; but Russia is obliged to ask Europe for permission if it quarrels with its neighbour.[52]

So the passage continues, concluding with *We can expect nothing from the West but blind hatred and malice, which does not understand and does not want to understand.* Figes tells us how much Tsar Nicholas agreed with this text. These Russian sentiments are perhaps as true today, and the passage as relevant now as it was in the mid-19th century.

The naval skirmishes between Britain and Russia during 1808 were caused by an instruction from France while the Russians had not wanted to break off relations with Britain. In the Crimea, both parties should have communicated and played their hand better. Without the 'football hooliganism on a national scale' stirred up by the Britain press, the misunderstanding following the warmth of the 1844 visit to London, and events on the ground running ahead of both parties' intentions, it is probable that war could have been very easily avoided. The Russian and British intentions in the region were not so far apart. Perhaps we can simplify that a heavy dose of 'Empire jealousy' provoked the tragic loss of 900,000 lives in the Crimea. Although 47,000 died in combat, the vast majority died of cold, hunger and disease.

---

[52] Orlando Figes, *Crimea*.

This book is not big enough to describe any culture, let alone one as vast as the expanse of Russia. We cannot even scratch the surface of such a land representing one sixth of the world's land mass spread over 11 time zones. It is hard to get our brain around the scale of the land. If everybody in the world moved to Russia, including of course all of India and China, the resulting population density would be about the same as England's.[53] The future of the world requires us to rethink relations with Russia. There are many lessons of history we need to re-examine.

As explained by *The London Times*, after a decline of the culture of Stonehenge, the new inhabitants of Britain were 'Beaker folk' who arrived around 2,450 BCE from the Crimea and Asian steppe. *Anyone who's got British ancestry going back a couple of hundred years will have a predominance of steppe ancestry*, as *The Times* says. About 90% of the British population four thousand years ago were 'Beaker folk' from north and east of Crimea. Thus, both Britain and European Russia have a core of common ancestry. We both share ancient experiences of many warring tribes, before being enslaved and sold which remains in the psyche. While Britain was 'exporting slaves', the Slavs were being likewise exported to the Greeks.

Although tribes lived for many millennia in Central Asia and the lands of European Russia today, modern Russian history begins with the city-principality of Kiev, 'Kievan Rus', the forerunner of the Russian state. The Vikings became the rulers of Rus, the first united East Slavic state, in 882 CE. Predominantly Swedish merchants continued to sell Slavs, from whence the word 'slaves' derives, to countries south of the Black and Caspian Seas. We are still suffering from the forgotten traumas of the Viking behaviours.

Somehow, during my history lessons as a young boy, either my attention was misplaced or my teacher forgot to tell me that William the Conqueror was not French, but a Viking who had won a foothold in the North West of France and named his dukedom 'Normandy'. In Russia, they refer to being ruled by the Normans knowing full well that the Northmen were Vikings. Had my history teacher instead shown me the picture below, courtesy of Max Naylor, the influence of the Vikings in Europe would have been more clearly retained by my visual memory.

---

[53] Taking 7.6 billion people with Russia's land area of 17.1 million square kilometres makes 440 souls per sq km. England's population was 56.29 million in 2019 with a land area of 130,279 km² making a density of 430 per km².

Viking settlement in the 8th (dark red), 9th (red), 10th (orange) and 11th (yellow) centuries. Green shows frequent Viking raids without significant Norse settlements. By Max Naylor

The orange Rus' state is as clear as the other Viking expansions into the Black and Caspian Seas with their accompanying slave trade. The Vikings also settled Sicily and Southern Italy in the same period. This map also shows the extent of Viking settlements in England with most of Ireland, Scotland, Wales and Cornwall suffering raids without Viking settlement.

The Encyclopaedia Britannica says *the Normans retained many of the traits of their piratical Viking ancestors. They displayed an extreme restlessness and recklessness, a love of fighting accompanied by almost foolhardy courage, and a craftiness and cunning that went hand in hand with outrageous treachery. In their expansion into other parts of Europe, the Normans compiled a record of astonishingly daring exploits in which often a mere handful of men would vanquish an enemy many times as numerous. An unequalled capacity for rapid movement across land and sea....*

The Encyclopaedia continues: *A truer explanation of Norman success would be that they combined a boundless self-confidence with a marked capacity for adapting to their own purposes the institutions they found in newly won territories.*

This all sounds rather familiar, while thinking of my small island, and explains a lot. The Vikings 'exported terror' and relied on the 'smell of terror' running ahead of them to facilitate conquest. In due time, the Mongol conquest had a similar tactic of a great terror exported by a few.

Thinking about Russian culture made me wonder if the subject would be like asking a fish to look for water. But we can simplify the task by comparing some characteristics of Britain and Russia, knowing how we share some common ancestors and the influence of similar Viking rulers. We can see where we are alike and where we are different, and what we might be able to learn from this.

Our Norman rulers were kind enough to abolish the export of slaves, but instead replaced this crime with Europe's harshest version of feudalism based on the design of the Carolingian Empire.[54] Our ancestors had only jumped out of the frying pan into the fire. In the map below, the birth of the Indo-European culture is firmly in the underbelly of modern Russia. Escaped slaves were subjected to perhaps no better treatment than that which their ancestors had run away from while Nordic merchants sold them back again to lands south of the Caucasus Mountains.

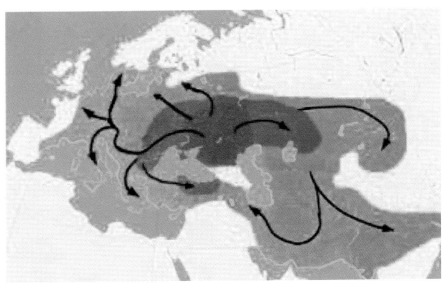

Map of the Kurgan hypothesis of the migrations of Indo-Europeans originating north of the Caucasus Mountains between 4000 and 1000 BCE (Wikipedia)

---

[54] The Carolingian Empire ruled the Franks from 751 and the Lombards of Italy from 774. In 800, the Frankish king Charlemagne was crowned emperor in Rome by Pope Leo III. The 'Northmen' imitated and adopted a harsh version of the feudalism initiated by Charles Martel, the grandfather of Charlemagne.

A question which often interested me was to ask Russians what they thought about Russians. The answers often contained two distinct types along the following lines: *our customs are traditional and orthodox. We are very reserved and closed. I can recognise another Russian from his face showing an inner anxiety, he is thinking all the time about something, deep behind the eyes. But there is another type who is very hospitable, who invites people home and offers the best accommodation and a feast.*

The two characters just described seem to be the escaped slave who has met the nomad of the steppe, as Martín Prechtel explained to me. My many wanderings have taught me that nomads always excel at hospitality. Nomadic generosity sustained me through my North African and Central Asian journeys.

Both Britain and Russia have a core foundation of 'Beaker folk' and warring tribes before suffering vicious enslavement followed by very little relief when their Viking rulers changed slavery to brutal serfdom. However, both went on to build vast empires. Whereas the British had to use Viking seafaring skills, the Russians could conquer on horse or by foot, overland.

For Britain, the last vicious invaders were the Vikings. But the Russian suffering at the hands of invaders continued. Long before the idea of empire building began, there was much more trauma to endure which has deeply affected the Russian psyche.

Kievan Rus' suffered brutal invasions by the Mongols from 1223 which largely destroyed the cities of Moscow and Kiev. Almost half of the population were massacred. The invaders took advantage of quarrels between Kievan Rus' principalities which sparked the division into Ukraine, Belarus and Russia. These lands were subjected to Tatar-Mongol rule until the invaders were finally defeated and pushed back to the East by 1480.

THE MONGOLS

Genghis Khan, named Temujin as a child, is an interesting man to study. Adrian Raine's research discovered that a combination of warrior genetics and a 'messy' upbringing can lead to an exponential increase in violence.[55] One morning, during a conversation with Meredith, this subject had come up.

Mark: *First of all, although we know Temujin's father was a warrior, we are not certain which warrior, or even from which tribe. Temujin was either the son of the Merkit chief, Yehe Chiledu, or he was the son of the Borjigin chief Yesugei.*

Meredith: *Why don't we know his parentage?*

Mark: *Because Yesugei defeated Yehe in battle and took Yehe's young bride, Hoelun, as a 'spoil of war'. A boy was born almost nine months later. He was named Temujin after a Tatar chieftain, Temujin-üge who had also just been captured by Yesugei. This might suggest that Yesugei saw his 'son' as a 'captured enemy'. On its own, this ambiguity must have created a tricky childhood. My conjecture is that there was a fierce ambivalence when one considers that his mother, Hoelun, had wanted to be with her original husband, Yehe. There is no doubt that Temujin had warrior parentage, but we don't know for sure which particular warrior among these two rival chiefs.*

Meredith: *This is certain to have had a significant effect on him.*

Mark: *But his life got messier. In about 1170, when Temujin was nine years old, Yesugei took him to visit the Onggirat tribe where a marriage was arranged to Börte. Temujin fell in love with Börte and remained devoted to her for his entire life, but had to wait at least three years until he could marry. As he and Yesugei returned home from this outing, they ran into their enemies the Tatars. Yesugei was poisoned and died. When Temujin arrived back home, he tried to claim Yesugei's tribe as their*

---

[55] Adrian Raine, *Anatomy of Violence*.

leader, but the tribe abandoned him instead. They took all their animals and yurts and moved on without him. Some historians claim this was because Temujin was too young to be their leader. It seems more likely to me that he was abandoned because his tribe knew he was really the son of the Merkit tribe and not one of them.

Following the abandonment he struggled to survive with his mother and younger brothers, hunting and foraging. At the age of 14, Temujin killed his half-brother Behter who was definitely Yesugei's son. The following year Temujin was captured and enslaved by the Tayichi'ud tribe. He managed to escape which was the springboard for his subsequent leadership career.

Meredith: *I see what you mean about a tricky childhood.*

Mark: *I think one of the worst parts of Temujin's background, in terms of how he must have been affected, came next. At the age of 16, he went to claim his bride, Börte, with whom he was still besotted. She was equally devoted to him and they began a life together. The Merkit tribe then came for revenge. They invaded and kidnapped Börte. She was made pregnant by the Merkits. Temujin had to build an alliance with Toghrul Khan of the Kerait tribe to have sufficient forces to attack the Merkits and reclaim Börte. Thus, history may have repeated himself. Temujin's eldest 'son', Jochi, was probably not his true son. There is a Mongol story that he was prevented from killing Jochi at birth by his mother Hoelun, who reminded him that if his father had behaved likewise then he would not have been alive. I am not saying all this to excuse or justify Genghis Khan's subsequent butchery, or that of his sons. Morality is not really my point. There seems no doubt that we have a case of warrior genotypes combined with a very messy upbringing which could lead to an 'exponential increase in violence' as Adrian Raine suggests.*

Reading that conversation again reminds me of the depth of fury which could have been around Temujin's heart. What about the traumas felt by his mother Hoelun and his wife Börte? How much was Temujin also affected by their burden? Another train of thought, which sometimes comes to me, is that extremely difficult and conflicting feelings in early life can make one construct very elaborate defences to overcome the rising passions. But these defences, whilst being almost sufficient to protect against external events are much more at risk against something which rises like a volcano from the inside. Seeking to protect against the inside might make for an ever increasing attempt to control the outside. Could this be why some of the most damaged leaders have not only a strong desire for control, but also develop an aggressive hunger for leadership because they *need it*. Especially, among those who produce harsh or despotic leadership. Leadership is mostly genetic. As James

Hillman said, *the oak is in the acorn*. Leadership is *'in the acorn'*, but what kind of leadership is heavily determined by the childhood summers and winters; particularly the traumas.

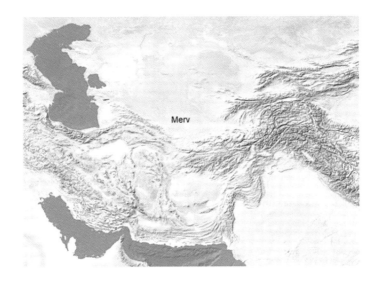

The worst example in the history of the Mongol empire is the destruction of Merv. The story of Merv is so tragic; there is no way for us to metabolise the brutality of her fate. By the time King John signed the Magna Carta in 1215, Merv had grown to become possibly the largest city in the world. She had, for sure, no equal outside China. She was once the centre of everything; in the middle between Kashgar and Baghdad on the Silk Road and in the middle of the Karakum Desert. Weary travellers wrote about this most splendid of oases; neat streets and pretty gardens; her sweet melons and thriving bazaars, exquisite baths and unrivalled libraries to entertain them. There was even a giant 'fridge', or cold room, to chill out from the heat.

The earliest evidence shows Merv emerging from the Bronze Age around 2500 BCE. She grew so fast because of her unique location. She was more than a vast Karakum oasis. She was a major cultural centre of the world, with a civilisation to rival any of the Middle East, Egypt or Persia.

For centuries, rulers and religions came from the East or the West like winds over the desert; they mingled together. She welcomed and feasted them all. Some consider Merv as the birthplace of Zoroastrianism. She made Jews welcome. She became Buddhist with many temples and monasteries. Cyrus the Great took a fancy to her and expanded her influence in his Achaemenid Empire. Alexander the Great, an admirer of Cyrus, also came to Merv and she took Alexander's name for a while. She adopted Nestorian Christianity.

During the Sasanian Empire, from the 3rd to the 7th centuries, Merv minted their coins. She was colonised by fifty thousand Arab troops. In the 8th century a new Abbasid dynasty was declared at Merv. In the early 9th century, the Caliph chose to have his residence in Merv and she became the temporary capital of the Islamic world.

Tughril Beg came from the steppe, united the Turkmen tribes, and founded the Seljuk sultanate in 1037 at Merv. By the end of the 11th century, the Seljuk empire controlled all of the Eastern Mediterranean, including Jerusalem, lands on both sides of the Persian Gulf, and stretched through the 'stans' on the Silk Road all the way to China. Merv became the calmer eastern Seljuk capital whilst the western Seljuks were busy repelling the European knights and their crusades. As in all her previous reincarnations, she was expanded and further adorned by her rulers and by the importance of her station on the Silk Road.

In the middle of the 12th century Merv was known for the manufacture of crucible steel. Her life became turmoil after the death of Sultan Sanjar and the end of two centuries of Seljuk governance. She entered the evening of her life with sudden and frequent changes of rule. Opposing tribes from all around possessed her successively, but could not repel the next tribe who sought to own her charms. She had witnessed almost four millennia's worth of sandstorms with competing warriors but could still take these inconveniences in her stride.

In the early 13th century, Merv was a jewel in her last empire, the Khwarazmian dynasty. This empire was not new to her. The founder, Anushtegin, was a former slave of the Seljuk sultan. Anushtegin and his successors expanded their vassal state within the Seljuk sultanate for over a century and grew to occupy most of the former eastern Seljuk territory.

At the dawn of the 13th century, two empires were facing each other across a 'shared' border: Genghis Khan's Mongol Empire to the east and the Khwarazmian dynasty, ruled by Shah Ala ad-Din Muhammad II, to the west.

Merv was at her busiest and most populous. A hundred camel caravans entered on a busy day, with some as large as 500 camels. The Arab historian, Yaqut al-Hamavi, in 1216, wrote that Merv had ten libraries richer in outstanding works than any other city. Little did he know how quickly there would be nothing left of this sumptuous Karakum oasis. Just five years later, she fell like a giant tree savagely cut down to the ground; the worst example of the butchery of a city in history.

I went to visit this tragic location on my 60th birthday, using up some air-miles and filling a gap in my senses of the Silk Road. The endless scrub reminded me of Afghanistan and Iran many years previously, and of vast caravans of Bactrian camels. There is something about Bactrians; they have so much more than the extra hump. They are not only made for surviving in searing sandy heat but are also equipped for the high altitudes and extremely bitter temperatures of the mountain passes in winter. Bactrians look more regal than dromedaries – there is something about their darker colour and humps tufted with black hair. Without bactrians, the Silk Road's deserts and mountain passes would not have been navigable.

My guide said, "Unlike Bokhara and Samarkand which opened their doors to Genghis Khan when he swept through, and therefore retained some of their fineness, Merv tried to resist. She shut her doors and was destroyed after a siege." He continued, "The ruler of Samarkand was smarter. He told the people not to worry about Genghis Khan; as he was a nomad, he would not stay long. So they should make him welcome for a while. The Shah had a different approach because he thought Merv was much stronger."

But, I had also heard a different story. A few years before, Genghis Khan agreed a peace treaty with Shah Muhammad, the ruler of Merv, to improve trade between their empires. A year later, a Mongol caravan of several hundred arrived at the Khwarezmid oasis of Otrar, a hundred miles from Tashkent, to establish ties. They were massacred on the orders of the Governor, an uncle of Shah Muhammed. Genghis Khan sent three emissaries to the Shah demanding that the Governor be handed over for punishment. But the three emissaries were executed instead. Mongol revenge was inevitable. This revenge was served by Tolui, the fourth son of Genghis Khan and the love of his life, Börte; Tolui was the butcher of Merv.

We don't know exactly how many lived in Merv, but some say seven hundred thousand and other historians say over a million. In addition to Merv's settled population there were so many incoming refugees and travellers that a million is very possible. In the butchery, there were just four hundred artisans spared for their useful craftsmanship; they were put to one side to be taken elsewhere. All the others were butchered.

That afternoon, in 1221, each Mongol warrior was ordered to butcher three hundred men, women or children. A million put to the sword. The scale of the slaughter is unimaginable. Some cities in history were burned, bombed, reduced to rubble by cannons or starved in a siege. But a million individual executions by sword cannot be metabolised. There sits the ground that had to drink all the blood, silenced by what happened. Standing there in silence is overwhelming.

The history of Merv reminds us that the two hundred and fifty years when the Mongol Empire stretched across the Central Asian steppe and included all of Kievan Rus', as well as those on all sides of the Black Sea, were not an easy time for the Rus'. On the one hand the Mongos 'rode through' and did not settle there. They had little ongoing dealings with the people they conquered. Genghis Khan, his children and grandchildren, remained nomadic pastoralists. They believed in meritocracy, respected all religions and did not object to the Rus' Christianity. But these opportunities were only afforded to those who survived the initial destruction, of course. Cities which were burned to the ground with the population annihilated missed these kindnesses.

This was a time for Russians to get 'a grip on themselves' and surrender absolutely, perhaps even hiding their terror. Although, hiding terror was not always wise, since the currency of the Mongol overlords was terror. Maybe the locally designated rulers wanted to see a little of the terror in their subjects to feel safer themselves. Could this practice have 'caught on' and prevailed? There was always the threat that a Khan would return if… But, according to my Moscow travel guide, if one accepted the Mongol supremacy all could be well. Perhaps we can take this comment a little tongue in cheek since Moscow gained her supremacy over the other princes of Kievan Rus' in 1327 when Prince Ivan I of Moscow joined the

Mongols to repress a rebellion by the Rus' of Tver. The Encyclopaedia Britannica's description of Viking characteristics as *'a craftiness and cunning that went hand in hand with outrageous treachery'* were flourishing. Fights for supremacy among princes are familiar to the British, particularly the Hundred Years' War with France which coincidentally began only ten years later in 1337. Clearly the mid 1300's were a good moment to sort out some princely pecking orders in Britain, France and Russia. But the weaponry which had by then evolved was rather more potent than any pecking order squabbles in the I-Kiribati ancestry. Many more of the civilian populations were caught in the crossfire.

Whilst Britain and Russia share genetic ancestry with 'Beaker folk' from the region of Kievan Rus', share tribal infighting and slavery followed by Viking rulers and brutal serfdom, those living in the Kievan Rus' had the extra Mongol brutality still to endure. Generalisations are difficult and dangerous, but it is not unreasonable to wonder whether the subsequent expansion of Russia and her Empire, with some harsh rulers, had been inspired by previous events.

After two and a half centuries of occupation, Ivan III liberated Kievan Rus' from the Mongols in 1480.[56] After many years of raids, it took until the 1550s for Ivan IV, known as Ivan the Terrible, to stop raids from Kazan by extending Russian territory eastwards.[57] He conquered the Khanates of Kazan, Astrakhan and Sibir. By 1556, Russia, with these extra Khanates on the Volga, had grown to a size of 4 million square kilometres, representing a quarter of the size of the Mongol Empire. Astrakhan, where the Volga meets the Caspian Sea, was the largest slave market in Central Asia. This notorious market, together with the Crimea slave market, had operated over centuries. The two markets are estimated to have traded over six million slaves from Finland and Russia to lands south of the Black and Caspian Seas; a greater number than were sold by any pair of West African ports in subsequent centuries. In 1550, 20% of the population of Constantinople were slaves who had been traded through the Crimea.

Many feelings must have been evoked as the Russian army finally destroyed such a vile place. It took another century to continue

---

[56] Ivan I was succeeded by two sons (Simeon and Ivan II), then by the sons of Ivan II until Ivan III (after 4 generations) and Ivan IV who was grandson of Ivan III.

[57] The English word 'terrible' derives from 'causing terror'. Fearsome or formidable would be a better modern translation from the Russian.

eastwards to surround Lake Baikal where the Russian / Mongolian border still stands.

The 'rolling back' of the Tartar and Mongol invaders during the 15th to 17th centuries had the effect of extending the influence of the Kievan Rus' further east than they may have dreamed of before the Mongol invasion. Perhaps, just as the first Samoan chief after three centuries of Tongan rule had wanted insurance by 'throwing everybody else out', the Kievan Rus' wanted protection by going after all the others who had attacked them. The island of Samoa could more easily 'throw out' their invaders, but the Russian steppe has no natural border like a coastline for protection. Enemies could simply ride back on a horse a few days later. The chosen alternative was to suppress them instead.

Both empires were of a comparable size, with both in this instance being the Mongol Empire on the one hand and the much later Soviet Union on the other hand. But, while the British were colonising indigenous peoples in all four corners of the earth, the Russians gathered 185 ethnic groups within a contiguous neighbourhood in what became 'their back yard'. When the British abolished serfdom, transferring energy to enslaving foreign indigenous people and transporting millions of slaves by sea, was it so different from the Russians extending serfdom across a much greater territory and transporting large numbers of serfs across the steppe to another part of their vast land empire? Russian serfdom was finally abolished in the emancipation reform of 1861 by Tsar Alexander II, which was not so long after the British finally abolished slavery. The parallels are uncanny. No wonder we struggle to get along because looking at each other has too many aspects of an unknown mirror.

The British and Russians were the architects of the two largest empires in the 19th century, amounting to a total of 40% of the world's land area. It was inevitable that there would be frictions and jealousies. What is remarkable, in retrospect, is how few direct conflicts resulted; in fact only one in Crimea which they could have avoided easily.

What some Russians have said to me is that what stands Russia apart is the cruelty towards her own people. But maybe they did not think of them as 'their own people' at the time. They might have thought like some British buccaneers felt about the transported slaves. Or, thought of them as the descendants of a people who had attacked them. Alternatively, perhaps such a long history of multiple sufferings and massacres has entrenched in the culture one of the harshest traumas to digest. Perhaps the Russians continue to suffer this trauma, whereas the British have found a different method to 'dissociate from it' in the Humpty Dumpty vein.

It is ghastly to admit, but such brutal points can explain some aspects of the complex relationship between Britain and Russia. Back as a twelve year old, there is only one useful memory retained from the priest who unsuccessfully tried to persuade me to be confirmed in the Anglican Church. He said, "remember when you point your finger at someone, there are three fingers pointing at you." I thought that was clever. It would be much easier if both nations admitted the shocking similarities of our past traumas and actions. This could be a different basis for moving on.

The genetic data tell us that the Western Russians are part of a cluster together with the Hungarians and Poles. Just like a genetic cluster of the English with the Dutch and the Danes.[58] But Western Russians also have some Finns and Tatars in the mix. Finland is a linguistic 'outlier' in Europe, with an Altaic language. During my work in the Finnish Arctic circle, on the top of the Gulf of Bothnia, they made quite a number of impressions on me.

On the first occasion, running a leadership workshop for the managers of a mine, they all seemed to be facing me like stone statues. There was no emotional feedback at all. The grit, resilience and determination with which they looked made me feel as if trapped down in the mine. Nothing could 'wake' any glimmer of an emotion. The prospect of spending two or three days blocked in a dry conversation filled me with dread. Suddenly I asked them to help me. Explaining my feelings that their bodies were in the room but everything else felt to me as if still a mile underground in their mine; I asked them to come in the lift to the surface, or there was nothing more I had to say. Their response was not immediate but since my mouth didn't move either, they had to respond or we would have had a stalemate. After that, the workshop was just like everywhere else. On my journeys in Russia, sometimes a look reminds me of this same resilience, which might also be a character of my silent years.

---

[58] L.Luca Cavalli-Sforza, Paolo Menozzi, and Alberto Piazza, *The History and Geography of Human Genes.*

The Finns have a word for this enduring grit, *sisu*, as an important trait in their national character. There is no equivalent word in English. Some say *sisu*, is like a white-knuckle form of courage to enable one to survive overwhelming odds. Having chewed on the idea for a long time, it seems this might inform us, and them, of their ancient resistance to overwhelming oppression. This was how they survived long ago, but the mind has 'hung on' to this state long after the immediate need has passed. This reminds me of the English 'stiff upper lip'. We know what it is but not what to do about it. A little spontaneity would be much too risky, although the English stiff upper lip wavered and trembled when Diana, Princess of Wales, posthumously taught the British something about grief.

While Britain lost any possibility for an indigenous population having a relationship to nature because of the deeply frozen temperatures causing everybody to leave or perish, Finland retained her descendants of indigenous culture, and therefore perhaps it is harder to 'dissociate' from the trauma. We could perhaps say the same of Russia. In both cases they have traditions of tribes who have been indigenous for tens of thousands of years in the Arctic and Siberian regions. People who lived in harmony with nature and their environment knew well the elixir of the 'third layer' and have retained stories from a time long ago when 'wishing was having' before any brutal oppression.

Words in a language can tell us much about a culture. Apparently Mandarin has 113 words or characters for shame. In English we would not come close, having chosen to keep shame at arm's length. On the other hand the BBC tells us that, in English, there are over 3,000 words for being a little or somewhat drunk.[59] Are they kidding? We share with Russia a difficulty with alcohol consumption; perhaps we both drown out what we cannot allow to be brought back into memory. But, by keeping the memory buried we continue the self-destruction. Our ancestors knew what they were doing when they polished the word 'spirit' to include alcohol. Not finding one can make us reach for the other.

Whenever asked about the European Union, my response was always that there was insufficient vision. The only goal which made sense to me was a free European market from Portugal to the Urals. Moscow is, without doubt, a European city. St Petersburg was one of the finest

---

[59] Susie Dent, BBC culture, 31 January 2017.

European capitals. The best chance we have for fruitful coexistence is to make this project our aim. Nothing else makes sense. One of my favourite ancient expressions is: *a favourable wind only comes to the ship that knows where she is going.* Over time, we can become friends of Russia again. We often were and we have so much in common.

Maybe once Britain is 'outed' by Brexit we can dream of a new arrangement including the Western and Eastern flanks of Europe; a wider and better Europe which includes the 'exiled' Britain and Russia. My vote had been to remain in Europe. But a knowledge of my island's history helps to understand why so many have an unknown desire to keep escaping westwards. Looking back, Britain was never truly welcomed into the Europe of a Franco / German alliance; but maybe they never wanted a welcome. The European Union began as a 'marriage' between French shame and German guilt over the 1940s while Britain had always been the 'gooseberry'.[60]

On several occasions we have missed our chance to be friends with Russia. After 9/11 President Bush had a chance to build a bridge to Moscow. The hand was offered but not properly grasped. At other times we could have been close again. The time has come to plan a route towards friendliness. With this aim on both sides, we should be able to solve the irritations and mistakes that keep cropping up. After all, these irritations are not on the same scale of the misguided 900,000 deaths in the Crimean War. With such a tragic history, Russians will always have some different feelings from ours, but we share so much trauma that we should be able to work together. Having asked Martín how to protect myself from the destructive urges handed down by my ancestors, he had replied: *You can't. You have to work with someone else, with your hands, and make something of beauty and then you metabolise it.* The time has come for the British and Russians to plan such a future. With the right vision our differences will melt and perhaps we can jointly metabolise our traumas.

The current plan for Europe does not do justice to the aspirations of the next generation. It makes no sense to maintain a stance towards Russia which smells just like the years before the Crimean War. We know very well that Crimea has been part of Russia since the Kievan Rus' and that Kruschev, in giving Crimea to Ukraine as a gift in 1956 to celebrate 300 years of friendship, had not anticipated the prospect of Ukraine

---

[60] A 'gooseberry' is an early English expression for an unwanted third person who is present when two other people having a romantic relationship, want to be alone.

wandering west. We should have known better than to cry foul and should take much responsibility for the 'stand-off' there. Simply and calmly suggesting a free referendum right from the outset would have been the gracious response, knowing full well that the majority in Crimea are Russian.

A goal to have Russia and Britain together with Belarus and Ukraine in a new and fresh version of the European free market may inspire the next generation. We can find a way to iron out many transgressions and overcome many grievances. If not, we will have learned nothing from the history of the last few millennia. The other Central European countries would have doubts due to their more recent relations with Russia, but the strains are beginning to show in their relations with Europe. We could perhaps arrive where we began the chapter on Russia, by being able to 'just catch a train to Moscow' one afternoon without a passport.

* * *

I wrote the chapters about Russia and the Mongols in 2020 before the catastrophe in Ukraine. Whilst the invasion cannot be condoned; NATO and Ukraine, as well as Russia, are complicit in activities which made an armed conflict more likely. Why did they all sleepwalk into this disaster? Why could they learn nothing from history? The seeds of future difficulties were obvious in the 2004 Ukrainian elections which showed how many in Western Ukraine see their future with Europe, whilst many in South-Eastern Ukraine feel they belong with Russia. A different and non-violent process must help find a way out of this madness quickly.

A wider vision of friendship between France, Germany, and other European Community nations was necessary for Alsace Lorraine to breathe freely after four centuries of trauma. Likewise, perhaps we need a new vision of a future relationship between Europe and Russia to enable the Crimean region to settle down while respecting her links to the East and the West.

PAUSE FOR THOUGHT

In *Mannership*, focusing on self-destruction in the individual mind, I made much use of the imagery of the Genesis story 'Cain and Abel' to represent two aspects of our mind. I wondered if Abel, who offered the 'first born animals', could represent our animal nature and spontaneity. Then Cain, who offered the *cultivation* of the land, might represent how our culture can 'kill' our nature. A message from history is that, if our ancestors suffered slavery, then our culture may have a tendency to drive our nature underground.

My musing included: *There is an interesting aspect of the fairy tales of two brothers in their instant forgiveness. We might be tempted to suspect that Abel remains furious because of his suffering at the hand of Cain. In the stories, this is not what happens usually when they meet again. There is instant gratitude as well as forgiveness following their recognition. We can look at their reunion from another angle. If Abel is very calm and submissive by nature then his taming by the culture will be easier. Cain would thus be experienced as a gentler brother to him. If, on the other hand, Abel is very fractious and fiercely independent then Cain will need to be even firmer in some way.*

China was also overrun by the Mongols, but their experience was very different from the Russian one. On the one hand, we can simply say that perhaps they had a different experience. But there is another possibility. Just like the previous paragraph, the experience and the oppression might have been felt differently because of who they were to begin with. Because the Chinese possess a less aggressive culture genetically, the Mongol yolk did not need to apply such constant brutality. The Russians, with their long history of suffering slavery, serfdom and Vikings would have reacted to the Mongols quite differently.

Sometimes, personal stories illustrate the history of parts of the world better than historians can. The next two chapters, in Uzbekistan and Tajikistan, share some lessons from my wanderings in Central Asia. I hope my reader can tolerate a brief diversion from weightier subjects before a light hearted meeting with ancestors.

Uzbek Ancestry

On my first visit to Uzbekistan, I was introduced to an exceptional guide called Nadya. Everyone said she was so knowledgeable and helpful that one couldn't find better. I could not disagree; all the arrangements were perfect as we passed through Tashkent, Bokhara, and Samarkand on the Silk Road. She was also delightful, and I was pleased to learn her son was a Chelsea football supporter. Over many years, Nadya has helped me prepare for a dozen visits to lands in the underbelly of Central Asia. She has an encyclopaedia of priceless tips and a vast spider's web of contacts across her region.

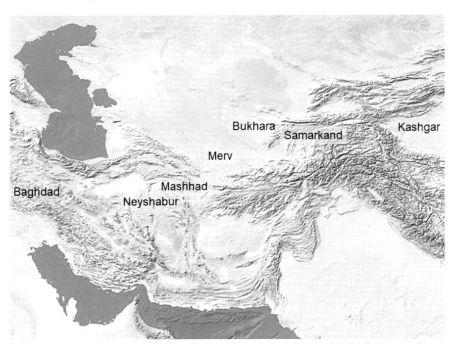

Bukhara and Samarkand to the northeast, Mashhad and Neyshabur to the southwest, with the oasis of Merv in the middle of the Karakum Desert.

113

Decades had passed since my last visit to the Silk Road at Mashhad in Iran. I was only eighteen then, and on my way back from India. Bukhara sits on the other side of the Karakum Desert from Mashhad. The camel caravans used to take twenty-five to thirty days to reach Mashhad from Bukhara with the giant oasis of Merv between them. I remembered, in Iran, the great trains of Bactrians with their distinctive double humps topped by dark haired tufts looking about to sprout.

Bukhara is charming and bewitching. Nadya knew all the legends as she introduced the fine mosques, squares and of course the bazaars. My attention was immediately captivated by a silk carpet. We passed by the seller twice each day to try and obtain an acceptable price. The silk played tricks on our eyes. From one direction the carpet was desert sandy beige, but from a different angle she changed to the colours of a rich green oasis. This couldn't be the same carpet, but she was. I knew the seller saw he had me hooked like a thirty pound trout on a five pound line, but we both enjoyed the lively banter with tea and sweetmeats.

As the afternoon cooled and a gentle breeze returned before our evening meal, I asked Nadya about her ancestry. More specifically, how had she come by her blonde hair and blue eyes?

"My great-grandmother was from Germany." She said. "My great-grandfather bought her." I wondered if I had heard correctly, but Nadya nodded.

"Gretchen was born in 1905, in Simmelsdorf, that's twenty kilometres from Nuremburg. She had blonde hair and blue eyes. Her father, my great-great-grandfather, was a merchant trading between Germany and Azerbaijan." I asked what the merchant was trading, but Nadya didn't know. Instead, she continued, "In 1918, he took Gretchen with him on a trip. She was thirteen then. On the way from Istanbul to Azerbaijan, they were both kidnapped and then sold in the slave market of Neyshabur in Iran."

Goose pimples ran up my arm; how fate throws the dice with our teenage lives. I imagined Gretchen's young terror on such a forced journey east. I remembered passing through Neyshabur on my way from Mashhad to Istanbul as a teenager. That's quite a distance, over three thousand kilometres. Nadya hadn't a concern for how this came about. What mattered was that this was the girl who became her great-grandmother. She was as keen to continue as I was to listen.

"My great-grandfather Ali was from Neyshabur." I wondered about his profession and Nadya explained. "Ali was a wealthy landowner. He found Gretchen and her father in the slave market in 1918, and bought both of them. But, soon after, Gretchen's father became ill and died. Ali decided to take Gretchen as his third wife; he changed her name to Miriam."

I was curious about the other wives, as well as the young teenage bride.

"Ali's first wife, Aliya, was Iranian and bore him three sons. Ali's second wife was an Azeri woman, but the marriage was childless. Miriam became pregnant soon after, and she had a son, Bayram, in the spring of 1920." Just to make sure that I was not losing track, I confirmed that Bayram was Nadya's grandfather.

That evening my mind was filled with Bukhara's exquisite sights, the irresistible silk carpet, and Nadya's ancestry. I needed to ask her more. I shuddered with the brutal thought of a thirteen-year-old kidnapped German girl being sold in a market. Nadya had reminded me that these kinds of events are still happening all over the world. I came back to earth realising how she would see her great-grandmother's abduction differently. For her, there could not be an idea that this shouldn't have happened. Without this kidnapping, Nadya would not be here. Of course, she had a different perspective. At once, I also understood why 'history' is perceived so differently in neighbouring cultures. History is only partly based on facts. A culture's relationship to the past is more important than the actual events.

At the earliest convenient moment, we continued with her family history. Of course, I had enjoyed Nadya's descriptions and legends of Samanid's Mausoleum, the many Mosques and Madrassas. But, a personal story from these lands helped me understand much more.

Nadya was eager to resume sharing her ancestry. "Ali was closely allied to Ahmad, the last Shah of the Qajar Dynasty. In 1921, when Ahmad Shah was deposed following a coup by Shah Reza-Khan, Ali had to escape Iran quickly. He could not take his whole family with him. He took his first wife, Aliya, and their three sons, together with Miriam and their son Bayram. They escaped through Azerbaijan and crossed the Caspian Sea. During their journey, Miriam had a second son, Rustam, but she died soon after."

I realised that Miriam was just sixteen when she died, leaving two sons.

Bolo-Khauz, the main Friday mosque from 1712 to 1917, Bukhara

Entrance to the madrassah of Abdulaziz-Khan in Bukhara.

The courtyard of Poi-Kalon Mosque, Bukhara.

"Ali brought his family eventually to Uzbekistan. They were refugees. Bayram had blue eyes, dark skin and a typical Azeri face. Ali started to produce and sell ice-cream from home, but any kind of business was forbidden by the Soviets. They were in big trouble. As non-citizens, they were told to accept Soviet citizenship and move to a village that was supposed to become an industrial town, or the family, including the children, would be imprisoned. This was how they became employed in a cement factory at Kuvasay, Fergana valley. When he was old enough, Bayram also worked in the cement factory. That was where he met his wife, Anna. They were both young factory workers."

"Anna's father was an Amish Siberian blacksmith, but her mother was from high society. Anna's mother had lived lavishly, owning lands in the west of the Russian Empire before the revolution, until the Bolsheviks took over and sent her family to Siberia. This was where she met her husband. But, in 1921, there was a famine in Russia. Many people, including Anna's parents, were sent south to grow food in the Fergana Valley of Uzbekistan. My grandmother, Anna, was born somewhere in Altay on their way south."

117

'The Ark'; the fortress from ancient Bukhara.

Registan Square, Samarkand. The scale is so extraordinary that the people appear to be the size of ants. A magnifying glass is helpful to see them.

I was struck by a few similarities between the stories of her grandparents. Both Anna's mother and Bayram's father had been wealthy landowners, and close to the aristocracy. They had lost everything suddenly following a change of power. Different circumstances forced them to flee during the same year, 1921, and their journeys brought them to Uzbekistan. Nadya resumed the story. "Anna was from a conservative Christian family and Bayram was a devoted Muslim. Their parents were against the marriage but, as Soviets, had to ignore religious differences. They had twin sons, Sergei and Alexander. Sergei is my father."

I thought that the family story, together with a swathe of history woven in, was complete and extraordinary. But, a few years later, I was to hear more. I was on another journey in Central Asia and came by the Silk Road from Ürümqi and Kashgar in China, through the walnut forest of Kyrgyzstan, to the Fergana Valley. Nadya met me at the Uzbek border and took me to her family house where I met Nadya's uncle, Alexander, her father's twin.

We were enjoying a family dinner while Nadya continued the story with more details from her uncle. "In April 1986, after the explosion in Chernobyl, the authorities announced a total army mobilization. Both Sergei and Alexander had army experience, but Sergei was invited to be head of a special team to 'clean up' in Chernobyl. Sergei understood the danger of radioactivity and knew he was facing his last days with his family and especially his young children.

"His twin brother Alexander, without telling anybody, went to a general in the Army and offered his candidature instead of Sergei's. He was unmarried and also an engineer. The general liked the idea and signed special papers which allowed the substitution. However, Alexander never told his brother. When the day came for departure, Sergei went to the meeting point with his backpack for Chernobyl. He saw his twin brother with a backpack too and could not understand why he was there. An army man called out names from the list, and Alexander's name was called but not Sergei's. Sergei went home. Only much later; he discovered what had happened."

Nothing compares with the raw instincts and selfless courage of Alexander who so willingly offered himself in his twin brother's place. The evening when Alexander and Nadya shared this part of their family story was especially moving. Sergei had recently passed away. Nadya was grieving the loss of her father, and at the same time remembering her uncle's loving gesture. We also spoke of how, despite the experience of working in Chernobyl, Alexander had outlived his twin brother. The only physical suffering which remained for him was feeling 'easily tired' but he enjoyed tending his vegetable garden in Fergana Valley.

Silk threads drying in natural red dyes, Fergana Valley

Finally, Nadya mentioned that Bayram tried twice to find the gold and jewellery which his father had hidden in Iran. He would never have received permission to travel there, so took illegal Gypsy routes. But he never found the place and took what he knew to his grave...

WALKING TO TAJIKISTAN

After the delightful dinner with Nadya's extended family, and the moving conversation with Alexander, my plan was to leave Uzbekistan towards the west and visit the Pamir Mountains and lakes of Tajikistan. Nadya suggested a Tajik guide she trusted, Shahboz. On the way to the border, there were two stops.

Knowing my love of bazaars, Nadya took me first to the Sunday market at Kumtepa. We enjoyed looking at their merchandise, bartering a little for fun, but mostly chatting with the people we met. For me, the market is primarily for gossip. With my natural gregariousness, in addition to an  insatiable curiosity, this chance to talk and learn is a highlight of my wanderings. The intrigue provoked others to join and the conversation became livelier.

After Kumtepa, Nadya suggested we visit Kokand, the old capital of the Kokand Khanate. We saw the Djama Mosque, Narbutabek madrassa and the Palace of Khudayar Khan which was built by sixteen thousand slaves. These days in Fergana with Nadya helped me to connect the dots of the Mughal Emperors whose monuments in India made such an impression on me as a teenager.[61] She explained that Babur ascended the throne of Fergana in 1494 at the age of twelve. Babur is descended from both Timur and Genghis Khan. His early rule in Fergana was troublesome, gaining control of one city only to lose another.

---

[61] Mughal derives from the Persian for Mongol. The Mughals are descendants of Mongol rulers such as Genghis Khan and Timur.

Unsuccessful in his homeland, he left for India and defeated the Afghan Sultan of Delhi, Ibrahim Lodi, at the First Battle of Panipat in 1526 to become the founder of the Mughal Empire. I was so grateful to Nadya for her help and hospitality, together with such a rich first-hand education. History becomes alive when I see the lands and hear the stories in context.

The time had come to bid me farewell, once again. We drove to the Uzbek side of the border crossing near Konibodom, arriving at about three in the afternoon. Nadya had, as usual, planned and checked everything. As we reached the Uzbek customs, she told me she had just called Shahboz. He was waiting already on the Tajik side. I smiled, knowing her careful attention to details and for ensuring all was well.

I walked into the Uzbek customs building and found an empty hall; clearly not a busy border crossing. From previous journeys, I knew that leaving Uzbekistan is sometimes harder than coming in. They would go through everything.

I knew how thoroughly the Uzbek customs would go through my photographs, check the films on my laptop, even question the book I was reading. I was prepared for that. I made sure that the last photo album I had 'visited' on my iPhone was one of nature. When the kind customs lady asked to see my photographs, and I handed her my iPhone, she touched the photo icon and the phone screen was filled with flowers and trees. She said, "I see you like nature." I nodded and smiled and we looked at a few together as she flicked through. She didn't feel the need to see any more. She was interested in my philosophical book, and we spoke of that for a few minutes. I told her I didn't have any films or videos on my laptop. She looked thoroughly inside my luggage, as if she did not trust the X-ray scanner, but was happy. Soon enough I had breezed through with the required stamp on my visa and customs approval.

My new nature loving friend waved me farewell as I walked towards the wire fence which marked the edge of Uzbek territory. The ground was barren, just a few tufts of grass. At the fence, an Uzbek soldier checked that I had the exit stamp in my passport. He did not speak but simply indicated that I was free to go through the gate in the fence. I was now in no man's land between the Uzbeks and the Tajiks.

At first glance the ground ahead looked like a minefield. Maybe I should be careful. There were some well-trodden paths, a little muddier than the grass, so I selected one of those for the few hundred yards to the Tajik side.

As I reached the gate in the Tajik fence, a Tajik soldier stopped me. His green uniform was rather smart. He had a Kalashnikov over his shoulder but seemed a little friendlier than the Uzbek soldier I had left behind. I greeted him warmly in English but he didn't understand my words. His smile, however, suggested he understood. He replied, but in a language I didn't understand. Then he spoke again and said something in a different language. I wondered if he had first spoken in Tajik and then in Russian.

I thought he would just wave me through. Instead, he indicated that I should sit on the grass. I wondered what the delay was, but obeyed his instruction. A few minutes later, I got up. He indicated I should sit down, rather like he was gesturing to a friendly dog. This didn't make sense. I looked at him again. He did not seem malicious. There was no sign of any reason for me to just sit there. I sat down and waited patiently. I could see a building which must be the Tajik customs but nothing was happening. Nobody was crossing the border in either direction.

After half an hour, I stood up and tried again. I attempted to explain my wish, by putting my hand on my heart, and demonstrating walking with my fingers towards the Tajik customs building. He clearly understood what I wanted. At once, he picked up his walkie-talkie and said something unintelligible before looking at me with another gesture that I should sit on the ground. He was a little firmer than the last time though. More like a traffic policemen indicating a red light as he held up the palm of his right hand. At first, while he was speaking on his walkie-talkie, I had felt hopeful. The customs would now know I was waiting. But, why were they keeping me waiting? My perplexity increased to despair. My guard was still friendly though. Was I misunderstanding him? I wondered if he was about to come to the end of his shift. Had he just called his replacement and not customs? Would the next guard be as friendly?

I knew I needed to stay calm. But, acting like a dog on a leash was not comfortable. I continued to sit on the grass with my leash right before me, the shoulder strap holding the guard's Kalashnikov. My ordeal was clearly not going to be just a matter of a few minutes.

I regretted there were no other travellers attempting to cross this border. I could have asked them for help. There were two hours' light left. I wondered if I would still be there in the dark, or all night even. I was mad at myself for not having brought a small bottle of water and some biscuits. What was I going to do, just sit here? I wondered about returning to see the kind Uzbek customs lady who spoke a little English. But, I realised that my single entry Uzbek visa had now expired. The Uzbek soldier would bar me. Besides, the Tajik soldier hadn't indicated that I should turn back. He had only indicated that I should 'stay put'. Not rudely, not kindly, but matter of factly.

As I looked at my phone to check the time, I saw that I had sufficient mobile connection to make a call. I wondered if the Tajik guard would let me telephone someone. But, who would I call? I did not want to worry Nadya.

I wondered if the Tajik customs had already closed for the day. Maybe that was why I hadn't seen any other pedestrians in either direction. Was that why he wouldn't let me in? This possibility did not seem likely. My instincts were that, if the border was no longer open, the Tajik guard would have gestured differently. He would have found an easy way to let me know the border was closed.

I looked through my notes from Nadya and found the mobile number of the Tajik guide, Shahboz, which she had given me. I decided to call him instead. I hoped he had not given up on me and gone home after such a long delay. Calling him to ensure he was still there, and would continue to wait for me, would be wise. I wondered if the soldier would mind if I used my mobile phone; I mustn't let him think I wanted to photograph him. Tentative steps would be wise.

Still sitting on the ground, I swivelled slowly to face him and very gently gestured the idea of making a call. He didn't seem to mind. He just nodded. I called Shahboz and he answered immediately. Having introduced myself, I asked where he was.

"I arrived at the border over an hour ago and am waiting for you behind the gate just beyond the customs building." He said. I could see roughly where he meant, although too far away to recognise anyone. That was comforting.

I explained, "I am stuck in no man's land between the Uzbek and Tajik sides. I can see from here where you must be. I can see a gate after Tajik customs where a few people are waiting. But, a soldier with a rifle will not allow me to walk to the customs building."

Shahboz understood and didn't seem concerned. He said he would see if he could find out what I needed to do. He asked me to call him back in fifteen minutes. I added that I seemed to be the only person trying to cross the border in either direction so he would recognise me easily. I thanked him for being there.

The next fifteen minutes were easier after speaking to Shahboz. I felt sure he would wait and help me through. I smiled at the soldier with a friendly glance, but neither of us knew what the other was thinking. What did he know that I didn't? Was the situation more serious?

After waiting and glancing rcpeatedly at my watch impatiently, I indicated to the solider that I would like to make another call. He nodded, so I called Shahboz back. He replied, "I have just been to the customs building and there is only one man who works there. He has gone for dinner." He added, "We will just have to wait."

I smiled more warmly at my guard, with a happy glint in my eye now I knew. A few minutes later, the soldier's walkie-talkie came to life. He spoke to someone and then immediately gestured that I should continue to the customs building.

The solitary officer, who combined the customs and immigration roles, greeted me politely. He spoke good English. I thought it wiser not to mention that I hoped he had a good dinner.

I was very relieved to meet Shahboz. We drove on to reach the northern Tajik city of Khujand at dusk and went immediately to the Arbob Cultural Palace. A wedding was about to begin, and I wondered if we could take a look. Shahboz asked the groom's family if a foreigner would be allowed to see something of a Tajik wedding. "Certainly, and you must both sit with us at a special table," they said. As the evening continued, just as in Uzbekistan, leaving was harder than coming in. They also wanted to see all my photographs from Central Asia.

At the banquet, Shahboz and I had a chance to talk to each other as well as the wedding party guests. This was the last day of August, a very busy time for mountain guides, I learned. Shahboz had been on the road every day of the month and had not seen his wife Guldasta or his infant daughter Amina for a few weeks. The wedding made him miss them more.

The Arbob Cultural Palace, Khujand at dusk

The morning after the wedding, we visited the Panjshanbe Bazaar. Walking through Asian markets always brings me to life; the sights, smells and tastes; the laughter and smiles, lush fruits and pretty children.

The Thursday bazaar, Panjshanbe in Khujand

After the bazaar, we began our drive towards the mountains. Shahboz had planned for us to hike in two different mountain ranges. Firstly, we should drive to Panjakent via the Shahristan Pass and Zarafshan Valley before walking to seven beautiful lakes. Secondly, he would take me to the Fann Mountains and stay by Lake Iskanderkul, where we would walk. Iskander is the Persian name for Alexander. Shahboz shared the local legend; Alexander and his army were camping by the lake on his way to India; his horse, Bucephalus, dived to the bottom of lake never to return again.

Soon we discovered that the Aini - Penjikent road was closed following a landslide. There was no access to the seven lakes. Shahboz was distraught. He was making frantic calls to try and rearrange our journey, by leaving for the Fann Mountains first, but this proved extremely difficult. He was tearing his hair out. Meanwhile, I occupied myself looking at maps, taking into account everything I had learned since he picked me up from the border. I asked him to pause for a second. He explained the difficulty of finding accommodation at short notice when so few had a mobile phone and anyway the mountain region had poor signal. He was most anxious that I would be upset. But, I told him, "This is the least of your worries. I am used to challenges like this and happy to do something else. I am sure we will find easily a plan which makes sense."

Looking at maps, the answer seemed obvious to me. But, this involved a solution he would not have thought to suggest. I decided to see if we could come to the same conclusion gently.

I asked him: "I think we should leave all your arrangements for our visit to the Fann Mountains as they are. Would you agree?" He agreed instantly, realising how difficult mobile phone communications were with the mountain regions.

"So, all we need is to think of somewhere else to go for a couple of days?" He also agreed but could not immediately think of anywhere which would please me. Having studied the maps, I had seen that his home village, Basmanda, was just an hour and a half away. The next question surprised him.

"If you imagine that I was not with you, and you only had to take me to the Fann Mountains in two days' time, you would use this free time to go home and visit your wife and daughter, wouldn't you?" The way he responded with excitement was not a surprise. "Then, if you can find a place for me to stay, even on a floor in your village, why don't we do that? I would be very pleased to see a Tajik village." He asked if I would be willing to stay with him. "Nothing would please me more, as long as this is not a burden," I said.

We decided not to warn his family; we would just turn up and surprise them. This was going to be more fun for me than hiking around the lakes. The first planned hike was easily forgotten.

With a little extra time on our hands, we stopped at Istaravshan with her beautiful Madrassa of Abdullatif Sultan. Then we climbed the hills to chat with families cutting up apples. Left to dry in the sun, these lasted for months. They tasted the same in winter, or so the ladies said.

A couple of hours later, after a long and bumpy track, we arrived in Basmanda. His family were so kind, and treated me royally. Two days later we set off for the Fann Mountains.

While driving to the mountains, I realised how many accidents of history were caused by a small detail which one culture had misunderstood of another. Had the Tajik soldier been able to explain from the outset that we needed to wait an hour, no anxiety would have arisen. By not knowing, our imagination can conjure up so many other possibilities including threatening ones. Our own history determines how our imagination works. Misunderstandings like these caused the Crimean War, fuelled by warrior and tribal tendencies from our British history.

Cutting apples for drying and preservation on the sunny hills.

Lake Iskanderkul

Fann Mountains

ANCESTRAL LESSONS

To help us understand our history, there are many important messages from our ancestors which they want us to hear, or see. They are still speaking to us, if we listen. A hearing person experiences words as sounds. Perhaps there is less need to *look* at words or to wonder where they come from. Our ancestors come to life when we start to investigate words with a different listening ear, and take a fresh look. All of a sudden we can find mysterious aspects of our culture which are very much alive. Like a rock in the garden. As we move her, all kinds of insects and beetles can be seen scurrying about. They must have been there a very long time but we hadn't looked before.

Not only may secrets of our own culture be revealed, but similarities and differences with different cultures might also appear. For example, take the English word 'liver'. The word hints at living. But why is life attached to this organ which we call the 'liver'? In Chinese, a liver is written as 肝. The left hand character, in ancient times, was used for a 'person'. 肝 could therefore be anciently understood as *'person stand up'*. A liver is connected in English with living and in Chinese with a 'person standing up'. Not so dissimilar after all. Perhaps the coincidence reminds us that to be a real person we must 'stand up' and live spontaneously.

Watching with the eye of a deaf person, and listening with the ear of someone whose hearing has returned, made me aware of a frequent misfit in the phrase, *I will try*. Uncannily often, when someone told me *they would try,* my deaf sight told me they were not even going to bother. Their speech and their body language seemed quite disconnected whilst uttering this specific phrase. Suddenly, it dawned that the verb 'to try' has opposite meanings in English. The meaning can either be 'to attempt' or 'to frustrate', as in a child who is 'trying'. The question of why my ancestors gave this word a double meaning seemed an intriguing line of inquiry. Also, how fascinating that people *unconsciously,* but frequently, use this particular phrase when quite ambivalent about their likely future effort in the subject.

Was this a one off, like a lone beetle under the rock? Or was there lots of life, which had been missed, under similar rocks? The only answer was to look under more rocks which reminded me of my childhood in the woods. The range of beetles and other insects in their colonies fascinated me.

In the English language, we have a significant number of words which contain two opposite meanings, known as 'contronyms'. That we have even a name for this family of words is relevant. We may have more contronyms than all other European languages combined. Why would a language, which can be so precise, have so many words implying opposite meanings? The 'surprise' is even more telling when we discover that many of these words relate to subjects of the greatest significance in our lives. Many of our contronyms include ambiguity on whether we are being helped and free on the one hand or to whether we are being hindered, obstructed or made captive on the other hand. These are not small nuances. On the contrary, the most common subjects of our contronyms are perhaps the most important desires of British culture; individuality, independence and freedom of expression. Immediately, this reminded me of my Viking and Victim roots and of Martín's observation; *you come from a people that wrestles with that.* Have our ancestors been sending a clear message, and have we been deaf?

The first family of contradictions relate to whether we are free or the opposite, whether we are helped or obstructed. Just a few examples are considered below:

> **Bound** means 'heading for some destination'; and can even imply joy and anticipation as in 'leaps and bounds'. Except that the word also means 'tied up'.
>
> **Fast** means either quickly or tied up, like 'made fast' as slaves often were, showing that the two opposite meanings in 'bound' were not an exception;
>
> To **bolt** means both to secure and to flee;
>
> A **trip** is both a journey as well as an obstacle which makes us fall;

Left can either mean departed (as if on a trip) or remained as in left behind;

To *buckle* means both to 'connect with' as well as 'to bend and give way under pressure';

To '*hold up*' means both 'to lift and support' as well as to 'attack for gain' as in a bank robbery;

To *fix* means either to repair or to neuter by castration or spaying.

Some of our contronyms are connected with importance and hierarchy:

A *peer* is both a person of nobility and an equal colleague;

A *custom* is both a common practice for everyone as well as a specially made treatment for a few;

A *variety* can be either a specific type, or alternatively an indiscriminate number of types;

A *model* is both an exemplar as well as a copy.

When we speak of management or leadership the ambiguity in our language continues:

To *overlook* means both to supervise and to neglect;

Oversight can mean either to have supervision of, or forgetting to look;

To '*give out*' means both to provide as well as to collapse due to insufficiency;

To *flog* means to sell or promote as well as to beat with a whip;

Finished can either mean successfully completed or ended by destruction;

To *screen* can be to exhibit as in a cinema or to hide and shield from view;

Likewise *transparent* means both invisible and obvious at the same time;

To *sanction* means to give permission as well as to punish or boycott;[62]

To '*wind up*' means either 'to end' or 'to begin' as in provoke or wind up a toy.

An ambiguity is also found in the expression 'to fight with France' which can mean both to fight alongside France as well as to fight against France. Considering how often we changed alliances in European wars, perhaps this lack of clarity is unsurprising. Apparently, in the last thousand years, the number of wars between Britain and France is the same number as those in which we joined to wage war on a third party. In our history, fighting with or against France is clearly much of a muchness as the words in our language can imply.

The Latin word 'sanguine' has evolved in English, perhaps because of our Viking invaders, to mean either confidently cheerful or bloodthirsty. Most of us might say that 'sanguine' is therefore a contronym. Erik the Red from Norway, whose murderous activities caused him to be regularly expelled westwards until he settled in Greenland around 982 CE, might have felt the two meanings of sanguine went hand in hand. Perhaps Tolui, Genghis Khan's son who butchered Merv, would share the sentiment.

The English also have a famous butcher, Dick Turpin, who 'operated' primarily in the 1730s. When he wasn't relieving animals of their skin and bones, he made a living fleecing folk on their journeys. He is perhaps our best known 'highwayman'. If English is not my reader's first language, the word highwayman does not mean someone who collects tolls on the turnpike but the meaning is not dissimilar. We English love our double negatives; they allow more ambiguity to creep in. We prefer the term 'highwayman' because someone who indulges in '*highway robbery*' is much too definite a term.

The early 18th century was a time when one could travel comfortably by horse drawn stagecoach, if one had the means. Unfortunately, Dick Turpin and his gang descended upon such travellers with regularity. Like vultures taking easy pickings. The records say he *relieved Mr Godfrey of six guineas and a pocket book on Hounslow Heath*. Relieved? Were the six guineas

---

[62] Some contronyms, like 'sanction', are of Latin origin and we share this word with many of our European neighbours. Perhaps the Romans enjoyed this ambiguity too.

and the pocket book so heavy that Mr Godfrey needed relief? Dick struck again in Epping Forest *depriving a man from Southwark of his belongings*. The word 'depriving' seems chosen for ambivalence as if wishing to highlight the elegant way the skin of belongings had been masterfully removed from a lamb. Where is the rage? Or was road rage something which only came in our current generation? Dick became more audacious, with more blood involved, until he was caught and executed at York in 1739. He was romanticised in English folklore, together with his magnificent horse 'Black Bess', as if many in our culture wished they could have done the same. Actually many did, but more often overseas where the arm of the law was less of a burden.

Writing this chapter, and listing some contronyms, immediately reminded me of Dick Turpin. Beginning with the era of *fast* stagecoaches and horses; travellers *bound* with free spirit on an exciting *trip*; until one bumps into Mr Turpin. Quite a *trip*. All of a sudden the passengers are '*held up*'. Some unlucky enough to be tied or bound with rope while relieved of objects of more interest to Mr Turpin.

The word 'coach', as in stagecoaches, comes from Hungary. Specifically from the village of Kocs, pronounced coach, where steel spring suspension was invented in the early 1400s. The more comfortable ride was much in demand across Europe and gave rise to 'coach' in most European languages. In Oxford University slang, 'coach' was first used in the 1830s to denote a tutor who carried one smoothly through the examination phase. This meaning caught on and prevails today.

One has to smile deliciously at the way our ancestors polished these words like smooth pebbles on the beach. Perhaps they chuckled as they knew all along what they were up to. There is another ancient possibility. Could contronyms have originally meant only one thing, but our desire to 'run away' from something fearful had introduced the idea of an opposite meaning? The opposite meaning may have offered some safety from the truth. It is much safer to keep in mind the idea that confidently cheerful and bloodthirsty are polar opposites, and instead go to movies where these two can 'only' be 'paired' on the screen.

There seem to be so many lessons from our ancestors waiting to be found once we are willing to look underneath the rocks. We might even remember that a rock is both a noun for something immobile as well as a verb for an action of doing the opposite, like rocking a baby. Rocking a baby is not entirely benign; there is a sense of something unsettling about the activity…

Martín often recommended we take more interest in etymology. However, this was the only example of his advice which was not needed in my case. Ever since my silent years, the origins of words had always aroused my curiosity. He also suggested we look out for irony, which the English have in abundance, to see what we can learn about our cultures. However, the examples of contronyms above do not seem to have any suggestion of humour. On the contrary, they seem more of a signpost to our culture's tragic wrestling with our past.

The English, Dutch and Danish form a close genetic cluster. One of the traits we three nations share is sarcasm. My family name, Goodwin, is a very ancient name for 'a protector and a friend' but this name is also used for the *most sly and treacherous* part of the waters off the South-East coast of Britain. These shifting sands which are constantly altered by the tides and currents are sarcastically named the 'Goodwin sands' and have sunk over two thousand ships in the last thousand years.

The thought which occurs to me is whether my island culture has found a way to dissipate fear with laughter, packaged as a silent pair. Is this why sarcasm is so important to us? Because sarcasm enables a biting and cutting remark to be sugar coated with humour? And the 'deadpan face' can preserve our stiff upper lip while serving delicious malice. Is sarcasm a very precise and directed form of irony?

This selection of some English contronyms might seem to my reader a fun interlude while writing more serious matters one morning. Except that the ancestors clearly want to be heard. We really cannot ignore how many of our 'contronyms' relate to whether we have freedom or not, as to whether we are helped or hindered. These words contain metaphors in our island psyche which are serious matters. It is, however, comforting to realise how many previous generations shared my internal struggles and contradictions. We clearly come from a people that 'wrestle with that".

On my travels, an interest in etymology often made me ask why a word in another culture meant what it meant. Since their language was unknown to me, we jointly explored like detectives until we made discoveries such as the Chinese character for liver. For someone like me who speaks no Chinese, etymology in China is like doing a jigsaw puzzle in reverse. Having started with the full picture of a character, one can disassemble the components until each piece of the puzzle has only a part of the original. Next, one can ask, what does that part mean? Mirth and enthusiasm can follow. So far, my Chinese hosts have always seemed to enjoy the game. Let me give an example.

While in Hohhot, the capital of Inner Mongolia, my curiosity asked how to write the name Goodwin. To which the reply was simply to draw the image shown here. Undeterred, the next question was how to disassemble the parts. First of all, my host explained that there were two characters. The one on the left, pronounced 'Hao', means 'good' and the one on the right, pronounced 'in' means 'win'. Simple enough, except my curiosity runs much deeper. How then does the one on the left mean good? The patient answer was that 'Hao' is also made up of two characters, for female and male, which is good, they said with a sweet smile. That seemed easy enough. Just to check, the left-most part, 女 means female. My enthusiasm for this new game encouraged my hosts to play more. The character on the right was explained as made up of five other characters. On the top, sits the character for *death*. Below death is a character looking like a post box which is *mouth*. Then under, mouth, is a triplet of characters, meaning *moon, money* and *normal*. It was quite natural for me then to ask how one derives "win" from *death, mouth, moon, money* and *normal*. This caught my audience off guard and led to much animated banter between them. The answer was not obvious and instead a reply at breakfast was promised.

The following morning's breakfast included a delicious reply. Well, they said, the character 月 which is usually translated as moon or month, used to mean a person in ancient times. They had discovered overnight that, during the time of Chairman Mao, this character had changed her meaning from person to moon. They showed me many other characters relating to the body such as waist, muscle, and of course liver, which included a moon or month. They were more surprised than me. The discovery of the meaning of liver was just a bonus along the way. Finally, having asked again how these five characters make up win, their response was amazing. *Death on top means that one's mind has 'overcome death' so implies alertness of mind; the mouth in the middle means a good communicator. The three characters underneath suggest supporting features. The former 'moon' represents the support of people, the shell refers to the support of many assets rather than just money, and the character for normal comes from one of our fairy tales of a fairy who came down to earth.* Altogether, *'In'* means *an alert mind, a good communicator with the support of the people, both tangible and intangible assets and down to earth.* Wow, quite a winner.

Naturally this is a joyous memory and can often be shared. Just a few days ago, meeting a Chinese couple on the train to Cambridge, led to the opportunity for me to offer this knowledge. They seemed as amazed as my hosts in Hohhot. Or were they just being polite?

By contrast, the English word 'win' comes from our genetic cousins, the Dutch and Danish. The verb has origins in *strive, struggle and fight*, presumably successfully. Clearly, 'win' means something quite different to the ancestors of the English and the Chinese.

Other cultures have very different lessons in their etymologies. The range of paradigms is much wider than we realise 'in the West'. Perhaps the most important lesson for us is to jettison completely the idea that one way of life suits all. We have spent far too long promoting our ideas of leadership, governance, political systems, and values. We need to help build a future on the premise that different paradigms are equally valuable.

In English, racism is a noun meaning "prejudice, discrimination, or antagonism directed against a person or culture on the basis of their ethnic group". The meaning should perhaps include a few extra words such as 'on the basis of their paradigms or beliefs'. Attacking beliefs, and calling them 'heresies', has also been poisonous. In *Mannership*, I discovered that different religions share much more than they differ. We need all of them to understand the planet, just as we need all the plants.

The Relationship between America and China

We do not know when the United States became the world's largest economy. Some suggest more than two centuries ago. Others suspect the time when her population exceeded that of the UK in the 1850s. The surge since the Great Depression of the 1930s confirmed the trends.

China has, by contrast, hosted the position of the world's largest economy for most of the last 5,000 years and is bound to regain her 'normal' place before too long. Maybe she has already done so.

On paper the relationship between America and China should be something to celebrate. But, for some, the idea is fearful.

The good news is there is much that both America and China share. They became strong as a result of the size of their domestic economies and their own ingenuity. Their entrepreneurial artisans have freely produced much that the rest of us admire. They are both 'civic' cultures who have sought to govern with a code of ethics and justice. They both have strong faith in meritocracy. Neither has a state religion, thank God, and both tolerate religious practice within reason. Both seek equality for women, universal education, and have relied on the success of independent families. Although not obvious, they share a 'National shyness', and have been introverted on the global stage for much of their history.

This is quite unlike most of the last eight thousand years when strength in many parts of the world was usually measured by conquering, enslaving, or plundering the treasures of others.

In a perfect state, the world would benefit enormously from a marriage between America and China. That is obviously going too far, but a 'civic partnership' would be equally good. There is no reason why this could not come about. The obstacles are mostly a potential misunderstanding of the other's paradigms. If the US plays a 'straight bat' they are likely to find the Chinese will play ball.

During my travels in the USA, it was not uncommon for an American to be suspicious of China. My role was to remind them that, in reality, China is very low on the 'warrior index' and does not have much history of external aggression. She doesn't think the way an American does. There really is little to fear. This reminds me of the American Scrub Jays. Only those jays with a history of pilfering from others relocate their food cache if they feel another noticed their hiding place. What we fear in others is often a part of ourselves. We should remember how reluctant America was to join the two World Wars of the twentieth century. It took quite some provocation by Japan to get the USA engaged in war. China could sympathise here. My response was to remind Americans of their own history, and their more peaceful nature before Pearl Harbor. Therefore they should not provoke China. China has never sought to be a global policeman as such a role is not a part of her nature. Whenever she was open to the world, she only wanted to trade.

Meredith's five key genotypes provide a useful yardstick to compare the US and China.

- Both cultures are very strong on civic and service behaviours.
- Neither culture is comfortable with tribalism.
- On the primordial genotype, China is above average. Although the USA exhibits a lower percentage of primordial behaviours, they have this in abundance if they could just make a fresh alliance with the Native Indian traditions within their land.
- Whereas the USA would score high on a warrior index, China would score very low here. This is a real opportunity for misunderstanding between them. Many Americans suspect that China is being doubly devious in hiding their future aggression. It is not part of the American paradigm to accept that China could simply be low on the warrior genotype, and that they are not seeking to hide violent tendencies. It will take more persuading to convince most Americans that China is not dangerous. Over the last four thousand years, China has rarely been aggressive beyond her borders.

In summary, the USA exhibits a 'warrior civic' culture whereas China's traditions are more 'primordial civic' governance.

One aspect of the 'civic' Chinese and American philosophies warrants a mention - the shared values implied in the 'Square and Compasses'. The writings of Mencius around 280 BCE teach that *men should apply the Square and Compasses figuratively to their lives and the Level and the Marking Line besides if they would walk the straight and even paths of wisdom and keep themselves within the boundaries of Honour and Virtue.* Mencius continues *A Master Mason in teaching his apprentice makes use of the Compasses and Square; ye who are engaged in the pursuit of Wisdom, must also make use of the Compasses and Square.*

George Washington was a prominent freemason as were many of his generals in the revolutionary war. Most of those who wrote the US constitution were freemasons sharing similar values to the Confucian *Compasses and Square.* Many masonic symbols figure on the US Dollar bill.

In the case of China, Confucian principles were taught to civil servants and emperors alike. The principles of leading while following paths of virtue are deep and ancient in Chinese history.

In the case of America, the masonic principles came from England and Scotland. As John Dickie writes in *Craft*, Freemasonry is a fellowship of men bound by a goal of self-betterment. Although political or religious discussion is not permitted in masonic lodges, there is no surprise that men seeking 'self-betterment' should also seek a more libertarian form of society. In many countries masonic lodges were a fertile ground for libertarians seeking individualism, free association and political freedom, together with a skepticism of authority and state power. In a lodge, kings and princes become equal brothers without superior rank which appealed to the writers of the US constitution. A masonic acceptance of a 'superior sovereign' without discussion of religion ensured that America was founded without a 'state religion'.

Following the Great Fire of 1666, London was rebuilt with stone. Although true stone masons were much in demand, the growth of 'Free and Accepted Masons' or freemasons was also rapid in the same period.

British history in the 17th century includes a metamorphosis in the relationship between parliament and the monarchy including questions of religion. After the English Civil War, King Charles I was executed on 30 January 1649. Eleven years later, in May 1660, parliament decided to restore the monarchy by inviting his son Charles II to become the King. During the subsequent reign of James, the younger brother of Charles II, parliament decided that 'King James had abdicated'. The throne was passed instead to his daughter Mary, and her Dutch husband William, in the Glorious Revolution of 1688. From this time onwards, British kings and queens ruled on condition that they needed approval of the Lords and the Commons to make law.

The British parliamentary party, the Whigs, was instrumental in following the public demand for political reform including the development of a constitutional monarchy and a reform of voting rights. As Dickie found in his research, there was a strong correlation between the Whigs and the growth of freemasonry in the same period. These libertarian ideals also became enshrined in the US constitution. Sadly, the early masonic lodges in America did not initially admit men of colour. Instead, the English Grand Lodge granted warrants to establish Prince Hall masonic lodges including black men in North America.

Both China and USA recognise that they have 'work to do' in improving their civic governance and their treatment of minorities. Rather than criticising the faults of the other, it helps to understand the current state. The USA has a quarter of the world's prison population. China has fears of tribalism and religious fundamentalism due to her history with the Mongols as well as bearers of fundamentalist religions.

There is a possibility that the fear of a shortage of water originating in the Himalayas might have been part of the motivation for the consolidation of Tibet. Could the friction between China and India have any relationship to the potential scarcity of water resources for their vast populations?

In terms of the future relationship between USA and China, the analogy with Britain and Russia in the 1830s is relevant. Britain feared Russian designs on her Empire, which fear was manufactured and misplaced. Russia had concerns about British aggression which was very real. This summarises well the military position between the USA and China currently. Just as Britain attacked Russia in the Crimea, any conflict between USA and China could only be started by the USA.

As a civic partner, an improved relationship with China might therefore nudge America away from a fascination with exotic weapons. We would all benefit.

We must be conscious that these potential civic partners have a few significant differences.

The USA does not have a long history of respect for Government. On the contrary, many went to America to 'escape Government' and become a law unto themselves. By contrast, 4,000 years ago, during a great flood, Yu organised the necessary civil works and founded the first Chinese dynasty, the Xia. Thus, they share a 'polar opposite' of origins and will always have different paradigms with respect to Governance. The secret surely is simply to recognise the difference. It will not be possible for one to 'understand' the other on this subject matter. We should therefore not be surprised if America lags behind China in terms of infrastructure; particularly new roads, bridges, fast trains, airports and so on. The American tradition is less of infrastructure built by Government, more built on the individual horse or automobile.

The USA is a champion of two British traits - individuality and freedom of expression. They might see these traits as 'hand in hand' and inseparable. China has admiration for individuality too, but their history since the Great Flood of 1900 BCE and other differences, such as the cultivation of rice, have made the family and wider groups in the community more important for survival. A culture's freedom of expression is one of her most defining traits; change is feared by both sides. The Dutch are very much 'in your face' with their directness, while other cultures are reluctant to raise subjects which might cause offence. Such differences should not matter if both parties understand where the other is coming from. There is no sense in attempting to change the other's perspectives. As time has gone by, the increase in China's freedom of expression was, however, noticeable by both Meredith and me independently on our journeys to China.

Because of their different histories, these two countries will never have similar political systems, but they can both share the desire to be prosperous and strong. With most political leaders it is not hard to realise that this could be a win – win for both of them. The unique cultural history and traditions affect the potential courses of a river's developmental path. When President Xi Jinping speaks of "deeper reform and opening up," he is not starting from the same paradigms as Indo-Europeans and therefore will have other ideas in mind. But we can admire the sentiment even without knowing what exactly.

There are positive and negative aspects of different paradigms of Governance. On my last trip to Cambridge, a lady taxi driver complained of the disastrous layout of the station taxi stand. She is right, actually. She went on to grumble about many other failings in our infrastructural design. My response was to remind her that this is the price we pay for our desire for individuality. We have been speaking about a third runway at Heathrow airport for seventeen years and might need another ten years to build, assuming all the individual opposition is overcome. China is hoping to build another 136 new airports in seven years. But, they are bigger than us so the comparison is not fair. The comparison is defeated by the realisation that our ancestors came to this island because individuality is what mattered to them, not the speed of runways. That is why some cultures have an inbuilt resistance to change. We love our eccentric professors, our punks on the Kings Road and many other exotic traditions. Runways can wait.

Instead of trying to negotiate a trade-off between Asian deference and avoidance of embarrassment and a Western belief in individuality and self-expression, perhaps we can have both. We might find that, actually, having both is what Confucius and Aristotle propose.

In summary, both America and China want to trade. President Xi Jinping seeks new relationships and a resurgence of the Silk Road Economic Belt. The truth is that we all want the same, really. Let's not let egos and paranoia distract us from an intelligent outcome. Travelling together we might absorb some new ways to solve issues by borrowing from each other's paradigms and thinking differently.

Assuming that America and China develop well, while Europe understands the need for a wider partnership including Britain, Russia, Belarus and the Ukraine, life ought to be simpler for everyone around the world. Together, we could then address more easily the much deeper issues within modern society. The destruction of our planet and self-destruction of our young children is much more important. With sane minds, global politics is the easy part.

Following a more fruitful conversation between America and China, perhaps they could agree how the 20th century taught us that both Capitalism and Communism have their failings. We know how easy it is to get lost or to take the wrong path. Greed in a culture, and greed among some business leaders can cause ethics to disappear.

My worry is that capitalism does not clearly distinguish between profit which is honourable or criminal. However, consensual leadership is usually more honourable. The most outrageous buccaneers who took slaves from West Africa to the Americas were warrior leaders. But the problem is much older than the Vikings as we will see in the next chapter on when and where the madness began.

We cannot simply blame the Viking or warrior leaders who took slaves to the Americas. We should remember how Governments did not always discourage the activity. Nicholas Draper has said that a third of those investing in the London docks in the 18th century were reaping benefits from slave trading, if we include the transport, insurance, and produce.[63] A few months ago, a newspaper article pointed out that the stock exchange in Mogadishu, Somalia, was now functioning again. But the best opportunities for capital gain were in companies involved with piracy. Not much has changed.

There has been much publicity showing the extent to which slavery is still operating in modern society. The UK Government estimates there are tens of thousands enslaved in Britain today. But we also miss something else completely; the extent to which something similar to serfdom is still prevalent within society. Have we become numb because it is such a large part of our history?

Companies tend to be led either in a 'civic or consensual' manner, or in a 'warrior' manner. The warrior companies treat their employees and customers like serfs. If we start looking, they are not so hard to find. Remember the contracts that take so much effort to escape from. Just try to transfer your business to someone else. The civic companies are easy to leave; they regret the loss and learn from losing us. The warrior companies make escape difficult; they construct obstacles and extra forms or letters to be filled in before we are even eligible to depart. The 'cancellation of subscription' button is impossible to find on their websites, or it doesn't work, or we have to wait on a long phone call to find out the first step of a procedure for escape. Remember those refunds we were due but the effort was overwhelming and we gave up. The civic companies seek to improve service and effectiveness. The warrior companies calculate the maximum they could increase their annual fees by before you take your business elsewhere and increase their

---

[63] N. Draper, *The City of London and Slavery: Evidence from the First Dock Companies, 1795-1800* in *The Economic History Review*.

charges just a little less than this 'trigger amount'. What about overcrowding on rush-hour trains? Does this remind us of being treated like serfs?

The UK Competition and Markets Authority reported that the British public are paying an additional £3.9 billion pounds annually as a result of 'loyalty penalties' to companies that 'keep *loyal* customers in higher priced contracts'. This is made up of £1.1 billion in savings, £1 billion in cost of broadband, £800 million in mortgages, £700 million in home insurance and £300 million in mobile phone contracts.

In the United Kingdom, we have suffered for centuries from our misguided support for 'warrior companies'. They may have higher annual returns and higher share prices which some fortunate members of the public enjoy. Some of them contribute more tax, which the Government appreciates. But these companies are not paying for the grief they provoke. Such companies created most of the atrocities of what became the British Empire. We need complete transparency so that we can weed out the warrior leadership from society.

As said before, as a culture "we wrestle with that"; the warrior and the victim. Until we are willing to stand up and state that we want the consensual part, the civic part of capitalism but not the warrior aspects, we will not have the leaders we need. China has also identified her challenge to overcome corruption. Her leadership is now committed to zero-tolerance with regard to corruption by both "tigers" and "flies". So we should be committed to root out the Vikings and Serfdom managers within capitalism. Maybe our two cultures will then meet half way.

Having more individuality and self-expression, we can use the internet to find a way to highlight those warrior companies treating us like serfs. A few extra whistle blower laws protecting those who tell the truth could come in handy. Also, a law entitling the public to compensation from a list of serf-like annoyances would sort the wheat from the chaff. Eradicating these behaviours will let the market reward those who improve honourably instead of the reverse which is too often the case, thus tempting weak leaders to take the wrong path as the Hoppers found in their *Puritan Gift*.

This is our responsibility to demand an end to Viking and serfdom activity within capitalism. Warrior skills can instead be better employed finding ways to attack society's diseases; the poacher can become a gamekeeper. We will not solve our problems with Vikings at the helm. But a reformed Viking might be priceless. Robert Bly overcame his Viking ancestry and he made a wonderful teacher.

When and Where the Madness Began

Since the Indo-European culture began in the under-belly of Russia, there is much that Russia, Britain and the settler culture of the USA share. China has quite different cultural beginnings.

Britain and Russia colonised 40% of the world in the 19ᵗʰ century. Combining this with activities of other European countries, most of the world was affected. This chapter broaches possible origins for particular tendencies which have been primarily spread by Indo-Europeans in their colonisation of others, wondering how the Imperial madness might have begun.

As seen in the small atolls of Tungaru in the I-Kiribati group, differences between neighbouring cultures can give clues to their origins and evolution. Their experiences led to the effects of some particular traumas, including 'marriage by rape' on two islands, the crusade on Tabiteuea, the reign of terror on Abemama, and others.

Cultural detective work in the case of Indo-Europeans is not so difficult; lots of finger prints and documentation of early events are surprisingly available. It is easier to see where the history of destruction might have began, and when, but why is more difficult to answer. Perhaps we will find out 'why' if we are successful in turning the tide of the self-destruction of our young children as well as the destruction of our planct.

Before examining sources of destruction in cultures, it may be helpful to summarise the clues to self-destruction in an individual mind as recounted in *Mannership*.

Adrian Raine's career in studying the brains of murderers on death row in California found that neither genetics nor childhood abuse was sufficient to produce a violent destiny. As he says, "biology is not destiny."[64] He found that the nature versus nurture debate came out as a tie. The relationship between these two factors was more important than either of them.

Adrian Raine also highlights a number of other factors which potentially influence the outcome including our birth experience and the quality of maternal reception. Raine convinced me with a study published in 1994. This involved 4,269 male births at the Rigshospitalet in Denmark in 1959. A record was made of whether these boys had suffered birth complications or subsequent maternal rejection within their first year. Maternal rejection was defined as to whether the mother had not wanted the pregnancy, had tried to abort, or the boy had been placed in a public institution, for any reason, exceeding four months in early infancy. Eighteen years later the court records were studied to see which of these males had been arrested for violent crimes. The conclusions were dramatic, and supported by other studies in North America.

The small percentage that became violent before the age of eighteen was similar if they had neither maternal rejection, nor birth complications, or had just one of these two indicators. However, among the boys who suffered both a complicated birth and maternal rejection the percentage becoming violent was three times higher. Moreover, even though the percentage of the boys suffering the 'double whammy' was only 4.5% of the sample, this small group accounted for 18% of all violent crimes perpetrated by the 4,259 boys. Interestingly, Adrian's study found that the increase in this effect only applied to violent behaviour and not to criminal behaviour in general.

My curiosity was aroused by an analogy with the extraordinary navigation systems of birds and ocean creatures. They have a number of independent navigational senses which resonate and enable them to find the same nest or spawning ground after many thousands of miles. I wondered if their different navigation systems also 'came out as a tie' to help the precision of navigation. If two or more separate senses or systems were clearly indicating south there would be little hesitation in flying that way. But if one suggested south and the other north, then other factors must be brought into consideration to resolve an internal conflict. Homing pigeons that make regular journeys between the same lofts do not always take the same route. Their flight path seems nudged

---

[64] Adrian Raine *Anatomy of Violence.*

by the separate impulses from their different systems. Perhaps our minds try to do the same, except that for many of us, because we remain stationary in our anxiety, we don't have any fresh air to help improve our directional guidance. We just go around and around in mind circles.

I understood at once that if a boy suffered a traumatic birth and was rejected by his mother, the young male mind would sense this world was not a good place. If two navigation systems are awry, it is very hard to navigate a safe course.

My interest in the birth experience led to a conversation with a midwife, Stella. She captured my imagination with her humbling warm observation of the new-born ability to look through her, communicating with eye contact, 'speaking' like a whale. This reminded me of the ancient meaning of the word 'beneficence'; to promote a feeling of wellbeing in others. The young of all species are specialists in beneficence. This ability enhances a new-born's chance of survival.

In the womb we cannot communicate with our eyes. But, from the instant we emerge we can reach out to others with the language behind our eyes. The loss of my hearing at fifteen months, and a silence which lasted until I was seven years old, caused me to continually rely on the 'language behind our eyes' which I named 'deaf-sight'. All over the world, the eye contact language looked the same to me and led me to wonder whether this was the meaning behind: *And the whole earth was of one language.*[65] On my journeys, it is always a pleasure to greet young children with this primordial language. The smiles in their eyes reach my heart easily.

Self-destruction implies that there is a part of us being harmed or destroyed by another part as in the Biblical story of Cain and Abel. I wrote in *Mannership*; *I have chosen to refer to this instinctual genius as the part of me from birth which is 'able', or Abel. Abel 'speaks' the common language and can offer up his communication with other first born creatures. Abel thus stands for my 'essence'. Our cultures affect us in many diverse ways. Soon enough we are able to start internalising the demands of our culture in exercising self-control. The part of us which plans and maintains vigilance on our abilities and impulses is the domain of the pre-frontal cortex, but includes more. Over time our self-control restricts and constrains the Abel part, or canes him to ensure cultural compliance. This other brother can be called 'cane' for short, or Cain for simplicity.*

---

[65] Genesis 11:1.

Bruno Bettelheim, in *The Uses of Enchantment*, explains that our oldest fairy tales are of two brothers. He adds that there are over 770 versions of this story in different languages during the last three thousand years. In all variations he suggests the two brothers symbolise opposite aspects impelling us to act in contrary ways; the nature nurture interplay in shorthand. Bettelheim concludes that a successful existence is only permitted following a thorough integration of these contrary tendencies.

The two themes of nature and nurture seem clear in the Cain and Abel story. Abel offers up the first born animals whereas Cain offers up the cultivation of the land. The animal spontaneity or 'first born animals' is linked with Abel. The culture, or cultivation, is linked with Cain. Following on from the brothers Cain and Abel, there is a similar theme in the twins Jacob and Esau.[66] In this case Esau acts impulsively which belongs with nature and Jacob studies in tents which belongs with culture. I became convinced that the Cain and Abel myth was not about jealousy, or murder, or fratricide, but about self-destruction. In the old stories, Culture is always triumphant over Nature.

During my explorations into these Genesis stories, I encountered the writing of Samuel Noah Kramer, a world-renowned expert in Sumerian history. Kramer suggests that the Cain and Abel story is an abbreviation of a much earlier Sumerian poem of two brothers Emesh and Enten. This is how my cultural enquiry led me to the Fertile Crescent and Sumer in particular. After some background to the history of this territory we will return to the import of the myths.

The Fertile Crescent agricultural revolution did not, initially, disturb the egalitarian nature of primordial society in this region. Around 8,500 years ago the Ubaid people arrived in southern Mesopotamia. Their indigenous neighbours, the Halaf, occupied the land further upstream including the foothills of the Euphrates and Tigris River headlands.

Marcella Frangipane explains the evidence of their egalitarian styles in the 6th millennium BCE.[67] Both communities had dwellings of similar size and style arranged haphazardly in their villages. A scarcity of communal buildings suggests the importance of extended families. While both cultures had essentially egalitarian burial procedures, there was more diversity in style within the Halaf. This might reflect different

---

[66] Genesis 25.

[67] Marcella Frangipane, *Different Types of Egalitarian Societies and the Development of Inequality in Early Mesopotamia* in *World Archaeology*, Vol. 39(2).

traditions among the peoples who had joined together in the 'upper river' region. Both societies managed agriculture and livestock. Each developed their distinctive styles of painted pottery. Both peoples were Semitic.

In terms of differences, whereas the Halaf had distributed decision making, the Ubaid had some guidance from a Chiefly family. Perhaps the Ubaid were more homogeneous and had arrived in the lowlands as a group with a leadership family. While some Halaf hunted gazelle and onager, the Ubaid fished but hardly hunted. The Ubaid were tighter communities with less influence over a wider area. The Halaf were able to expand significantly with new 'off-shoot villages' maintaining close cultural contact with their origins and continuing to share their sophisticated pottery.[68]

There is one particular difference between the Halaf and Ubaid cultures which became subsequently very important. The Halaf region had sufficient rainfall for their agriculture, but the lowlands occupied by the Ubaid could not prosper without irrigation. This aspect will be considered a little later.

The Halaf culture developed centralised stores with an administrative system. This enabled them to specialise, exchange products, and preserve resources in cooperation.[69] Perhaps the Halaf were one of the earliest examples of a 'primordial and civic culture'. In this regard, their development was more like early China than Indo-European. The Halaf do not seem tribal and neither developed a warrior nor slave culture. Despite the apparent advantages of the extended Halaf society, when the Ubaid people sought to expand upriver it was the latter culture which prevailed. By around 5,200 BCE the Ubaid culture had expanded from the Persian Gulf to the Mediterranean. *(map overleaf courtesy of www.ancient.eu/map)*

Marcella informs us of two other differences which the Ubaid developed and may have enabled them to impose their less equal culture on the Halaf. Firstly, there was a progressive 'widening of the gap' between the Ubaid population and their leadership resulting in more 'chiefly control'. Secondly, the sequences of 'temples' at Eridu reveal special buildings always rebuilt in the same place suggesting a 'religious'

---

[68] Marcella Frangipane, *Different Types of Egalitarian Societies and the Development of Inequality in Early Mesopotamia* in *World Archaeology*, Vol. 39(2).

[69] Idem.

authority. Maybe these two features went hand in hand; religious authority and more powerful chiefs. Roman Emperors and Roman priests come to mind, albeit five millennia later.

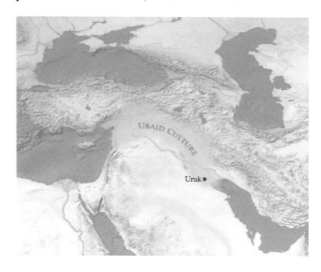

Around the 4th millennium BCE, the Ubaid culture became impregnated by a people from the east, the Sumerians. Since they wrote the world's earliest stories in cuneiform on clay tablets, much more about these new arrivals in the Fertile Crescent can be revealed. In the 1850s, Jules Oppert discovered that the structure of the Sumerian language had close affinities with Turkish, Finnish and Hungarian thus suggesting a common steppe ancestry.[70] The Sumerian word Edin, meaning 'steppe' is found in the beginning of the Book of Genesis as *in the land of Eden, to the East* which Kramer suggests is the land of their origins. Kramer noted that the names of the local rivers in Sumer are Semitic and predate the Sumerian language. This reminds me of the indigenous Indian names for rivers throughout American New England.

We can say, with safety, that the Halaf period was 'primordial civic' using Marcella Frangipane's evidence. The self-incrimination of Sumerian writing tells us they were 'warrior tribal'. Sometime around the 4th millennium BCE saw the first documentation of an early over-running of indigenous consensual primordial civic culture by a foreign hierarchical warrior tribal culture. The challenge for us is to find a way out of six thousand years of corruption.

In the meantime, there are many lessons to uncover. In terms of where this trauma originated, the evidence points rather firmly to the most important Ubaid city, Uruk, which is shown on the map above.

---

[70] Samuel Noah Kramer *The Sumerians.*

Uruk's 'civilisation' subsequently boasted many 'firsts' although, with the advantage of hindsight, many of these firsts are shocking. The thought reminds me, with delight, of an interview given by Martín Prechtel. He was asked what he thought about American civilisation, and he replied, "I think this would be a very good idea." Back to the early Mesopotamian stories, Samuel Noah Kramer has written an entire book on the 39 'firsts' of Sumer.[71] On a positive note, they had 'the first schools' known as *edubba* or tablet houses but in parallel they boast the first caning of schoolboys. The cuneiform tablets say that boys were caned for lateness at school, lack of neatness, missing elements in their tablets, loitering in the street, not straightening their clothes, talking without permission, rising without permission, leaving without permission, not speaking Sumerian and other transgressions. Many indigenous societies around the world might recognise the inclusion of many of these, particularly the last transgression; the use of their indigenous language, as a result of their colonisation by Indo-Europeans. The trait in British schools of a punishment by caning, quite 'disproportionate' to the 'crime', thus began over five millennia ago and was still in evidence during my British childhood. There is something rather sexually perverted about a teacher needing to demonstrate control over the life of a child in such a brutal and humiliating way. My time in indigenous society, in different parts of the globe, taught me that using a cane, or something humiliating, for education would be unthinkable for them.

Uruk had stone architecture on a grand scale, mass production of pottery bowls, and cuneiform writing among her 39 'firsts'. Kramer informs of professions such as philosophers, teachers, historians, poets, lawyers, reformers, accountants, architects, sculptors, ambassadors, statesmen, governors, city fathers, temple administrators, military officers, sea captains, high tax officials, priests, managers, supervisors, foremen, scribes, archivists and many others we would still recognise. However, most of these achievements pale into insignificance when we remember that Uruk was built in parallel with brutal slavery, mistreatment of both genders, the destruction of feminine rights as well as defilement of the sanctity of Mother Nature. The Sumerian impregnation of those who had enjoyed peaceful coexistence with neighbours was perhaps the beginning of a warrior culture, including revenge, which has still not ended.

---

[71] Samuel Noah Kramer *History Begins at Sumer.*

We cannot simply conclude that the problem began with the Sumerians. Already, before the Sumerians arrived, the Ubaid had achieved the 'upper hand' on the Halaf. But, the addition of Sumerian characteristics turned the tide much faster in a direction of inequality. The difference between sufficient rainfall in the Halaf region and the Sumerian dependence on irrigation may have been a critical catalyst in the subsequent history. Irrigation projects require administrative control and cannot be achieved on a grand scale by individual farmers. The culture which evolved in China also depended on a relationship to the civic achievements of those who conquered the great floods around 1920 BCE. But this challenge from Mother Nature did not make the Chinese into warriors. Instead, in the case of China, this led to respect for Government.

Since neither genetics nor nurture is sufficient to produce a violent destiny in an individual mind, perhaps cultures are similar. How the different contributors combine is far more significant than either of them and the relationship to challenges determines a culture more than the challenge itself. Therefore, the relationship between the Sumerian nature and their dependence on irrigation may have been a determinant factor.

In the land of Sumer, agriculture was not possible without irrigation. But with irrigation and the rich silty water of the rivers, their harvests were magnificent. The subject is also brought out in their mythic poetry. Kramer suggests the ancient Sumerian stories were designed as philosophical treatises on the human condition or to address humanity's place in the world. In the 'disputation of silver and copper', copper retorts: *Silver, only in the palace do you find a station... If there were no palace, you would have no station; gone would be your dwelling place... In the ordinary home, you are buried away in its darkest spots, its graves, its places of escape from this world... When winter comes, you don't supply man with the firewood-cutting copper axe; that's why nobody pays any attention to you... When the harvest time comes you don't supply man with the grain-cutting copper sickle; that's why nobody pays any attention to you...* This 'disputation' story seems to be referring to an aspect of our humanity in the difference between the two metals.

These Sumerian creation stories recorded on clay tablets include the debate between 'Summer and Winter' or Emesh and Enten. Kramer suggests that the Cain and Abel story can be seen as an abbreviation of the 'disputation' between the two brothers Emesh and Enten as there are many similarities. In the dispute between Enten and his brother Emesh, they came before Enlil, the Father of the Gods, in the House of Life with their offerings. Among his arguments, Enten says "Father Enlil, you gave me control of irrigation; you brought plentiful water. I made one meadow adjacent to another and I heaped high the granaries." Enten is declared the *farmer of the Gods* as he is 'in control' of the life-producing waters and irrigation on which Sumer depends.

Seemingly, irrigation is the critical factor. Without 'control' of the waters since winter, the harvest in summer is not secure. Apparently Culture always triumphs in the old stories, and the irrigation aspect of Sumer is critical. Following Enlil's pronouncement, Emesh bends his knee before Enten, offers him a prayer, nectar, wine, gold, silver and lapis lazuli to acknowledge his superiority. However, unlike Cain and Abel, the two Sumerian brothers then dwell in unity representing winter and summer respectively. This was the outcome which *Mannership* suggests as a cure for self-destruction.

Is there any possibility of a link in the Sumerian psyche between the overarching need for 'control of the life producing waters' and other aspects of control, particularly of sexuality which is also life producing? Can a historic need to control the water of life on a grand scale become corrupted to become the control of life everywhere, including in the bedrooms of adults? The idea stated like this sounds absurd. But, realising their rewards from the Gods in terms of bounteous harvests following their control of the waters, could give rise to feelings of great potency. Somehow man's control of nature might delude him into thinking he may be elevated among the Gods.

The south of Mesopotamia had no timber, just reeds and mud. Although, as a result of their silt laden irrigation, they were able to build up vast granaries, they had no minerals and had many other deficiencies. They needed either trade or conquest to develop further.[72] By the 3rd millennium BCE the Sumerian poems contain the names of other lands including India, Egypt, Ethiopia and the Mediterranean highlighting their trading connections. We cannot simply blame the Sumerian genetics for what flowed. Their relationship to their need to control nature's water, combined with their need for many other items they did not possess were critical drivers in how their culture expanded. Perhaps their ability to produce vastly superior granaries to those of their

---

[72] Samuel Noah Kramer *The Sumerians.*

neighbours might have given them the idea that they were entitled to more than others. Large granaries also enable a culture to feed a slave population.

The Sumerian cities fell, in the 24th and 23rd centuries BCE to the Akkadian ruler, Sargon the Great. But the Akkadians absorbed almost the entirety of the earlier Sumerian myths according to Kramer. Much of Sumerian literature thus became adopted by the Akkadian state of Babylonia before the Hebrews wrote down the Torah during their Babylonian captivity in the 6th century BCE. The writings of the Hebrews then became the main Western source of many of these much earlier stories. Of particular interest is the similarity between stories of the infancy of Sargon the Great and Moses. Both of these men, towering in their respective cultures, were found in a basket, or small 'Ark', among reeds in a river. Sargon was found floating on The Euphrates, and Moses was found floating on The Nile.

Speaking of the Ark, The *Epic of Gilgamesh* poem is believed to be among the world's oldest known 'written literature'. Gilgamesh was the 5th King of the 1st dynasty of Uruk, which dates his reign a little after 3,000 BCE. This poem tells us much about the Sumerian culture in these ghastly times with boys and girls treated brutally. Gilgamesh used the women as he pleased, including the *'Droit du seigneur'*, a practice which continued in Medieval Europe as 'right of the first night'. This entitled the Lord of a village to sleep with any bride on her wedding night. The outrage was rather more widespread in subsequent history than many are willing to admit, and not just in Europe either. It is hard to imagine another 'habit' which could provoke greater internal fury. Many of the world's worst cultural practices may thus have originated in Uruk.

It is helpful to know when and where wicked traditions began if we seek to address them. We have arrived in a time when the news has been more public about the extent to which men of power could still just snatch women they fancied. We might wonder why this rather precise English verb, snatch, which means *to take or seize hastily, abruptly, without permission or ceremony* has evolved in America to imply a delicate part of a lady's anatomy. The language tells us that not much has changed since Uruk for some people. We mustn't forget that the UK is also guilty of the same linguistic crime. The worst four letter word in the English language, cunt, also refers to feminine sexuality. On both sides of the Atlantic the languages have maintained a similar affliction to the feminine spirit as described in Sarai and Abram's relationship to their 'Egyptian slave', Hagar.[73] Our use of the word 'afflict' has become much too benign, nowadays we imply to 'bother' or 'annoy'. Instead, we should remember what 'afflict' used to mean, which was 'tortured' or 'thrashed' and completely 'struck down'.

Not only was the feminine spirit thrashed at Uruk, but the Sumerian poem, the *Epic of Gilgamesh* also contains the oldest written story of a wanton attack on the sanctity of Mother Nature. Martín reminded me that, before Gilgamesh, the headwaters of the Euphrates were covered by a sacred cedar forest. In the Epic poem, Gilgamesh sets out to kill the guardian of the cedar forest, Humbaba, and to return with substantial lumber. After all, they only had reeds and mud to begin with. The story of 'The Deluge' appears afterwards, with the flood survived by Utnapishtim, the son of the last King of Shuruppak before the deluge.

The discontinuity of settlement between Shuruppak and Kish on the Euphrates River, which has been confirmed archaeologically in roughly the same time period suggested by the poem, was chronologically spawned by upstream 'deforestation' according to the flow of the Epic.[74] By cutting down the forest in the Euphrates headlands, they brought the deluge upon themselves. The attack on Mother Nature therefore backfired rather spectacularly. Such cause and effect might well make a culture conclude that the Gods were displeased. The 'noise and wickedness of humankind' could refer to the felling of sacred cedar. Cutting down trees is a noisy business.

Malidoma Somé has a line which has just come to mind. Something like, "our relationship to Mother Nature is the same as our relationship to the feminine spirit." The history of this city of Uruk supports Malidoma's clarity. Violence towards women and violence towards Mother Nature are apparently connected. By contrast, indigenous societies revere Nature, honour their dependence on her, and respect the feminine which 'makes live and life'.

Perhaps Martín's teaching of lost meanings in the Gilgamesh Epic resonated so easily with me because of a memory in Jamaica. In 1984, Booker Tate was asked by the Jamaican Government to manage the state owned sugar industry. Luckily, we had an exceptional leader in Bobby

---

[73] Genesis 16.

[74] Shuruppak is 25 miles north of Uruk and Kish is 10 miles east of Babylon.

Campbell who was managing the sugar estate in Zambia. He was thrilled to return to his Jamaican homeland. Every three months, I travelled to Jamaica to review his progress and attend the board meeting in Kingston. One of the many stories which Bobby shared with me was how the slave ships stopped at Port Royal on their way from West Africa to the Southern States. The most violent and difficult slaves, who were sometimes 'too hot to handle' or thought to be unsaleable were dropped off at Port Royal.[75] Bobby thought this might explain why Jamaica has a little more violence in her genetic pool. I noted this extra detail of events which can spawn cultural variants.

After a couple of years, we discovered that the sugar cane at Monymusk in the Clarendon Plains was regularly suffering from long droughts before being swamped by floods. Over a beer, we wondered if this was a cycle which had taken place over the centuries. Perhaps we could find out how long these maddening cycles lasted. Luckily, sugar agricultural managers record the rainfall daily. Together with our neighbour, the New Yarmouth Sugar estate, we had two centuries of daily rainfall figures to explore. 73,000 days of rainfall figures. We found that the droughts and floods had only recently appeared. There were none for the first 190 years. Then, all of a sudden, both appeared. At once, the farm managers made the connection. This was immediately following the felling of trees in the hills to the north of May Pen to make way for housing. By cutting down the trees, there was a double effect. Firstly, transpiration from the trees used to be taken up the hills by the breeze producing a regular gentle rainfall. Secondly, the firm support provided by tree roots used to contain the rains so that water was released gradually without flooding. What was particularly fascinating was the immediacy; not years or months later, but almost the same afternoon as the tree loggers came back down the hill.

A few days later we shared the data with Michael Manley, Prime Minister of Jamaica. We explained that to save the sugar production in Clarendon as well as protecting those living in the plains it was essential to replant trees on the hillside among the new housing. Of course, the Government did not follow our advice; one cannot be too ambitious with politicians. The story remained with me, like a dormant seed, until suddenly rehydrated by a teaching from Martín on the *Epic of Gilgamesh*.

---

[75] In passing; 'dropped off' is an English contronym either benign as in 'dropping off a friend', or 'throwing overboard'.

The Gilgamesh story of 'The Deluge' is also found in the book of Genesis as 'Noah's flood'. James Kugel, in *How to Read the Bible,* highlights the major similarities. He says: *In both texts we find the divine warning and commandment to build a ship; the further commandment to fill the ship with animals as well as the hero's family; the account of a great storm and then its abatement; the ship's landing atop a mountain; the trial release of birds to determine if the waters had receded; the offering of a sacrifice and libation on the mountain.*

More compelling than the similar major facts are a number of other details highlighted by Kugel. He says; *the two stories do not just agree on the events themselves but also on the way the story should be told.* Genesis records that *God smelled the pleasing odour* of Noah's sacrifice, using similar words as the *Epic of Gilgamesh.* Kugel points out, in the writing of Genesis, that the use of exactly the same words for these details is 'odd'.

Kugel goes on to say that, on *even the most friendly interpretation of historical dates,* it is not possible to place the Gilgamesh story after Genesis as the oldest Cuneiform copies found are several centuries before the birth of Moses. Further, he adds, *there is another concrete reason for believing that the Bible had borrowed a Mesopotamian story as much of Israel is mountainous and rainfall is sparse. By contrast the flat plain between the southern Tigris and Euphrates rivers could certainly have allowed whole cities to be inundated.*

Kugel's analysis of the Torah, *Genesis, Exodus, Leviticus, Numbers, and Deuteronomy,* highlights that many Hebrew scholars now believe the first written books of the Torah were a product of several authors during their Babylonian captivity. This could explain why a number of Mesopotamian and Sumerian stories appear in the Torah in addition to their oral traditions.

In addition to the enslavement of the Hebrew tribes in Egypt and Babylon at different times, Abraham's family, or at least his younger brother, was said to have been born in Ur. Since Ur is a Sumerian city, it is not impossible that Abraham's family and ancestors also had an earlier experience of enslavement during their time in Sumer. Thus, it is no surprise that we can learn much about these terrible times from the sacred texts. In my explorations in *Mannership*, I came to the conclusion that the split in an individual mind, as suggested by two brothers, Cain and Abel, was spawned by slavery. A mother would reluctantly but lovingly 'break her son's spirit' to give him the chance of surviving the enslavement. After all, if he could not control his impulses, he would be sure to be killed by the enslaving authorities. Thus could originate the criticality of Cain being able to keep his natural brother underground.

Martín had another teaching which gobsmacked me. He has quite a few of these. This one was how to tell if a culture has a history of enslavement; by whether the language has the verb 'to be' or not. A culture which had never been enslaved would have no need for the verb, he said. A culture with the split mind, the Abel and Cain culture which struggles to connect, is a 'to be' culture. Descartes was all excited about *I think therefore I am*. Well, if he really was, then he would not have needed to think about it, Amen. This reminds me of a great difference between many western philosophers and Chinese sages. The preoccupation of many western philosophers is to find answers; to explain everything. Perhaps one of my weaknesses lies here too. Touché. But, for the Chinese, it is instead important to help produce more sages. With more sages one can get on with a task instead of wondering what the task is.

Martín warned me that another language might appear to have this verb 'to be' when it doesn't really, because of translation into a 'to be' language. Checking this with my Chinese hosts one day, asking one of them to write "I am" produced the Cantonese answer as 我係. Armed with the piece of paper, I showed the characters to others and asked them, "what does it say." The answer was always, "I am". However, with my persistent interest in etymology, I asked help in undoing the jigsaw puzzle by disassembling the characters. They agreed that a truer translation was "I belong" or "I relate" instead of "I am". Martín was right. Without a period of enslavement the verb 'to be' would not have come into existence. China does have some enslavement in her history, but only in a few dynasties and usually as punishments for a crime. By contrast, Indo-European cultures have many instances when the majority of the population was enslaved. The practices of the Fertile Crescent were continued in Rome and Greece. In the 309 BCE census of Attica there were only 21,000 free citizens and 400,000 slaves. Corinth was said to have had 460,000 slaves.

'I belong' or 'I relate' is very different from 'I am'. In I-Kiribati there is also no verb 'to be'. They are too busy *being* to need a verb to describe their natural existence. But, with the continued encroachment of Churches strangling their natural spontaneity, while suggesting 'something better', they might need such a verb in the future if they are not careful. How can a Church believe in God on the one hand, and imagine there is something more whole than a life of true spontaneity? There seems to be only one answer here. Suggesting that the Church can offer something better than who we are gives a power to the Church which they would not otherwise have. Caning our nature as children to produce a more uniform culture in the last five millennia is not the answer. Threats by a Church are a form of caning.

At least we have an observation and a question. Disrespect for women and thrashing Mother Nature are apparently connected. Racism may also be connected with both. We may have found some origins in time and place. The question is how are we going to eradicate Viking, or Uruk, behaviours from Western society? As Meredith said, the challenge of the future is not so much about wars between nations, but more about the internal struggle between the warrior and the civic in society. The answer will be neither communism nor capitalism but something akin to a more egalitarian consensual primordial civic society.

In the meantime, we need a fresh paradigm to think about mental health.

Our Relationship to Mental Health

We might be making progress in the struggle against cancer; some can now be prevented and others treated successfully. Overall cancer deaths, since their peak in the 1970s, have mostly declined. But, when we look at mental health in modern society we are becoming overwhelmed. Unlike many cancers which can become more prevalent in the second half of our lives, the crisis affecting mental health has exploded among our children and adolescents.

We are not just losing a struggle against psychic afflictions. We are barely treading water in the face of an advancing tsunami. The surge in difficulties among young adolescents as they approach child-bearing age can only be a portent for a disastrous outcome.

This chapter surprised me. I was surprised by my ignorance and inattention. In the late '80s, towards the end of my tropical farming years, I struggled with African civil wars in several countries where Booker Tate was active. A head-hunter suggested a different career for me with the recently merged CarnaudMetalbox or CMB, based in Paris. He was persuasive and there were a number of intriguing 'fits'. Both companies, Carnaud and Metalbox, had been my clients as a consultant in the '70s and I knew them well; my experience of founding Booker Tate as a merger of two farming organisations would be useful in this new merger of CMB; and the new President of CMB, Jurgen Hintz, did not speak French whereas I am bilingual. Following a long discussion with Jurgen, I accepted a position as his right-hand man with a responsibility for changing the leadership culture in a company with 160 factories around the world.

I had not been involved in manufacturing before, was not an engineer, and therefore was out of my depth in many respects. This never troubled me when I changed careers as somehow, like my teenage wanderings through Africa and Asia, I thought I would figure things out as I went along. I 'knew' someone would help me or guide me if I asked properly. Jurgen liked the three aspects which the head-hunter suggested would make a good fit. He recognised the depth of my interest in different cultures around the world and my observations on critical aspects. Following the recent merger, the opportunity to create a new culture based on open leadership, employee empowerment and engagement, was appealing to both of us.

This experience with CMB taught me a great deal. As in my earlier observations on cultures, lessons don't just come from who we are, or the circumstances of our career, but opportunities can be thrown up by something we hadn't thought about. Like the importance of irrigation to the Sumerians affecting their thinking, or the rice plant leading a culture in a different direction from the influence of wheat or barley.

CMB was Europe's largest producer of metal packaging. This included all kinds of metal packages but usually made from steel or aluminium - Coke cans, soup tins, peanut packages, cigar cases, aerosol cans, biscuit tins, coffee containers, paint tins, oil cans, and many other varieties. I hadn't realised that the large number of CMB factories was caused by the cost of transporting air. An empty Coke can costs the same amount to make as to transport about three hundred miles. A '24 tonne container' of empty Coke cans weighed just 3 tons as most of the 'volume' was simply air. This was why it was necessary to build factories as close as possible to customers. Another surprise was that other overseas producers of metal packaging were not really competitors because of the cost of transport. Toyo Seikan in Japan, possibly the best can manufacturer in the world, was willing to share and show their production methods because neither they nor we could compete in each other's markets. On several journeys to Japan, I learned some paradigms which completely changed me.

There is a Japanese Institute of Plant Maintenance, JIPM, which was set up to promote and audit the best manufacturing methods throughout Japan. Just at the time of my joining CMB, JIPM was willing to start sharing some of their manufacturing thinking with other nations. The Chairman of Examiners of JIPM, Professor Hajime Yamashina, was willing to mentor me in JIPM's work and his invention of 'World Class Manufacturing'.

By now, my reader will be wondering what this has to do with mental health. The answer is a great deal and very fundamentally, but patience is required. Please discover this with me.

Yamashina was my mentor for ten years and long after my leaving CarnaudMetalbox. I am very grateful to him for many lessons. I enjoyed travelling to Japan to accompany him on tours or audits of advanced factories, as well as his visits to Europe when we would sometimes travel together.

Martín Prechtel, a shaman from the indigenous Tzutujil Mayan culture of Guatemala was also my mentor at the same time, but for completely different reasons. My fascination and joy in discovering more about indigenous society, and the role of shamans in particular, was just beginning. Martín used to come and stay at my house for about ten days every three months. He is still my teacher even now as, even after twenty-five years, there is still a lot to learn.

There is something which these two mentors said, in very different words, but which I did not connect as similar until I wrote this chapter on mental health. There is an unexpected paradigm shared by advanced Japanese production methods and indigenous societies related to 'health'. Perhaps it is also important to underline the basis of my relationship to mentors as a reminder of how our infancy keeps cropping up as we meander through life. During my silent years, I was always looking for a friendly face to tell me what was going on. I always knew there was a dimension that I was missing and therefore I was always completely open to receive whatever a mentor could provide. Since my silent childhood, I always assumed that others understood more than me. Perhaps my enquiring and innocent way of *looking at them* to learn was endearing and therefore they shared more.

First, I will explain the thinking from Yamashina's perspective.

The Japanese can be quite Socratic in their teaching. One evening, after dinner with Professor Yamashina in Kyoto, he said to me quite abruptly: "The trouble with you Westerners is that you throw away your spoilage." Soon after, he bid me goodnight saying we would meet for breakfast. His comment was puzzling; the tone of voice and abruptness quite unusual. Clearly this was an important lesson and intriguing. Was he suggesting we should have recycled the defects, or spoilage? Having tossed ideas around all night, I had to ask him in the morning.

He presented me with a completely new idea. Advanced Japanese manufacturers can understand almost everything about a production system from an analysis of the defects, especially from the evolution of different types of defects. Sensing I wanted him to expand, he continued, "when you go to hospital they will take blood for analysis. Then they will test again after some time to look for differences. You can learn so much from this analysis and the changes. For us, defects of a process are like a blood test. They contain some of the most useful information on the process. While visiting factories in Europe, I see they just throw away their defects or scrap. This is like pouring hospital blood samples down the drain without analysing them." The metaphor was perfectly clear, and fascinating.

This idea became a cornerstone of a new way of thinking and was the basis for a new culture of leadership and engagement in CMB. It was a pleasure to roll up my sleeves, don overalls and work with teams on the shop-floor to explore this new paradigm. Once, while spending a night shift in a factory producing metal cans for Fray Bentos Steak and Kidney pie, I saw the very same model of metal can which had exploded and terrified my cook Teimaua on the Gilbert Islands because I had forgotten to explain how to open the tin. My story went around the factory like a wildfire. Working on the shop-floor was thrilling and we all learned so much. Every different type of defect in the cans could be traced to a particular failure in the production process. Trends in the types of defects were especially revealing. This was like a new consciousness and we were fascinated. We learned that we did not have a 'scrap problem'; instead we had different trends of very specific diseases.

Let me share one specific case. We had a factory in the northwest of England that produced lids for beverage cans. The factory defect rate was 1.5%. Since each press was producing about a million lids per day, this was 15,000 defects per press per day which sounds much worse than 1.5%. Not having any industrial experience myself, I asked the factory manager if he would like to

volunteer for an experiment to 'understand the diseases'. We progressively analysed these in ever greater detail. Although it took three years, we managed to get the defect rate down from 15,000 per day to 45 per day on each press once we understand the faults or weaknesses in the process.

We created a team with operators, maintenance staff, engineers and the quality department. To maintain focus, we started on only one press and identified all the components of the process which could cause a disease. It was fun working together with operators and technicians. We called ourselves 'detectives for defectives' and started to see the production process in a totally new light. Instead of just watching lids whirr by at ferocious speeds we started to learn. An important disease was misaligned score on the tongue of the lid. The 'tongue' is the part of the lid which is forced down so that you can drink from the can. We kept analysing until we found various root causes such as a drop in vacuum pressure or dirt in the guides. The Japanese also have an idea called 'Poka-Yoke' which means a technique to prevent the possibility of an error. Once we realised the critical level of vacuum pressure to hold each lid securely in place, we modified the press settings so that the machine stopped if the vacuum pressure dropped. In this way, progressively we were able to eradicate the root cause of each disease. Understanding led to cure.

This felt like hunting. But the essence was to treat any damaged lid as a sign of a defect in the process. Instead of operators thinking that they *made Coke cans*, everybody realised they *were engaged in improving the process* that made Coke cans. This is also an important philosophy of Japanese production systems; they think of operators as process engineers on the lines. Each time we were able to eradicate the root cause of a disease, the gain became sustainable. I liked the etymology of eradicate from the Latin 'to take out the root'. This reminded me of helping my mother remove weeds in the garden as a small child. I could only throw away the tops but she got the roots out. This new consciousness led to greater involvement and engagement. More importantly, a new language aligned all levels of the organisation. Not having a background in manufacturing and neither being an engineer, this change in culture excited me. The operators started to see themselves as more valuable; the absenteeism rate dropped and factories became safer because of a greater awareness and interest.

Another aspect which amused me was differences in cultural responses around the world. In Japan, and other rice growing cultures, the idea of daily checks was second nature because the rice plant required this attention. Leadership of the paradigm was less important because this thinking connected with something already in their psyche. In the USA we had to make the idea resonate with an American hunting culture with a new name; a 'hunt for losses', which was more easily grasped. My preference was always *detectives for defectives*. In a subsequent chapter, I will include a few other lessons of differences between Japan and USA which arose during this period with Yamashina.

During Martín Prechtel's first visit to London he told me that the Tzutujil Mayan culture did not have a concept of mental illness. When a member of the village 'exhibited symptoms', this was a trigger for Shamans to get all the villagers together to find out what was awry in the community; to find what had caused 'someone' to exhibit the village disturbance. Only while writing this chapter did I make the connection between Yamashina's eradication of weaknesses in a process through understanding trends of symptoms present in damaged lids and the Tzutujil Mayan culture of gathering a village to understand why someone has 'developed symptoms'.

We can only tackle the problem of mental health by thinking differently about the problem we face.

Each minute about 625 kids are born around the world. As Adrian Raine found, biology is not destiny. In the factory making Coke can lids, a coil of aluminium is cut into 'discs'. Each minute about 620 discs fly into a press as potential 'good lids'. The 'damaged' lids are produced by the same process as the 'ones that passed'. It is a matter of luck or timing as to which metal discs become 'damaged' by the process. It was just their misfortune that the glides were dirty or the vacuum pressure dropped as they came by. Perhaps their birth experience was messy or they were not 'held' sufficiently at a critical time.

It is a close run thing whether these lids or kids pass or not, sometimes. In previous generations, those with the 'stiff upper lip' may have thought; *it might not be the fault of the metal, but it is for sure a lack of mettle.* This kind of thinking has brought us where we are; on the edge of a cliff. Those with mettle made better Vikings, though.

Quite a few of those who consider themselves healthy are 'highly functioning defectives'. They have many of the same struggles but have found a 'work around'. During my time in Kiribati, and as a tropical farmer, many were not aware of the burden of my anxiety operating as a head wind. It had been possible for me to find a way to keep my distance, or dissociate, most of the time in order to be able to 'function'. But our denial afflicts others more than we can know. My girlfriend from Abemama Island sensed that she was missing something in her relationship with me, but could not express what. Someone from a 'whole' culture might not understand those of us with a messy or insufficiently held upbringing but they sense something missing quickly.

Many have tried to scream warnings in recent years by attempting to evaluate the cost to society of different failings. Adrian Raine, in *Anatomy of Violence*, tells us that gunshot wounds cost the USA $126 billion per year, homicide costs were over $300 billion in 2010, with cutting and stab wounds adding another $51 billion. As Adrian pointed out, the cost of homicide was *more than the combined budgets of the Departments of Education, Justice, Housing and Urban Development, Health and Human Services, Labor, and Homeland Security.*[76] Back in 1999 homicide was estimated to consume 11.9% of GNP.[77]

New Zealand has recently passed a 'world-first legislation' granting victims of domestic violence 10 days paid leave to enable them to leave their partners and find new homes while protecting themselves and their children. The cost of domestic violence in New Zealand was estimated at between NZ$4.1bn and $7bn a year. This would equate to NZ$430 billion at USA population levels.

Using the principle of Tzutujil Mayan villages or Japanese production philosophy we should rethink our paradigms. We will find that, whilst these figures are shocking, they are very wide of the mark. Even if we could estimate the cost of murder, suicide, self-harm, domestic violence and many other afflictions we will not have even scratched the tip of the iceberg.

As an example, in the USA in 2013, suicide accounted for 13 deaths per 100,000 souls. A massive error would be to assume that, luckily, 99,987

---

[76] Adrian Raine, *Anatomy of Violence*.

[77] Anderson, D.A. (1999) The aggregate burden of crime *Journal of Law and Economics* 42, 611-42 as quoted by Adrian Raine in *Anatomy of Violence*.

of the 100,000 were just fine. According to the 2011 Youth Risk and Behavior Survey, among high school students:[78]

- 15.8% seriously considered suicide
- 12.8% made a plan for suicide
- 7.8% attempted suicide one or more times
- 2.4% made a suicide attempt that required medical intervention

Percentages are misleading and affect our consciousness differently. It is much starker and truer when we say that out of every 100,000 souls, 13 were able to terminate their lives, 15,800 seriously considered suicide, 12,800 made a plan, 7,800 attempted more than once, 2,400 made an attempt which required medical attention. And these are the figures for one year. What about the following year for the same 100,000 adolescents?

Using a show of hands, when I asked at two psychological conferences, how many had experienced the fleeting thought that they could jump off a balcony or in front of a train, there were about 70% who were willing to admit the thought. So that makes 70,000 per 100,000. Hopefully the point is becoming clearer. The Mayans and the Japanese, in their different ways, grasp the issue correctly. They have understood how to view the afflicted souls or lids as gate-keepers highlighting the extent of our problem. Those who escape an affliction might have just been lucky. We 'wrestle' with so many afflictions. The problem will not go away by giving the 13 out of 100,000 all the help we can. This 'psychic cancer' affects most of our society and not just a few. In the UK, about 70% are 'wrestling' with unconscious challenges which can become suicidal in their most extreme manifestation.

We need a totally fresh paradigm, and will need to start by 'scrapping' the measure of Gross National Product or GNP.

How can we be guided by a measure which values and includes as 'production' the costs of homicide, of suicide and self-harm, of domestic violence and rape? A reliance on GNP is an absurd thought process and a major contributor to misguided governance. This thinking is like a bird having an extra navigational system which deliberately and always points in the wrong direction; much worse than an unnecessary headwind. All kinds of undesirables show up as benefits and

---

[78] Youth Risk Behavior Surveillance — United States, 2011.

improvements in the GNP. Even natural disasters such as earthquakes, floods, forest fires turning communities to ashes, tsunamis and hurricanes have a 'positive effect' on GNP. The calculation measures the economic 'boom' caused by the cost of the clean-up and reconstruction efforts but ignores the costs in terms of loss of what was already there.

The United Kingdom GNP almost doubled in the years between 1938 and 1944 when the island of Britain was ravaged by war. A feverish activity to defend as well as to repair caused the economy to surge using the GNP measure. In 1945, the year of peace, the sudden drop in industrial demand caused the GNP '*to tank*'.[79] Future recessions in our economy were often compared as '*Britain's biggest headache since 1945*'. Economists sometimes forget that 1945 was, in other ways, not a headache.

Suppose that a recommended healthy diet amounted to about 2,250 calories each day. Then a society which grew to consume over 3,600 calories per day will also show a 60% higher GNP. In a sense, it is the GNP which is obese. The costs of treating the effects of the obesity also show up as increased GNP. The average is misleading as some of our adolescents are anorexic and need help, whereas others are consuming very much more than 3,600 calories with a different need for support. Could eating too much as well as too little be considered a form of self-destruction and waste? Not something to celebrate in GNP. All addictions are likewise forms of self-destruction but are 'valued positively' in GNP.

At the very minimum, our 'measure of a healthy economy' is a misguided one. Getting rid of the GNP measure might be a useful step. At least, in Bhutan they try. The Bhutanese saw the defect in the GNP thinking as long ago as 1971. Instead, they sought to measure their Gross National Happiness. Bhutan is one of the most beautiful places on earth. They cannot tackle the Indo-European headwind alone. The global effect has swept them up too and the recent increase in suicides among Bhutanese adolescents is particularly alarming.

Martín reminded me that we should not try to throw away our 'Imperial minds' or they would become even more ferocious. Instead, we have to employ the Imperial Mind in creating the conditions where our indigenous soul might feel welcome again. Perhaps, following the wake

---

[79] The noun 'tank' can be a container for liquid or a military armoured vehicle. But the verb 'to tank' means to fall in value, usually disasterously.

of the *"Me too"* movement, we need to have some smart phone applications tracking our Gross Domestic Waste. At least the word 'Gross' then becomes more properly employed in the phrase.

Like advanced Japanese Production Systems, and Mayan villages, we will not be moving in the right direction until we focus on the root cause of 'the waste'. Everything which is good in society can take care of herself and does not need measuring. The waste must be our concern with the constant reminder of a system which has failed all of us. Those who struggle the most can sometimes help us to see the obstacles more clearly. We all have the same afflictions to varying degrees.

My first therapist, Robin Skynner, spent most of his career with hospital patients who suffered from a number of psychic afflictions. He had noticed that each time a new drug came out many of them got better. From the change of the drug, I wondered. He said not. He noticed that what made them better was the increase in interest shown by the doctors, because the doctors were curious about the effects. That is what made the difference. So, a genuine interest in those who struggle helps both of us. They benefit from the attention and we learn. As gate-keepers to the failures of our culture's processes they have priceless information for all of us. If we are frightened of their afflictions, then we are frightened of ourselves.

Before moving on to the next subject, the reminder of Bhutan's deliciousness and contribution to 'health' warrants a brief pause in the Himalayas with a short story.

Bhutan, Land of Hidden Treasures

In the autumn of 1973, after my arduous Sahara crossing, the most likely place to find me was in the travel section of Blackwell's Bookshop in Broad Street, Oxford. A small glossy coffee-table book caught my eye. The photographs were exquisite and enchanting. This gem, *Bhutan, Land of Hidden Treasures*, written by Gansser and Olschak was irresistible. Instantly my favourite, the book spent many years next to my Isle of Lewis chess set in my sitting room. I admired the photographs often and wondered when I could visit. Looking in my bookcase just now, this book jumped out at me again.

As a teenager, in 1972, I travelled to Nepal and trekked up to Nagarkot to watch the sunrise over Sagarmatha, or Mount Everest. The mountains made a deep impression on my young mind. After the struggles of the Sahara, my heart yearned for the tranquillity of the Himalayas promised by the Land of Hidden Treasures, just fifty miles to the east of Nepal. But, Gansser and Olschak had awoken my interest before the door opened. In 1973, Bhutan was still closed to visitors.

In the following years, even when not so far away from Bhutan, I hadn't managed to visit her. In some strange way, this dream was never far from my mind, a latent desire, but I never made a plan to go. Was I saving the best for last? Or was I waiting for fate to find the right time?

Fate was not in a rush. She waited almost forty years. Suddenly, and this word suddenly is one of fate's favourites, an American client asked me to conduct a leadership workshop at one of their factories in Guwahati, Northeast India. The client had a specific date in mind, 4th October, just over a month away. I accepted at once. A visit to India was long overdue and the possibility of spending a few extra days there excited me. I imagined all the cricket analogies which could be added to my workshop which Indians would love. But, I still hadn't looked at a map to find where this factory was exactly.

Guwahati is beside the Brahmaputra River, in Assam. Childhood memories of geography lessons came running back to me. The Brahmaputra had captivated me since a small boy; the river in flood could be as much as thirty-seven eye popping kilometres wide. Philip's School Atlas had graphs of the Cherrapunji rains. They had a record annual rainfall of more than a thousand inches; more than twenty-six metres of rain. The town also boasted the record rainfall for a month, 370 inches in July. I cannot recall why these black columned rainfall charts at the back of the atlas fascinated me, but the memory of them is as fresh as the smell of my grandfather's pipe tobacco. My father used to buy him two ounces of 'Digger Shag' for sixpence.

Savouring these memories distracted me from noticing that Guwahati is the closest Indian city to Bhutan. The border is just fifty miles north of the Brahmaputra River. My heart jumped. Was fate finally beckoning me to Bhutan? My friends told me that planning a visit to Bhutan at a few weeks' notice was quite impossible, ridiculous even. There were no foreign embassies and the only way to obtain a visa was to contact the office in their capital, Thimphu. I contacted several travel agents. They were kind and helpful, but all said the same; it would not be possible to get a visa at such short notice. They tried to discourage me by suggesting that there was insufficient time to find a hotel, a guide or transport, let alone the visa.

These kinds of challenges seem specifically designed to spur my activity. There had to be another approach. I took a first step and discovered the only airline flying into Thimphu was Royal Bhutan Airlines, called Druk Air. I called them and asked for a ticket in the days before my workshop. Initially, they were kind but not encouraging. There were no seats on the days we checked, so I suggested another, and another. Suddenly the assistant said they had just one spare seat. In my excitement, I reminded her that I only needed one seat. A few minutes later, she found another flight with only one free seat for my return. She said that I was very lucky to have found a seat. I told her how delighted I was, and how this visit was a long held dream.

I imagined she would know her country well, and I said, "Now that I have purchased a flight, how can I find a hotel, guide and the 'impossible' visa."

She was so calm, and said, "Do not worry, we can do all of that for you, leave it to us."

My anxiety intruded. "But there are only three or four weeks for you to organise?"

"There is no need to worry; we will manage everything in time," she replied.

In the next few days, Druk Air prepared my itinerary. When they sent their first suggestions, I liked the disclaimer; *we suggest that you use your itinerary as a guide rather than a fixed schedule. Unexpected stuffs always happen in Bhutan. One of our travellers met the King of Bhutan while descending from Taktsang Monastery and stopped to have a chat with him. Another went to a Museum that was unexpectedly closed as the guard was home for a nap. As Bhutan has just opened up to the world, do not expect the service to be the same standard as visiting a Museum in London. However, they are one of the friendliest and jolly people you would ever meet.* I had no hesitation in leaving all the planning in their hands, particularly since they possessed the only key to my visa.

Each time another email arrived with exciting additions to my programme, I thanked them so warmly before asking gently how my visa application was 'coming along'. Their immediate response was always the same kind reply, "Not to worry. Your visa is well underway." Reading these emails again reminds me of the contrast between Bhutanese calmness and my impatience.

Just six days before my flight, an email arrived from Druk Air. "Your visa has been approved. Good karma ☺. Your guide is Mr. Tshering Penjor." I smiled, thinking how easily and calmly they achieved everything. Why had I worried?

There was another surprise two days later. The last email from Druk Air said simply, "You are lucky because you will be arriving on the first day of the Thimphu Tshechu festival and will be able to enjoy the dances." I was dumbstruck. I remembered the dance photographs from *Bhutan, Land of Hidden Treasures*. This religious festival is the highlight of the year. In my excitement to find a way into Bhutan, the timing of this festival hadn't even been on my mind. Fate had certainly chosen her time well. I realised why all those travel agencies said the timing was not possible at short notice, but fate ignores what others say is impossible.

The flight from Delhi to Bhutan revealed breath-taking views of The Himalayas poking through clouds that looked like sea-foam tickling the mountains' toes. Suddenly a green patch appeared in the clouds. I saw an airfield. My first reaction was fear. I hope we are not going there. There is a steep mountain range all around so we would have to drop like a stone to arrive; like landing a plane inside a volcano crater. The aircraft banked. I hoped there was another airfield that I hadn't seen; surely the one I saw was only for helicopters? But we banked more steeply and turned, and turned even tighter like a corkscrew to lose altitude on the spot. Finally an access to the runway appeared feasible. The relief was palpable when we touched down. The captain told me that only nine pilots in the world were qualified to land a plane at Thimphu. I had no doubt he was right.

The Himalayas to the west of Bhutan, the Land of the Thunder Dragon.

I stepped off the aircraft in a crisp fresh air, in bright sunshine, greeted by the ground staff in their unique Bhutan uniform; long white cuffs, jacket and kilt. The immigration officer's smile was the warmest ever welcome to a country. After she stamped my passport, I asked if I was allowed to take photographs of the airport. She replied, "But of course; feel welcome." I wondered where else I had experienced an airport so friendly; perhaps on a Pacific Island.

Tshering Penjor was waiting for me. His delight and the warmth of his hand-shake made me welcome. Driving into Thimphu alongside children walking home from school in their neat red and dark green uniforms alongside the rice was delightful. I turned to Tshering and said, "I have a really good feeling about your country, she is wonderful. How have I missed her all these years?" My enthusiasm was infectious. We knew we were both going to have a wonderful time.

The Thimphu Tshechu dances in the courtyard of the Tashichho monastery.

Tshering described his homeland as the 'only country in the world that is actually a living museum'. He is right. The dances contain many tales of morality to cleanse the mind. The audience were dressed up in all their finery to enjoy the blessings.

Thimphu Tshechu festival dances.

The dance depicting the Day of Judgment lasts for five hours.

Tshering explained how the remoteness of Bhutan, free of roads until 1962, enabled them to preserve their culture and style over many centuries.

The next day, Tshering drove me over the 10,000 foot Dochula Pass to Punakha, the ancient capital of Bhutan.

'Palace of Great Happiness' built in 1637.

The air is so clear and fresh with scented pine and cedar forests. This wonderful kingdom, the only 'officially' Buddhist country, has much to teach us, particularly in the realm of happiness as their ancient capital was so aptly named. As long ago as 1971, they realised that the 'Western economic measure' of GDP was fundamentally flawed. Instead, they sought to improve their national happiness. Tshering and I enjoyed our meandering conversations, and he found in me a kindred spirit. I remembered, during many visits to Asia, the lands where I felt most at peace were the Buddhist ones.

After a few days together, Tshering told me that the best of my visit to Bhutan was saved for my last day. I could not imagine anything more special than we had already seen. Normally, he said he would like to surprise me, but he felt the need to warn that we would have to climb quite high tomorrow. Was I ready for this? I wondered about his sore ankle, and how he would manage. When I asked where we were going, he replied, "To the Taktsang Palphug Monastery, the Tiger's Nest."

I told him that I had read about this climb and thought much of the way could be undertaken on a horse. He nodded. When I asked how much a horse cost to rent for a day, the answer was $8. That seemed a bargain. I suggested he let me rent two horses so he could ride with me.

The following morning, we were up early and found the owner of a few horses. Our two were ready. Immediately I noticed there were no reins.

Surprised, I asked, "How do I steer."

The owner was amused by my question. "You talk to him," he said.

I realised that he was serious. I was just about to say that I don't speak Bhutanese before I paused to think. The horse would not speak English either. The owner added, while I was digesting my predicament, "The horse knows the way."

On my leadership courses, I used to explain that the horse was one of the most emotionally sensitive and attuned animals. He could smell what the rider was thinking. I used to tell them that if you ride a horse fast down a hill and attempt to jump over a fence, then if you have the slightest doubt whether you can get over the fence the horse will smell your doubt and back up. So, you might still go over the fence, but not with the horse. But, now I was going to have to put my own teaching to the test on a narrow mountain path with a sheer edge dropping down thousands of feet. I would have to rely on the horse knowing what I felt.

At first this was straightforward; the path was wide and the horse knew the way. But, after a short while with steep climbing, he started to pant, breathing very fast. I feared his heart and body would explode. I reassured him, and suggested he should stop for a few minutes to cool down. He understood immediately. I was not in a rush, and very grateful for my ride. Once his temperature and level of exhaustion reduced, I suggested he could start again. He did. We had a few more stops for breath on the way. I told him he was such a fine horse and I liked him. He understood me very well. We had only one area of disagreement, however. Much higher up the mountain, the path was very narrow and the drop on my right was precipitous and sheer. I could not bear to look.

I wanted the horse to stay close to the left side of the path, nearer to the rock face but he preferred the right side close to the edge. Several times I had to ask him to move left and he did. But then surreptitiously he moved again towards the right. I wondered why.

Noticing that the ground near the edge was soft mud, whereas the ground near the rock face had sharper stones, I told him that I now understood. Could we walk more slowly so that he could avoid the difficult stones but still stay on the left side where the path was less scary for me? He agreed and helped me to relax for which I was immensely grateful.

I was pleased to have a new horse story variant for my workshop on leadership in Guwahati the following week.

The Tiger's Nest, Taktsang Monastery, Bhutan,
just holding on to the cliff at 10,232 feet.

This visit reminded me of something which James Hillman taught me. "The most beautiful moments of your life are always when you are out of control, and yet you spend most of your life trying to stay in control." My experiences of wandering around the world taught me how 'the balance between control and spontaneity' is a rather particular hallmark of cultures.

In the case of Bhutan, Hillman was spot on. Fate had been the guide for this visit, and had achieved more than I could have dreamed of. Perhaps this was why I revelled in my unexpected journey from the memory of the Cherrapungi rains and the smell of my grandfather's tobacco all the way to the Tiger's Nest. Maybe, somewhere or somehow, my heart knew that my time to visit this special Kingdom would be decided for me.

Lessons from Japan and USA

Writing the earlier chapter on 'our relationship to mental health' reminded me of other lessons and learnings during a decade working with Professor Yamashina.

After a couple of years at CMB, I decided to follow a different course from full-time employment. I was captivated by beginning an inner journey and decided to train as a group therapist. I loved the work of indigenous shamans – Malidoma and Subonfu Somé from the Dagara tribe of West Africa and Martín Prechtel from the Tzutujil Mayan culture of Guatemala. They stayed at my house and all noticed immediately my different way of watching as well as my curiosity and eagerness to learn. I wished to continue coaching leadership, employee engagement and empowerment, but preferred to branch out on my own and offer my support as a freelancer. Recognising the benefits of the Japanese thinking on processes, I wanted to continue learning from Yamashina who was keen to share more.

Very early on, I realised that my mind did not work in the same way as my different mentors. My 'thinking process' was different. This could be linked to my childhood and the culture of Britain, I thought. When Yamashina was tired of teaching me, I would share some of my observations on the differences between the Japanese way of thinking and Western thought processes.

During the early '90s, just after the fall of the Berlin Wall, the fastest growth in my client work was focused in Central Europe with organisations seeking advice on a 'life outside the Soviet Union'. Watching their thinking helped me to understand more about Russia.

Yamashina introduced me to the idea of the importance of the rice plant to his culture in terms of daily checks, and also to their belief in continually seeking to 'improve a process'.

As I began to weave these aspects of Japanese culture into my leadership coaching around the world, I was alerted to other global differences in the way the message was received as well as to some possible origins.

Realising that I had to explain the Japanese methodology as 'hunting for losses' in America suggested this was because the American culture was more like 'hunting' and less like rice farming. They were not process thinkers but opportunists. A culture with five millennia of rice farming would more naturally think of preparing and levelling the land, removing obstacles like stones and rocks, enriching the soil, managing the flow of water, planting in a nursery and then later planting out, controlling weeds, watching for pests and diseases, continually comparing with neighbours, monitoring the progress of each step, and then harvesting. By contrast, a Northern European culture or an American culture with a strong history of hunting would think differently. They first learn of or imagine a possible target, decide how to approach, prepare weapons, approach carefully based on experience, aim at the first realisable opportunity and make a second attempt if the first fails, before relaxing once successful until hungry again.

These are very different thinking processes and affect not just rice farming or hunting but many other aspects of daily life.

I noticed trends on Wall Street and the Tokyo stock exchange which reflected these differences. A farming culture is used to harvests depending on the weather. Good and bad years are normal and not a sign of failure. For a farmer, longer term growth can come from either improving the process or farming more land. Companies on the Tokyo stock exchange seemed less sensitive to the effects of a temporary drop in profitability, as if this was just 'weather'. Instead, stock prices grew following increases in market share as if the farmer now had 'more land', and for improvements in their processes.

On Wall Street, the thinking seemed to be that a hunter should be able to hit the target in any weather, so a drop in performance was a sign of weakness and not weather. Not only that; but Wall Street demands quarterly publication of profit trends which is not needed in farming cultures. Sometimes the link between a culture and everyday aspects of their history become easy to see, just like the little islands of Kiribati. Perhaps the Sumerians, who hardly hunted, were the first 'process thinkers'. They improved their irrigation and farming to produce vast granaries.

In the year 2000, at the end of almost ten years of learning from Professor Yamashina, he was invited to present his thinking on World Class Manufacturing in Brussels. He asked me to join him. We agreed I should present a lecture titled "Using Japanese techniques to enhance employee involvement and empowerment." This presentation included a mixture of lessons from Yamashina, from CMB, from my eight years of tropical farming with Booker Tate, from the American men's movement led by Robert Bly, from shamans, from the lessons of my inner therapeutic journey, from experiences of indigenous cultures and my wanderings. Somehow, everything in my life seemed to offer a different ingredient in the jigsaw puzzle of cultures.

The illustrations included Booker Tate's management of cotton in Swaziland and an African gazelle to visualise the differences between farming and hunting.

One aspect of my lecture, which originated in Robert Bly's teaching, was the effect of 'industrialisation' on the masculine psyche which resonated with me. Imagine a village blacksmith prior to the industrial revolution. He had a direct and personal relationship with his customers. He had control over his workplace. He had a relationship with his suppliers. He was involved in developing his task and teaching others.

But, once he was 'taken over' by industrialisation, his contact with customers was controlled by 'sales'. His contact with suppliers was controlled by 'purchasing'. His work planning was assumed by 'production control'. His workplace layout was controlled by 'methods'. His choice of machinery layout was taken by 'engineering'. His guidance of apprentices was controlled by a 'training department'. His innovations were ignored and controlled by 'research'. His pride and promotion were controlled by 'marketing'. He was 'salami sliced' and disempowered. Bly noted that the blacksmith's children no longer saw their father work and his position in the family declined.

My purpose was to highlight the importance of restoring the links that had been lost, which could be achieved in a teamwork environment. In some client factories we set up shop-floor teams in direct consultation with customers so that the employees adjusted the production in liaison with their clients. Motivation soared on both sides. The audience understood how teams could restore a sense of self-esteem that had been lost in the industrial revolution.

The presentation also included the effects of European wars on industrial thinking. In the 1950s, factory management styles were still influenced by war time methods. Strategy was made by Generals in secret. Front line supervisors were often considered 'one of them' just like sergeants in the army who were not officers. By the 1970s, in my first consultancy career, a focus was on 'management by walking around and being seen' as well as asking supervisors to cross the wall to become more like a middle managers. But, since insufficient guidance was provided, they 'straddled the wall' and did not know where they belonged. A more open approach to factory management did not begin until the early 1990s following greater understanding of Japanese methodologies.

Yamashina and I each devised a simple test, to alert leaders to their way of thinking. My reader can try them now. One morning, on the train from London to Doncaster to visit one of my clients, and after a traditional English breakfast served in the dining car, Yamashina produced a picture which had been drawn by his wife. This picture, or 'puzzle' is shown opposite.

He said; "Draw a continuous line from the top box A to the lower box A, then another line from the top box B to the lower box B without the lines crossing, and finally a line from the left box C to the right box C without crossing either of the first two lines and without leaving the light blue area of the picture or going through another box."

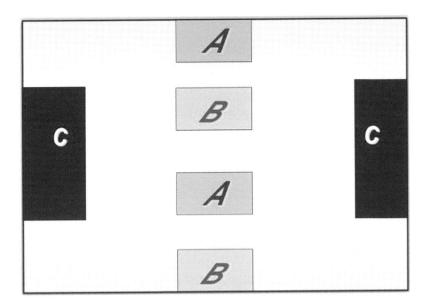

Immediately, I imagined a line from one A to the other, running down the left side of the B and a line connecting the B boxes on the right side. But then, sensing that I had blocked the way across to connect the C boxes, I paused for reflection. Yamashina sensed my reaction. He said; "90% of Western engineers will say it can't be done, but 90% of Japanese schoolchildren will complete the task within fifteen seconds." The programming of these different minds opens the door, either to an obstacle or a solution.

Later on, I created a different test. I asked leaders to imagine they had a sailing boat and were holding the steering wheel. My question was; "what are the three categories of things you need to know to be able to steer." For a Western hunter mind, the first two are easy but the third can be a challenge. By contrast, the Japanese mind often thinks of the third one first.

The answer to both questions is at the back of book. What is much more interesting than the answer is the awareness of one's own thinking processes.

HELPING OUR CHILDREN
TO KNOW AND BE KNOWN

Beginning my career on the other side of the world in Kiribati taught me what was missing from my upbringing. Subsequent experiences with other communities in the 'third layer' of connectedness, and working with indigenous shamans, introduced me to attributes which 'healthier cultures' shared.

Mental health challenges affecting different cultures are not the same. There can be no global recipe. But, since western cultures are the pushiest in terms of spreading trends among our children, we must address our own troubles first.

We seem to have two major crises; the destruction of our planet through global warming, and the increasing harm felt by our children in a 'chilling' of connectedness. Malidoma Somé told me that these two catastrophes are connected. Global warming is more widely understood, and efforts are being made to 'slow down' the hurtling towards destruction. But, the global crisis of mental health is less well understood and our plight is becoming much worse because we are essentially travelling in the wrong direction.

The chapter on 'When and Where the Madness Began' speaks of an egalitarian consensual primordial civic Halaf society around 9000 years ago in Mesopotamia which was overrun by the Ubaid culture with more 'hierarchical distance' and greater wealth for priests around 7200 years ago. Subsequently, the arrival of Sumerians and the invention of slavery in Southern Mesopotamia over five millennia ago caused a 'splitting of the mind'. This split is represented in Sumerian mythology as the 'disputation' between the two brothers Emesh and Enten. The story became abbreviated as Cain and Abel in the Book of Genesis. Unlike the Sumerian version where the two brothers dwelled in unity after Enten was declared the winner, the Genesis story has Cain burying Abel in the ground. Culture always 'defeats nature' although spirit cannot be killed.

The brutality and fear inherent in slavery meant that my ancestors could only survive by 'burying their nature underground'. An ability to 'get a grip on oneself' is an essential pre-requisite for survival. Significantly, Judean authors wrote the Book of Genesis during their captivity in Babylon.

The Indo-European cultures, born in the underbelly of Russia where the invention of the wheel met the domestication of the horse, also carried this fear of enslavement of their true nature on steroids as they overran nearly all the indigenous cultures of Europe. By running away from a fear, they committed the same crime – rather like Oedipus who tried to escape the oracle's prediction only to kill his father on the road. Much later, and once they had ships to sail across oceans; Indo-Europeans spread their dominion across most of the planet.

***

In Greek, *merimnao* or anxiety means 'a divided mind'. A very common trait of 'divided mind' cultures is anxiety. The problem becomes worse because Abel is terrified, and Cain is very anxious. The table tennis of anxiety between them escalates and can cause palpitations. As explained in Mannership, the fear and shame that Abel feels is so strong and so deep that we cannot 'go there' to repair the wound. The wound endures and is still very present in descendent cultures 5000 years later.

Susan Cain, in her wonderful book *Quiet*, says the Dale Carnegie Institute was *dedicated to helping businessmen root out the very insecurities that had held him back as a young man. Carnegie had written how ability in public speaking... is the indispensable weapon of those who would forge ahead in the keen competition of business.* The use of the word 'weapon' is significant.

Susan explains brilliantly how the American culture became one of the 'extrovert ideal' and shifted from what the influential cultural historian Warren Susman called a Culture of Character to a Culture of Personality. The social role demanded was 'to become a performing self'.

Western society was thus accelerated on a path to value the personality 'as demanded by our culture' at the expense of the character we were born with.

Susan also tells us how *this culture of personality opened up a Pandora's box of personal anxieties from which we would never quite recover.* She describes how

194

child guidance experts of the 1920s set about helping children to develop winning personalities and by 1960 a third of all prescriptions from US doctors were for Miltown or a similar drug called Equanil *for the anxiety that comes from not fitting in.*

During my deaf childhood, silence was not my greatest difficulty. Shame was much worse. Whenever I spoke, others saw me as deformed or 'handicapped'. A high wall of shame grew while inside I was drowning with *anxiety that comes from not fitting in*. Later, as a seven year old boy starting to hear, I was assisted by lip-reading classes and elocution lessons. But, looking back now, my greater need was for a friendly prison warder who could have helped me dismantle the wall of shame.

All of the help I received was for my brother Cain who 'had to make his way in the world'. Abel was forgotten. My teachers noticed the effects but did not know how to address the questions. One school teacher's report in my first year, aged seven, says; *it may not be entirely his fault that he has come bottom in this subject, as he is not always able to hear. He must watch carefully when spoken to and when listening to stories.* Another said; *he reads with speed and understanding but finds reading aloud with clarity and expression difficult.*

My shame in speaking after such a long silence was clear. Neither the teachers nor I knew that this was the subject to address. My example might seem extreme, but visiting schools nowadays there is scarcely a class without several who are hiding behind an inability to share their suffering, victimisation or bullying, or their burying of other fears. I needed another 55 years to metabolise some of this shame, once an indigenous shaman helped me understand the origin. He had noticed the curse at once. The greater surprise was how deeply this affliction remained hidden in my mind. I could 'function' as a businessman while being completely unaware of such a wound.

Instead of enabling the individuality of our children to flourish, we are instead giving their 'brother Cain' more tools to be successful in keeping 'Abel' underground. In so doing, our children forget who they 'really are'. We are a long way from *Katei ni Kiribati*. We are not teaching our children to know themselves, their genealogies, skills and knowledge. We might even need to examine whether we are justified in maintaining our Indo-European belief that we value individuality. Abel does not feel that we value him.

Cain's victory and Abel's burial did not begin at the founding of the Dale Carnegie Institute. But we can see how, a century ago, yet another way was found to strengthen Cain with extra skills and techniques to make his path a success. All along Abel continued to be forgotten, kicked along the road like a can. Perhaps the reason why some of the world's cultures do not learn from history is because they are unwilling to look inside themselves to find the traumas of their ancestors. By burying Abel they also bury their ancestral memory and thereby are condemned to repeat the errors of history. The phrase that 'ignorance is a form of self-destruction' is apt; and this teaching is shared by many of the world's religions. The advice should be a clear star in the night sky.

When you know yourselves, then you will be known, and you will understand that you are children of the living father. But if you will not know yourselves then you dwell in poverty, and it is you who are that poverty. [80]

What new techniques will we manufacture next to give more 'scaffolding' to Cain's personality? Or will it be too little, too late, as we may have destroyed our planet before we allow Abel to rise again? Is the current trend in social media the next wave of 'Cain promotion'? If so, we should not be surprised if an equal and opposite force which harms young children accompanies their Cain-like desire for social recognition.

Some children have expressed how social media means that they are now exposed to bullying 24 hours per day. There is no respite. This is a significant factor in the increase of self-harm among children. At least my childhood had 'time out' from 3 in the afternoon until 9 the following morning when classmates could not bully me, as well as a 'weekend off'.

Whilst I enjoy my iPad, we cannot expect that Abel will play with Cain's new toy. Apps and other tricks are good for Cain's amusement, or as a substitute nanny, but are not going to strengthen our connectedness with Abel.

***

Many therapists have commented how frequently new patients describe a 'happy childhood'. Maybe this apparent paradox can be solved by imagining that Cain had the happy childhood because the family conspired to forget about Abel. In this conspiracy, Cain has no guilt.

---

[80] Gospel of Thomas 3

A quick search of countries on a 'happiness' scale usually finds Finland, Norway, Denmark and Iceland topping the list. The first question is; can happiness really be measured? The second question is; why are there no indigenous cultures featuring anywhere on these scales?

Can Abel be measured? Or have our 'Cain-like' minds created a measure that conveniently forgets about Abel because our essence and infusion with spirit cannot be measured. The Choctaw Indians would not think of measuring the breadth or depth of their chuckles.

The Scandinavian cultures clearly emerge as the winners on the 'happiness scale'. But, and it is a very big but, despite Finland 'topping' the World Happiness Index in 2018, their rate of suicide is above the European average. So is Denmark's. What is going on? Having coached leadership, empowerment and engagement in all Scandinavian countries, their 'happiness' does not scratch the surface on a scale of the joy found in some indigenous societies.

Once, while consulting a Swedish factory at Fjällbacka, I discovered that one of their obstacles was an inability to confront others when necessary.[81] We spoke about this for a long time together. Eventually, it became clear to me that the underlying root was a fear of anger. I suggested an exercise which Robert Bly had used to tackle my fear of anger. The Swedes were excited to experiment, and I found a perfect spot in a fjord for the experience. Afterwards, we walked back in silence to the factory and sat in a circle. They all said they had never felt warmer or safer. I wondered whether some of the consensual aspects of Swedish culture were a fear of anger, in disguise. Could this explain their expression that personal distance is 'one field' as some who have a fear of anger retreat far away? I was reminded of the African proverb; a person without anger is unborn.

We have to admit that Cain's happiness and Abel's presence are quite different worlds. Could we stretch our minds to admit that 'happiness surveys' have simply found a way to measure Cain's 'comfort'? I am always impressed that the Scandinavian societies are so comfortable, with an unusually strong support system for all – which is rare in Indo-European cultures. I take my hat off to them. My hope is that, with Cain so relaxed, they might lead the way in helping Abel return and share a

---

[81] Perhaps this is what the I-Kiribati mean by: *He or she is emotional, friendly to strangers, and can be the best of friends and the worst of enemies.*

great feast. Only then would we be turning the tide towards warming our connectedness.

Happiness is not getting what we want; it is wanting what we get.[82] Or, perhaps this phrase describes the split. Cain is happy when he gets what he wants. Abel flows and does not 'entertain' the idea of happiness. Just thinking about whether we are happy or not means we have to temporarily be sat 'beside ourselves'; only Cain can think about such a question.

If we have a sincere interest in Abel's rebirth, it is the lessons of indigenous society we need to relearn. They do not use the Cain and Abel story, but sometimes speak of an imperial mind and an indigenous soul. I always liked that, and saw many links in the metaphors. Once, I asked Martín Prechtel how I could lessen my imperial mind. He spun around: "You can't. If you try to lessen your imperial mind you will make him much more ferocious. You must train your imperial mind to create the conditions so your indigenous soul is more welcome." That made sense to me.

Early on, in my work with Martín, one of my tasks was to decorate a clay bowl before baking her in an open fire. The challenge was to carve thirteen diamond shapes around the perimeter in the warm red Apache clay. Naturally, the clever part of my mind tried to use the length of different leaves to see which leaf would fit thirteen times around. But, by the time my pot was turned to measure her other side, something prevented me from measuring thirteen times with any leaf. My frustration soared. Something in me was determined to thwart any measuring. My frustration grew so strong there was a danger of throwing down and smashing my unfired pot. Begging Martín for assistance, explaining how my internal conflict was about to destroy my pot, he tapped me gently on both temples saying one temple was fighting the other. "You are so competitive. Why can't you let the holy measure? Why can't you trust your hands?" This was a new experience for me. A number of such challenges made me feel physically sick until I allowed my hands to complete the task without interference from Cain's measurement system.

The beauty of indigenous teaching is that we do not need to 'get well' in order to help our children. We just need to be travelling in the right direction, and then our children will help us. Together we can start the

---

[82] Rabbi Hyman Schachtel (1954).

repairs. We can find much support in many religions for indigenous traditions.

I shall always remember my first therapist's words. Robin Skynner told me that the part of me I feared the most might be the part I loved the most when I found him. Could this be Abel himself? Could Abel be a part of my mind that I had lost? Could the destruction of indigenous society be connected with this fear. Could the pain of the loss of our nature be so great that we cannot tolerate the aliveness of a culture with indigenous traditions? Could this account for a part of anti-Semitism? After all, Abel was a Hebrew translation.

The Indo-Europeans hastened their dominion across the globe in the 15th century once they had ships to sail vast distances. These ancestors left us a clue. The word 'assimilation' also arrived in the 15th century according to Merriam Webster, and is defined as: "*Assimilation* refers to the process through which individuals and groups of differing heritages acquire the basic habits, attitudes, and mode of life of an embracing culture." The dictionary's choice of words: 'differing heritages'; 'basic habits'; 'mode of life'; and last but not least '*embracing* culture', contrives to sweep the truth under a gentle silk carpet. To find an equivalent level of euphemism, we have to go back to the enslavement of the I-Kiribati; *Recruiting was not always popular in the island communities* and *The Micronesians quickly learned to fear the 'menstealing ships' … which began seeking recruits in Kiribati … (and were) taken by men who had great sport in the bush catching them and making them fast.*

Many of the indigenous were 'assimilated' in '*boarding schools*' – clearly the euphemistic department in literature was very busy with contronyms around the subject of enslavement. The legacy of five centuries of dominion includes an imprisonment of indigenous people around the world out of all proportion to their representation in society. For example, in Canada, the percentage of indigenous peoples in prison is about 10 times their representation in society for men, and 15 times for women.[83] Canada is but one example of a disease which still covers much of the globe.

Are the indigenous reacting to our imperial behaviour in a way like Abel would before he was 'domesticated' and we cannot tolerate being reminded of our own domestication? Are the indigenous seeking a measure of autonomy greater than we can tolerate for the same reason?

[83] justice.gc.ca.

Could racism be linked to a fear of Abel? In all cases, it is our imperial minds that need to be re-trained. There is much to study in the teachings of our ancestors, as well as learning from the traditions of other cultures.

***

Chapter IV of the Confucian analects tells us: 1. The Master said, *'At fifteen, I had my mind bent on learning. 2. 'At thirty I stood firm. 3. 'At forty, I had no doubts. 4. 'At fifty, I knew the decrees of Heaven. 5. 'At sixty, my ear was an obedient organ for the reception of truth. 6. 'At seventy, I could follow what my heart desired, without transgressing what was right.'*[84]

The length of time required by Confucius 'to follow his heart' tells us how difficult the journey can be, and suggests we need to start earlier or learn much faster. The greater our delay in starting to understand the extent of the earthquakes in young minds, the more building rubble we have to remove painstakingly to find signs of life.

Great philosophers, prophets and sages admit to the long-time taken to achieve this freedom, even after having realised their entombment. The two most important ingredients seem to be understanding and spontaneity. The teacher appears once we are ready.

In terms of understanding, Christ uses the word 'metanoia' which means 'changing our state of mind'. Confucius had a similar teaching in 'bringing the mind under new influences'.

Mencius says: *He who exerts his mind to the utmost knows his nature* and *the way of learning is none other than finding the lost mind.*[85] Perhaps the journey to understanding, and overcoming resistance, can also be identified by releasing our spontaneity. Maybe the circle is a virtuous one. The more that we allow spontaneity to rise in us, the more we learn about our resistance. As Gurdjieff pointed out, we cannot escape unless we admit first that we are in a prison. If we think we are free, we cannot escape.

There should be a warning on the bottle. If we think that we will get fully well in our lifetime then we have no chance. Those who are facing the right direction say that the best we can hope for is to work with others to create *a better and more enduring inheritance.*

---

[84] *Confucian Analects, The Great Learning & The Doctrine of the Mean*, translated by James Legge.
[85] The *Mencius* in Chan, Wikipedia.

My purpose was never to extoll the virtue of any particular culture or religion. But my heart leaps with joy whenever different religions or philosophies agree. Mencius describes Confucian thinking with an illustration of a child falling down a well. He explains how witnesses would immediately feel 'alarm and distress'. The feeling is not to gain friendship with the child's parents, nor to seek the praise of their neighbours and friends, nor because they dislike the reputation if they did not rescue the child. The feeling of commiseration is the beginning of humanity; the feeling of shame and dislike is the beginning of righteousness; the feeling of deference and compliance is the beginning of propriety; and the feeling of right or wrong is the beginning of wisdom. All of us have these 'Four Beginnings' just as we have four limbs. For someone to have these Four Beginnings, but to say they cannot develop them is to destroy themselves. [86]

This position of Mencius is further aligned with the Buddhist and Taoist teaching, as well as the Gospel of Thomas when he explains how humans do not need cultivation; they just need to accept their innate, natural, and effortless goodness. Thus these four beginnings can sprout, grow and develop, or they can fail. The object of education is the cultivation of benevolence, otherwise known as 'Ren'.

Confucius described Ren as: *wishing to be established himself, he seeks also to establish others; wishing to be enlarged himself, he seeks also to enlarge others.* [87]

Confucianism clarifies the responsibility of leadership. *All relationships should be beneficial, but each has its own principle or inner logic. A Ruler must justify his position by acting benevolently before he can expect reciprocation from the people. In this view, a King is like a steward. Although a King has presumably higher status than a commoner, he is actually subordinate to the masses of people and the resources of society. Otherwise, there would be an implied disregard of the potential of human society heading into the future. One is significant only for what one gives, not for what one takes.*[88]

We cannot expect young children to have an understanding which we do not possess. But, we can enjoy their spontaneity and allow them to reawaken ours. We can help them more once we increase our understanding. Our children can be our best teachers if we are attentive to our thoughts and feelings as the next generations grow through the

---

[86] The *Mencius* in Chan, Wikipedia.

[87] *Analects* 6:30.

[88] Mencius lived from 372 to 289 BCE. This passage comes from Wikipedia.

development stages we have forgotten. There is an African proverb: *the reason why grandparents and grandchildren get on so well together is that they have a common enemy.*

***

The list of what 'we must do' is too long and well beyond the scope of this book. Only a few of the measures we can think about in the short term are mentioned here.

Adrian Raine reminds us how much we have recently learned concerning potential damage in the womb from certain diets and other substances. He explains how some parents don't know that shaking their crying baby causes brain damage now and violence later. He suggests a clear need for education on parenting in young schools, particularly how to manage when a baby will not stop crying at night. Perhaps such early lessons will help the young remember their own experiences and learn how their path was perhaps 'not ideal'. Maybe the child has a little sister she can help.

Some of us can benefit from an awareness of the indigenous 'repair system' with their spontaneous enjoyment of 'known stories'. Living my life again would have taught me to enjoy my daughter's favourite bedtime stories until *she* wanted to change them instead of my thinking she needed a new one.

We need gentle counselling in schools from a much earlier age, and for everyone in class. As the Mayan villagers and Japanese production methods illustrate, we need to look at the entire process using the lessons of those who exhibit the cultural challenges more clearly. Adrian Raine has wisely proposed much greater attention to vulnerable children. However, we cannot afford simply to identify those in danger. All our children are at risk. Healing the entire class, or village, helps everyone. Those who might not need the help will naturally become allies to assist their peers.

If you bring forth what is within you, what you bring forth will save you. If you do not bring forth what is within you, what you do not bring forth will destroy you.[89]

The ages from 2 to 13 years seem the most critical to help our young generation to express themselves. If we do not address this challenge, we are failing to educate our children. Instead, whilst we might be training

---

[89] Gospel of Thomas 70.

them, we would not be 'leading them out' which is the true meaning of 'education'.

We must coach our young how to express anger without aggression, shouting, or any other form of violence so they are not 'unborn'.

***

To help our children understand, we must be honest about our culture's history which is not an easy task. My hope, in this book, is primarily to share the extent of our problem. The sins of 7200 years are not so easily purged. But, just as an understanding of our relationship to our life's traumas is helpful and healing, so a culture needs to share an understanding of the relationships in the culture's history.

Some primordial societies are not entirely free from violence, physical or sexual abuse. However, they manage these rare crises differently. Firstly, there is a much faster awareness that 'something has gone wrong'. Relations are so much closer that others will immediately realise a tragedy has occurred. The sufferer receives instant support from elders. In our therapy world we have learned how the 'absence of witnesses' makes the trauma so much greater for a child. A child can only accumulate mountains of shame if there are no witnesses to the crime. Many Western institutions have conspired to protect the perpetrators at the infinitely greater expense of the children who become traumatised and entombed. Hopefully, the increase in awareness of the extent of the 'cover-up' and the greater willingness of the oppressed to speak out might lead to improvements in our cultures.

In *Mannership* I recall watching a small child, Anna in a Spanish airport, abruptly petrified by her parents threatening her with abandonment because of her tantrum. The scene was riveting for me, but nobody else seemed to notice as if everything was normal. Somehow our culture has become oblivious to this aspect of 'taming' children and thus accepts the 'naturalness' of the 'experience'. This is how some aspects of culture are passed on. Anna's experience is a shocking illustration of the way our indigenous souls can become entombed without any apparent evidence of the crime. A handful of seconds can affect a child for a lifetime without any visible scars or evidence.

Perhaps the story of Cain and Abel is likewise glossed over and a potential lesson can be missed. By attaching to the story meanings such as fratricide, murder and jealously we can escape another meaning which is rather too 'close to home'.

Before concluding this chapter in a short discussion with Meredith, let me challenge the 'happiness winners' with a fresh dimension of new questions. Does their indigenous nature show up at the feasts? Are Abel, Esau and Hagar dancing at their feasts?[90] Is 'spontaneity in check' so the 'mind' can be happy? The questions are not envious ones. The achievements of Scandinavians in terms of peace, egalitarian and consensual life set them apart from most of Europe. That is beyond doubt and a considerable achievement in today's world; especially in the light of their Viking ancestry. I wondered how Scandinavian societies cleaned themselves of their Viking history until Meredith suggested that their strong women must have thrown the bad men out – I liked that.

In the annual gatherings of Inuit in Greenland falling about themselves with laughter, or Choctaws chuckling, there is something which most of us in Europe are missing; something which is more than 'significant', and which filled my heart with sweet warm water on Pacific Islands and in indigenous societies.

Returning to the imagery of Meredith's idea of the genotype struggle between the warrior and the civic, perhaps this gives us the hint of a key or a keystone. Like a beautiful stone 'civic' arch which would quickly collapse without a keystone. Could the keystone be a metaphor for our indigenous nature? What else could we be looking for on all our therapeutic endeavours?

This explains a culture's need for Shamanic leaders. They are the ones who, throughout history, ensured the cultural plumbing worked so the spirit flowed. My culture has long since lost these ancient traditions which enabled the two brothers to dwell in unity.

The subject had come up briefly in one Saturday morning's conversation with Meredith.

Mark: *The shamanic position has some similarities with our ancient pagan culture which had three roles, Druids, Ovates and Bards. The Druids were philosophers. The role of a Druid was a philosophy or thinking role.*

Meredith: *It's not a power role?*

---

[90] These three are representations of the healthier part of the split minds in the sacred texts as explained in *Mannership*.

Mark: *No, not a power role. The chiefs had power while the Druid was a thinker or philosopher.*

Meredith: *Who were the Ovates?*

Mark: *The Ovates had the connection with the other world. The Bards were keepers of the cultural stories, poems and dances. In native cultures, maybe the Shamans are both Bards and Ovates. The chief had a strong civic role, but this is a separate dimension. The Ovates' task was to find out where the tribe's spirit was either blocked or leaking.*

Meredith: *This is lovely.*

MEMES, ELBES AND TRIBES

Earlier in this book, before a discourse on the USA, we looked at Meredith's categories of genotypes to evaluate how the genetics of those who sailed to settle America were different from the tribes they left behind. A 'self-selection' had taken place among those with particular characteristics of behaviour. As Charles Darwin reminds us, selection is a much faster determinant of change than evolution.

Cultures are influenced by technology and inventions. Some technology came by chance like meteoritic iron, but other inventions grew as a response to unexpected challenges. The area where Indo-European culture was born, in the under-belly of Russia, witnessed a meeting between the domestication of the horse and the invention of the wheel which put this culture on steroids for conquering.

This book begins by highlighting differences between cultures in the islands of I-Kiribati. A people with the same language and genetics on almost identical geographical islands could produce significantly different cultural outcomes. The experiences suffered by each island are a strong determinant of the future culture. The way in which a culture diverges from a neighbour with the same genetics is due to the spread of 'memes'. A meme is an idea or a behaviour that spreads by imitation within a culture.

Like individual minds, either a culture can repress and forget the past, or a culture can remember and metabolise history. This is an effect of memes in the way history and experiences are re-processed. If a society maintains access to the 'third layer', revenge is unlikely to be on their dinner menu. As I learned with individual minds, although history is a huge factor, the relationship to the past can be more important than the actual events. The answer to the question, "why don't we learn the lessons of history" can be as simple as, "because we are not willing to learn about ourselves." We might be acting out a part of our history that we don't remember.

Language can influence us because our ancestors chose the words we use and thus the way we frame a subject. The languages which we inherit from our ancestors thus contain hidden memes. Meredith introduced the subject of memes to me one morning in a discussion on something else. Initially, I did not grasp the significance of memes but Meredith explained more.

Meredith: *In my career of management selection I learned early on that there was a particular pairing that should be avoided like the plague.*

Mark: *Which pair?*

Meredith: *Paranoia plus the warrior genotype.*

Mark: *You have stopped me in my tracks. If you look at how much of history has been contaminated by that pairing...*

Meredith: *Absolutely. But, as you say, the actual number of people leading destruction is not vast. It is the amount of destruction they cause which surprises us. Once the warrior genotype excites the tribal genotype they can run out of control. Don't forget that these genotypes are still around in society and the business world. It applies just as much in business life. Look at the banks. The people who got to the top were only interested in one thing, a bank taking over another bank. It was all to do with power, personal aggrandisement and so on. So this paranoia warrior combination is not just in history, they're there in the business community. They are an absolute menace.*

Mark: *Until relatively recently, business was under the control of nation states. Now it is becoming almost the other way around. If we are not careful we will have more crises like the last banking crisis. We need to preoccupy ourselves with the paranoia and warrior combination that can devastate so much of our lives.*

Meredith: *That's why I'm so interested in an alliance with the civic genotypes which are very thinly spread.*

Mark: *An alliance between the civic and primordial genotypes?*

Meredith: *Yes, the civic and primordial. The primordial is the foundation, but has never had power, and needs the civic in modern society. We need an alliance of the civic and primordial to compete against the warrior.*

Mark: *Are you suggesting that the tribal and service genotypes would otherwise be neutral.*

Meredith: *Yes. Tribal behaviours consolidate ranks very fast because people want to belong to something. They are joiners and want to join the establishment, whatever that is. Look at Europe's history. We have a very tribal nature. On the one hand, Europe has contributed massively to the world's civilisation, particularly since the renaissance. But every once in a while the warrior genotype comes along and provokes a monstrous tribal fight. Culture starts with a few genes reacting in a different way to the challenges of the environment.*

Mark: *Say that again? Culture starts with a few genes…*

Meredith: *Yes, particular genes responding to challenges of the environment.*

Mark: *So… any particular genes? Can you give me an example?*

Meredith: *If we take Greenland, for example, the people who first went to Greenland…*

Mark: *Were Inuits originally from Mongolia.*

Meredith: *No, I was thinking from Scandinavia. I am not talking about the Inuit. The first Viking colonists who went there showed almost no response to the rigors and challenges of the environment. As a result they died out.*

Mark: *You could also say the same about many of the first European settlers who went to North America. Many of them did not survive. It took a different group to get established.*

Meredith: *When colonists go to new places, they respond in different ways according to their genetic predispositions. I'm sorry to say that when German colonists went to South-West Africa, they engaged in genocide on a big scale. There was a tribe they almost completely wiped out, the Herero.*

Mark: *There are so many examples of this in European colonial history, with decimation of indigenous tribes and restricting the remainder to 'reservations' like the British in North America, the French in New Caledonia and plenty of other examples.*

Meredith: *I was very interested in your earlier point, when you talked about how the British had often colonised in a different way.*

Mark: *We had a very large number of colonies and protectorates, so there are more varieties of experience. Countries became colonies, settlements, dominions and protectorates for different reasons. Some were conquered outright. Some were invaded* by settlers supressing the indigenous population such as in America, Canada, Australia, and New Zealand. Some countries were effectively colonised by a company, like the East India Company, and subsequently joined the Empire. Many of the atrocities were committed by companies, as was most of the slave trade.

A few countries asked to join for protection against a neighbour or from fear of being colonised by someone else. Just like Armenia wanted to be a part of the Soviet Union in order to have protection against Turkey. The Cook Islands sought membership of the British Empire to protect themselves against the possibility of being colonised by France. Tonga sought to be a British protectorate to avoid the risk of being colonised by Germany. Once protected, Tonga had self-rule and was never actually colonised; her needs were satisfied by British protection which makes our relationship with them almost totally benign.

Likewise Botswana asked to be admitted in order to have protection against South Africa. However, a point we have to make is that it is critical to have a sense of shame about the atrocities. I have noticed that most cultures forgive Americans quicker than others as it is rarer for them to have initiated a conflict.

Meredith: *That is an interesting idea.*

Mark: *I think we had sufficient virtues in our colonial history to have helped many nations despite our wickedness in other cases. This is also borne out by the lower rate of military coups in former British colonies compared to other Europeans.*

Meredith: *These aspects affect a culture. The environment which is found, and the genetic response to it, starts a culture. Then the message is spread through memes.*

Mark: *You have reminded me about the culture of not eating pork in Judaism and Islam. We don't know exactly why. Some said it was because of the risk of diseases from pigs and others say because of the amount of water which a pig needs to remain cool. None-the-less it became a cultural taboo in the Middle East. But just a few months ago I was in Kazakhstan, and I accidentally walked into an enormous wedding party. Perhaps because I was a stranger on my own, they said come in. They sat me at the top table of this wedding. There I was...*

Meredith: *Wonderful.*

Mark: *This happens to me all the time as a lone traveller. I naturally asked a few questions. What's it like, and what's going on? This was a large Muslim wedding with an enormous feast. But the main dish was pork. I thought to myself, how interesting, a vast Muslim wedding, feasting on pork, but of course they're not in the Holy Land. They are neighbours of China where pork is important in the culture and has no taboos.*

Meredith: *Cultures start with genotypes or particular individuals who respond to the challenges when they move into a new territory. But other people, who do not have the same genetics can imitate them. This imitation is called a meme.*

Mark: *You are saying that a meme is a conscious adaptation to follow a gene?*

Meredith: *Yes, that's right.*

Mark: *Instead of having the genetics, you use the power of consciousness to follow someone else who has figured it out.*

Meredith: *Yes, but with a passive form of consciousness. Those who are pro-active, and particularly people who are intellectual, would ask the reason first and then follow. But those who are more passive in the way they respond to things just copy it. It's like a virus in the mind.*

Mark: *Maybe a better term would be a probiotic, or healthy bacteria. If you think of Darwin's evolution, most animal species cannot evolve fast enough to cope with the change in environment. The accelerant that enables animals to evolve fast is 'friendly' bacteria. Bacteria evolve faster because they can evolve within a generation. Perhaps we could say that bacteria have good memes. Bacteria can communicate with others to effect change within the same live generation. It's like they can tell their bacteria friends: "by the way there's this new antibiotic so you have to switch this and that to defeat it." Bacteria in our intestines break down food which we could not otherwise digest. It's interesting that we talk about culture in bacteria. Now I can more easily get my brain around this idea of memes in the evolution of culture. Those who don't have a particular gene can follow others through memes. Maybe memes can avert a danger like another Hitler.*

Meredith: *Yes, of course, that's right.*

Mark: *Perhaps that's why the Germans can be so scared of great orators, unless they are foreigners. They loved the oratory of both J F Kennedy and Barack Obama in Berlin, but they're terrified of a German orator because of the part of them that might follow; this mesmerises them.*

Meredith: *Yes. And they're terrified of the effect of being mesmerised.*

Mark: *Perhaps they now have a meme to watch out for great orators. But German opera singers can bring up the hair on the back of your neck more than others. Maybe it is safe as long as it's from an opera singer and not a politician. But other cultures love a politician who is a great orator, like the Americans for example. 'Wooden' politicians struggle in America. Perhaps that helps me to understand memes.*

Meredith: *Many aspects of religion arise because of how these memes grow in the mind. Religion is a great consolidator of memes. A culture can only change with new memes. For example, a culture begins to collapse when the pivotal belief systems that hold it together fall apart, as we found in Egypt.*

Mark: *What do you mean?*

Meredith: *Once you no longer believe that the Nile flows steadily as a result of a Pharaoh, who's born from a star and has to be reborn every time to ensure the Nile is flowing, then it changes everything. The culture then fragments. It breaks apart very quickly.*

Mark: *Where does the word meme originate?*

Meredith: *Richard Dawkins refers to it in his book quite late on. A meme is described like an idea, or behaviour, that spreads from person to person within a culture. A meme carries cultural ideas or traits that can be passed from one mind to another by imitation.*

Mark: *So, in one way they are like genes, as they can replicate. But they spread quickly. I had not realised that the idea and the word was originally from Richard Dawkins. He explains it very well.*

Meredith: *In some ways memes are like genes as good memes propagate and poor ones can become extinct.*

Mark: *Like the idea that the earth is flat. That meme became extinct. In your books, you introduce 'elbes'. Can you explain them?*

Meredith: *The human mind, like the eye itself, is programmed to collect smaller sensory inputs and to weld them into a broader 'whole'. An 'elbe' is a creation in the mind of a specific wider meaningful image; an image of dangerous thoughts in the mind of an enemy like heresy, treason or treachery. Then memes begin to lose their significance in the face of the larger elbe which becomes the centre of attention.*

Mark: *Who invented this word?*

Meredith: *I did. Or rather it was put into my mouth by my colleagues at Clare College because I pointed out that human society is driven by force. It's driven by what's in the mind – not necessarily by material things but by what's in the mind. The warrior genotype has produced things in the mind which are all about enemies, fighting enemies. But these are only enemies in the mind, not entirely enemies that are poaching on your territory.*

Mark: *So, perceived enemies?*

Meredith: *Perceived enemies – exactly.*

Mark: *So an 'elbe' is something in the mind that perceives an enemy when they might not actually be an enemy?*

Meredith: *That's right. My friends suggested it because it was like a corruption of the word Belbin. But, secondly it has a historical meaning. If you look through history, the forces divided by the Elbe take you through a lot of European history. They were pitted against each other because they were on the opposite banks of the Elbe. They all focus on the enemies on the opposite side of the river.*

Mark: *And it is amusing that the word Elbe is the middle of Belbin. An elbe is more than a meme, it overtakes the memes because our own safety is so primary and the 'elbe' constructs a threat from nowhere.*

Meredith: *Yes. But I am using the word for something even more specific. It's also the part of the person that sees primarily an enemy because of their possession of heresies. Heresy is much more serious than a difference. It's why often the biggest heresies are within people who belong to the same so-called faith. They've got the wrong bit of Christianity or the wrong bit of Islam – these are much worse enemies.*

Mark: *More of an enemy than someone who is Hindu or Buddhist?*

Meredith: *That's right.*

Mark: *When you spoke earlier about the first Viking settlers on Greenland, this reminded me of the very detailed analysis of their demise in Jared Diamond's book 'Collapse'. He points out how the first Vikings, led by Erik the Red in 982 CE, did not learn from the Inuit. So perhaps your model would suggest that they were unable to learn how to fish, catch ring seals and whales because of an 'elbe' considering the other's activities as heresies. As Jared explains, they were certainly hampered by a rigid version of Christianity and invested much of their resources in Churches which could instead have been better used for their survival. As to the first recorded meeting between the Vikings and the Inuit, Jared comments that "the Norse had a 'bad attitude' that got them off to a dreadful start with the people with whom they were about to share Greenland." From what we know about Vikings and the Inuit, the bad attitude is sure to be a Viking trait and not Inuit.*

So, can I assume that your idea of a 'super-elbe' is the anti-dote? Something which overcomes this tendency to fear heresies?

Meredith: *Yes, that's right, someone who's not prepared to accept enemies because they're on the other side of the river, or they belong to a different tribe. Super-elbes don't have any regard for heresy – it's the elbes that are concerned with heresy. So heresy is not a crime amongst the super-elbes because they are more tolerant.*

Mark: *Or open to new people and able to get on with them. Super-elbes would have instead made the Vikings friendly with the Inuit and they could have shared so that both benefited. I wonder how much of this also applies to the British settlers in the Americas.*

While we were walking around Meredith's garden, a ritual which we always followed to stretch our legs and 'get some air', I realised how much Meredith had discovered by observing the different characteristics of those who took his test, and how his results matched my instinctual observations of many cultures. Also, I realised the value of psychotherapy in 'vaporising elbes'. Perhaps paranoias come from elbes that are not known to us.

Returning to the conservatory, Meredith was curious about Africa and tribal differences which led our conversation in a new direction.

Meredith: *Going around the world, you should be able to make some comments about Africa. After all you crossed North Africa with native tribes, and you were the largest farmer in Africa for eight years.*

Mark: *The 46 countries of Sub-Saharan Africa are predominantly tribal. There are over three thousand ethnic groups in Africa. I often used to think that one of Africa's difficulties was related to the borders which were arbitrarily set by colonial powers without taking the tribes into account. If you make a river into a border then this splits tribes which lived on both sides of the river. Sometimes borders are simply lines of latitude or longitude which has nothing to do with who is living on the ground. There are very few Sub-Saharan countries which were designed around the territory of a homogeneous tribe. There are only eight countries in which one tribe has a majority, and in these eight cases the majority tribe represents over 80% of the population.*

Most countries have a very significant diversity of tribes, with the largest tribe being in a minority. The median would be something like a third of the population belonging to the largest tribe. Sadly, the eight more homogeneous countries did not always have peaceful coexistence within their borders for different reasons which was sometimes the fault of European influence. In the case of Rwanda and Burundi, which both have about 85% Hutus, the country was ruled by the 15% Tutsi minority. On several occasions this provoked intense ethnic conflicts. Perhaps we should start with the calmest three countries with a close correlation between the peoples and their tribal boundaries.

Meredith: *Which are these three?*

Mark: *The winner by far would be Lesotho with over 99.5% belonging to the Basotho tribe.*

Meredith: *You never hear about them.*

Mark: *With such a homogeneous society there is no reason to hear about them. Then Swaziland has 85% Swazis. Booker Tate used to farm sugar and cotton in Swaziland and the country was always calm. One of the Swazi chiefs was Chairman of the Board. He would come in a small leopard skin with just a red feather in his hair. He insisted we should have air-conditioning for board meetings otherwise we looked so uncomfortable even though he was always covered in goose pimples. His decisions were very sound and we really appreciated his chairmanship. Making us comfortable at his chilly expense was so gracious.*

Botswana's population is over 80% from the Tswana. Botswana is a very pleasant country. We never farmed there, but I enjoyed walking with the Bushmen to learn about their ancient Sān culture. The Tswana have been one of Britain's greatest friends in Africa. In 1872 Khama III became chief of Bamangwato. He, together with other chiefs, travelled to London requesting protection against a possible attack from his neighbours. Britain accepted his country as a protectorate in 1885. This is a good example of a country which wished to be a part of the British Empire. They returned the favour by sending over 10,000 soldiers to assist us in the Second World War, which I think is more than any other African country.

Meredith: *What about the other three countries among the eight homogeneous ones.*

Mark: *One is a country that I do not know, Equatorial Guinea, having never been there. The population is 80% from the Fang tribe. Sometimes I have thought of making a visit just to understand their Fang culture. I prefer to comment based on personal experience, either in the countries where Booker Tate farmed, or where I travelled extensively with tribes. Another example is Zimbabwe with over 80% from the Shona tribe. Using Adrian Raine's lens, we could say that, as a country, Zimbabwe had a very traumatic birth experience following the colonial period. The British did not help. We should have 'dealt with' Ian Smith when he declared a white supremacy Government in 1965. The British also behaved atrociously in the independence of Botswana by supporting South Africa's wishes to prevent the new King of Botswana, Seretse Khama, from marrying a white English girl.*

Meredith: *You have missed one country.*

Mark: *Yes. Not an easy one for me. Somalia is also an exception as they have 85% Somalis. However, they have a very strong clan culture which exacerbated their internal frictions. There were many difficulties in the late '80s and the Somali* economy collapsed leading to internal fights. Sadly a fine farm at Juba, which Booker Tate managed, was completely destroyed in the conflicts.

Somaliland, the part of Somalia which used to be a British protectorate, is apparently beginning to flourish peacefully on the Horn of Africa. By contrast with the rest of Somalia with several rival clans, Somaliland is mostly made up of the Isaaq clan. The Somaliland capital, Hargeisa, with a population of 1½ million is said to be calm these days. There are magnificent Neolithic rock art paintings in caves, up to 10,000 years old.

History reminds us that the British let down the 'Dervishes' of Somaliland more than once. We began by conquering them a century ago and ended by encouraging them to reunite with the rest of Somalia in 1960. The 'marriage' was almost a condition of their independence from Britain.

In addition to the tribal mix within poorly chosen borders in Africa, we have to factor in the religious mix. Sub Saharan Africa is one third Muslim and one half Christian with a roughly equal split between Catholic and Protestant. Many individual African countries have a very large mix of Protestants, Catholics and Muslims. Therefore the indigenous traditions, which grew up like plants to nourish the people were trampled underfoot. Adding the religious diversity further complicated the existing tribal mix. Most of their colonisation was very unhelpful, to say the least. Black Africans have suffered in unimaginable slavery for perhaps three millennia. Only a minority of tribes are significantly 'intact' to overcome their elbes.

During my time at Booker Tate, one of my greatest frustrations was the European Common Agricultural Policy (CAP). Africa's greatest potential asset is probably farming. The price paid to European sugar beet farmers was 26 cents per pound in 1990. We could have delivered surplus sugar from Africa at 7 cents per pound, but it was not allowed by the CAP as they wanted to protect the subsidised European farmers. Even apparent acts of generosity by CAP were destructive.

Meredith: *How do you mean?*

Mark: *I remember Europe sending its surplus beef to Africa as a gift. If you remember we had 'beef mountains' and 'mountains' of all kinds due to prices that encouraged over-production in Europe. This 'generosity' destroyed many cattle farmers in Ethiopia who had tended cattle for a whole season only to find themselves competing in the market with unexpected free beef given away by Europe. Some of them lost a season's effort. I am drifting off the subject. In terms of your genotypes we would have to say that there is a strong mix of tribal, warrior and service genotypes in Africa. The primordial is still extremely strong, but perhaps lower on the civic.*

Meredith: *If you looked for the civic genotype in Sub Saharan Africa, where would you start?*

Mark: *Definitely in Ethiopia. They have a very good education system. I was always fascinated by their religious history as it is unique in Africa. Their Orthodox Church was established in the early 4th Century, just after Armenia, and was in communion with the Coptic Orthodox Church of Alexandria. However, they also have a long pre-Christian religious tradition. According to their records, the Queen of Sheba had a son, Menilek I, by King Solomon. So this would have been about 950 BCE. This Ethiopian dynasty from Solomon and Sheba lasted until the death of Emperor Haile Selassie in 1974. According to Ethiopian accounts Sheba was persuaded by Solomon to give up worshipping the sun and moon, and to worship 'God' instead. A British Archaeological expedition to the Gheralta plateau in northern Ethiopia found a gold mine with inscriptions in Sabaean, the language of Sheba, a few years ago. There seems to be no doubt that there were regular camel caravans from the southern end of the Red Sea to Jerusalem at this time. Apparently the state of Sheba was on both sides of the Red Sea, which means her lands were in both Ethiopia and Yemen.*

If you allow me, and then we should move on, one of the tribes that really interested me is the Maasai. They have a high percentage of the warrior genotype, but they seem to direct this wisely to protect themselves and their traditions rather than to attack others. They are usually very open in sharing their practices. I would select them as one of the most fearless of the African tribes.

Life is very different in tropical Africa. The soil is sometimes so fertile that you can just push something into the ground and wait. Also, you can build a house quickly with the materials around. There is no issue with protecting yourself against cold. But, as we said earlier, perhaps one of the most important differences between tribes is the relationship to their primordial traditions. Some have retained this in full health and for others it is trickier. In conversations with elders of a tribe, I sometimes become distracted. This alerts me to a level of functioning among them which is much deeper or more primordial than I can manage. My mind has suddenly wandered in the conversation which, on reflection, indicates that they have passed into an 'altitude' of connection beyond my reach. The Maasai, who have a number of stages of traditional initiations, are a good example of this. After a certain point, in conversation with Maasai elders, suddenly my awareness that my mind has 'flown' alerts me to the depth of their connection with nature. It is as if the 'dissociation defence' steps into me. Humpty Dumpty has enabled my mind to divide and escape.

Perhaps there was no need for some of them to philosophise. On my trips to Africa, I always felt so alive. Once you are alive, why would you want to complicate things with thinking about a civilisation? Nature has her own 'civilisation'. The African way of life is a civilisation. One only has to read 'Things Fall Apart' by Chinua Achebe. This reminds me of one of my favourite African expressions, "when death finds you, make sure it finds you alive." Amen.

To remain 'intact' and healthy, a culture needs to remember their history and a tribe needs to rejuvenate links to their primordial origins. A role of shamans, or 'spirit plumbers', ensures the spirit of the tribe and individuals are neither leaking nor blocked. My global wandering showed me which tribes maintain harmony with nature and others which 'conquered' or failed to respect nature.

As Meredith taught me, some adventurous offshoots of tribal society gave rise to civic society in which pioneers in philosophy or technology laid the foundation stones of civilisation. Consensual egalitarian primordial civic society, like the Halaf in Mesopotamia five millennia ago, had neither warriors nor slaves. Many would suggest a development of civilisation after warriors and slaves, implying that all civilisations were built by slaves. However, without the Ubaid and Sumerian development of a hierarchy of chiefs and priests, without the development of warrior and slave culture, the Halaf would have continued to progress. They were more advanced than the Ubaid in many respects before they were 'taken over'.

If we go further back in development, there are other societies which may have been civic before warriors invaded. The grass-tuber and fish economy at Wadi Kubbaniya in Egypt began about 20,000 years ago. At Tell Abu Hureyra in Syria, which was first occupied by hunter-gatherers between 20,000 and 10,000 years ago, more than 150 species of edible plants were identified. In China, the earliest pottery was found in Xianren Cave and dated to 20,000 years ago. Since these different peoples broke new ground compared to everything else around them, and lived in a community which was not hunter-gathering, we could consider them as early examples of the primordial civic genotype.

Meredith suggested to me that, in tribal society, group identity is as important as personal identity and often more so. This is present in our cultures today. When lacking membership of group, a compulsive search for one's lost 'tribe' begins. Tribal loyalty can generate unquestioning compliance and obedience. Separation from the 'tribe' may lead to feelings of uncertainty and anxiety. Many of these observations were the foundations on which Meredith's research on team roles was built. He had noticed the particular behaviours which each of us brings to meetings with others. Meredith came to the conclusion that the struggle between warrior and civic genotypes within each nation will be greater than that between countries. This resonated with me strongly.

I saw then that, if we hope for the civic genotype to become much stronger than the warrior genotype, we should not threaten other countries as this helps promote their warrior genotype unwittingly. A good example is Iran. They have a wonderful culture and history. In the longer term, we would all be better served by an internal victory of their civic roots. But while we threaten them, the civic lose ground to the warrior in their society. There could not be a better case to illustrate a need to lead by example.

Before continuing with the subject of leadership, the conversation with Meredith on African tribes reminded me of my first visit to Botswana. This short story will be included in the next chapter.

The Bushman, the Dress and that Tyre

I cannot say that my first visit to Botswana was an accident, but a week earlier this idea hadn't been on my mind.

A couple of months before, I had agreed to travel to Rosslyn, near Johannesburg, at the request of Julian, an American client, to review the performance of a factory with him. Since the journey from Chicago to South Africa was long, and the flight cost disproportionate to the length of our visit, I purchased a non-refundable cheaper fare. Unfortunately, six days before we were due to fly, Julian emailed me to say he was sick and we would have to postpone the trip.

Julian offered to reimburse my flight costs. In that instant, I realised how much I was looking forward to being back in Africa, and there would be a 'hole' in my diary otherwise. I emailed him back, saying that I wished him a speedy recovery but he did not need to reimburse me. I would use the ticket and take a break in Southern Africa. That was how the long overdue visit to Botswana came about, one of the most peaceful of the African nations and gateway to the Kalahari Desert.

My energy surged with the prospect of another adventure. The internet offered a variety of local travel agencies, including some that resembled the No. 1 Ladies' Detective Agency of Precious Ramotswe. I chanced upon another simple website and filled in their online enquiry form. Meanwhile, finding a flight from Johannesburg to Gaborone, the capital of Botswana, was easy. There were eight flights a day to choose from for the fifty-five minute journey. Selecting which flight to take took longer than the time to buy a ticket. I paused to have a cup of coffee, savouring the smell of the roasted beans when the phone rang. The number on the screen looked very strange and foreign. Who could this be?

A gentleman by the name of Mr. Rowlands was calling in response to my online enquiry. He was a retired primary school teacher and sounded like he had his feet on the ground. The travel agency was his, he explained, and he thought to telephone as my planned visit was in a few days. I thanked him for taking the trouble to call. He confirmed that he could organise a trip for next week and had a driver available. He asked me, "What do you want to do?"

I was stumped for words. Without thinking, I said, "I haven't thought about it." The silence on the line was awkward. I realised he must be taking me for an incompetent tourist who didn't have a clue. That was not the way my Botswana adventure was supposed to start. Then I felt guilty that I was wasting his money on such a long distance call.

He broke the silence by asking, "What about a game safari?"

His question brought me to life. "Well, I used to farm in much of Southern Africa and was hoping for something different. Maybe something uniquely related to the local Tswana culture." I felt relieved; his impression of me must have changed.

"What about walking with Bushmen?" He offered.

"Perfect, I couldn't think of a better idea."

Mr Rowlands promised to find out if any of the Bushmen he knew were available and to let me know very soon. He said that a day or two might be necessary to raise them 'on the bush telegraph'. Two days later he emailed to say that all was confirmed. He had reserved a room at Kgale Lodge in Gaborone. His driver, Tich Mutanga, would collect me at seven thirty the day after my arrival to take me to the Kalahari. There, a Bushman by the name of Size would show me how to survive in the desert. Tich would wait for me in the lobby. I asked for one change to the plan. Would Tich join me for a cooked breakfast at seven so that we could meet properly face-to-face before our long drive side-by-side? Mr Rowlands responded that this would be very well received, and I was pleased that he understood my respect for local guides.

Just three mornings later, there we were sitting down to a full English breakfast of eggs, sausages, bacon and beans with plenty of toast and coffee.

Chatting with Tich was easy. We made an immediate connection and trusted each other. Soon it was time to go. Tich walked me out to his agency's four-wheel drive land cruiser in the classic camel colour. Suddenly, I noticed how unprepared I was. My rolling luggage bag was better suited to airport walks. What was I thinking in taking my laptop in a knapsack to the Kalahari? Climbing into the passenger seat, I noticed the odometer, 350,047 and even though these were kilometres, this was not a young camel. As we pulled out of the parking lot, the Toyota squeaked. Perhaps the ride would be quieter on sand, my mind was already wandering.

Tich said we had about a hundred kilometres to drive on a tarmac road, and then another hundred and twenty on sand or stones. My knapsack and computer would soon be full of sand. I asked Tich if we could stop somewhere, before the end of the tarmac road, where we could buy a plastic bag, or a sealable container of some kind.

About an hour later, we approached a village with a modest general store. There was nothing suitable to protect my laptop. Instead, we packed a cardboard box full of fresh fruit including some very juicy South African plums. Tich mentioned there was a Chinese store nearby. We could also try there. We did with no better luck. But, looking upwards suddenly, I saw high on the wall some rolls of beautiful and colourful cloth for making clothes.

"Tich, do you still have a phone signal?" I asked.

"Yes."

"Can you call your wife and ask her how much material she needs to make a dress?"

He looked at me quizzically but made the call. Three and a half metres was the reply.

"Right, now can you choose the material your wife will like best?" I insisted.

Having bought the colourful material, I swaddled my laptop and electronics carefully in the middle of the cloth as if binding an Egyptian Mummy.

We set off again and I was a much happier man. I had resolved my problem the African way, by going with the flow. My enthusiasm was infectious although Tich was still a little puzzled.

"The ladies don't think like us, Tich." I laughed. "We think they want a big gift, but they prefer lots of little ones, and we just bought your wife seven gifts."

"Where are the seven gifts?"

"Yes, Tich, seven! The first gift: you called, so you were thinking about her. The second gift, you were thinking of her in a new dress…"

"That's the same gift," he said.

"No, Tich, it doesn't work like that for the ladies. These are two separate gifts for her. Third, you asked her how much cloth she needs for a dress, that's another gift." Tich smiled. "Then you chose the material and that's the fourth. She will be wondering now what this new dress will look like. Her wondering is a fifth gift because she doesn't know but she will think more. The sixth is how she will imagine you carefully looking after the material until you see her again, and finally the seventh gift is the anticipation of the surprise when she receives the material."

"Yes, but she will have to make the dress," he said.

"I know, but she will have all the gifts again while her sewing machine is humming. I am sure of it. You will see. And I am happy too, thinking of all this. Of course, there is the bonus that her dress will meanwhile protect my laptop in the Kalahari." Tich smiled again. He said that I wasn't a normal tourist. I didn't mind that, asking him the last time he bought his wife some material for a dress. He understood my point.

We were now off the tarmac road and our banter continued for the next twenty minutes or so. Meanwhile the Toyota land cruiser was being thrown about on the sand and stones like a ship in a storm. The dust and sand were everywhere. Suddenly, Tich became silent. I looked at him anxiously. He said, "We have a problem with a rear tyre."

It wasn't just a puncture; the rear passenger side tyre was shredded. A six-inch nail had gone right through to the rim of the wheel. "Do you have a spare?" I asked nonchalantly to disguise any anxiety. He had. That was a relief, and Tich climbed onto the roof to unbolt the spare before passing the wheel down to me. The solution seemed simple enough; we just had to jack up the vehicle, and then take off the nuts holding our damaged wheel. Except there was a lock-nut; the kind designed to stop others from stealing the wheels, and this nut was more than very effective in deterring us. The 'key' spun on the inside and none of our tools could get a grip on the outside. We tried everything. I lay on the ground to push with my legs to give Tich more leverage and pressure on the wrench, but nothing took hold. We were defeated.

There was nothing to do except wait, in the African way, for another vehicle to come by. At least we had plenty of water, and even fresh fruit if needed. Two trucks came after half an hour, but their tools were no better than ours. Forty minutes later, a car came with a young South African couple. The boy, in his twenties, jumped out and looked. "Yes, I have a tool for that." His wrench was designed with a progressive grip and did the trick. We had 'broken the code' of the lock-nut and got the wheel off. But, the new tyre was fixed with only five of the six bolts since we could not use the broken lock-nut again.

Tich was quiet. He looked worried. Was he worried that we no longer had a spare? Or was that my worry? I could have just asked him directly, but respected his silence. Then, I remembered, particularly in Africa, how a vehicle's owner would often expect his driver to pay for a damaged tyre. "How much will a new tyre cost, Tich?" I asked.

He answered, "Three months' wages."

His answer said everything. I replied, "A six-inch nail was not your fault."

"Yes, but I should have stopped sooner. Then the tyre would have been repairable."

I saw his point. I could picture the scene with Rowlands. The shouting and screaming, and Tich having to take a beating, no arguing or he would lose his job.

I didn't feel much better. My entire journey in Botswana would be ruined if Tich suffered because of this tyre. I pledged that I would take care of this somehow. Tich was not reassured. He hardly knew me: why should he take my word?

During the next hour, we spoke less and watched the views more. The laughter and love of his wife's dress had evaporated.

It was mid-afternoon before we arrived at our lodge. The manageress brought us a very late lunch with a beer. With the coffee, she casually announced that there were lion on the salt flats just twenty kilometres away. I didn't want to ask Tich to drive further. But, when I told her we now lacked a spare tyre, she offered their own lodge Landrover and driver. Tich and I looked at each other. There is something about lion; one can never see too many of them.

The lodge driver knew exactly where the salt flats were. We were less than a kilometre from the lion when, suddenly, the wheels of the Landrover lost their grip and started to slip in the sand. Our driver jumped out, and immediately took his shovel to dig out the wheels. But, when starting the engine again, the wheels sank deeper. We had another ninety minutes of light left at most. We needed branches, strong twigs or anything we could lay down to make the ground firmer, and to help the wheels get a grip. But the Landrover sank even further until the chassis of our vehicle was resting her belly on the sand. The wheels were just hanging there, spinning uselessly.

"Does anybody have a mobile with any signal?" I asked. I certainly didn't, nor did the driver, but Tich had one out of the five bars on his screen. Not enough to make a call we found. We sat in our open Landrover, waiting and thinking. We discussed our options. Walking back would probably take us four or five hours. Maybe we should stay in our open vehicle overnight and walk in the very early morning.

Just five minutes later, another vehicle was heading directly toward us. They stopped and seven strong men jumped out. Their uniforms announced they were research rangers of the Kalahari National Park.

"What are you doing here?" one asked.

"We are stuck."

"No, you are not stuck. You just need a good push." Together we pushed our Landrover out of the soft sand onto firmer ground. What a relief!

They told us the lion were just around the corner and the ground was good so we really should make the most of the last fifteen minutes of light. We saw the lion in the twilight.

Dinner that night was excellent and the beer so refreshing, as we laughed about our day's adventures.

Yet Tich was still worried about Rowlands and the tyre. Since we were 'in this together', I suggested that Tich should warn him of the truth. That would soften the blow when the full story came out. Tich did as advised, but clearly was still apprehensive about the final outcome. "Let's sleep on it," I suggested.

The following morning was bright and sunny and the air was deliciously fresh. After an early breakfast we drove to meet Size.

The moment we arrived in the village, I felt as if I had walked through a veil to another world. There are times when I meet indigenous people who are so much at home with nature, and at home with themselves, that there is no option but to relax. I felt at home here.

The children loved the juicy mauve plums. As soon as they took a bite, the juice squirted out and ran down their chins only to be rescued in their small hands without missing a drop. They giggled with the utmost enjoyment. Their delight brought me back to the dress of Tich's wife.

With a lovely energy, we set off on our 'walk' led by our Bushmen guides. Size walked with a deep connection to the ground; as if the ground bowed beneath each footstep. I saw he was completely in harmony. He would nod to each plant as he passed, sometimes stopping to explain their particular use. Some were for nourishment, others for medicinal purposes. The plant that interested me most was for drinking. I could not imagine how one could drink from such a small leaf. Size proceeded to show me.

He began by loosening the sand under the leaf with his fingers to find the plant stem. Then, very carefully, he loosened the sand around the plant stem deeper and deeper into the ground using his fingers together with a stick which he carried. This was not a quick process as the plant

stem had to be preserved undamaged, he explained. As he continued, he seemed to be losing his arm. "The drink will be at the very end of my arm's reach," he said. Having found a tuber, he needed to dig a little deeper to ensure he also released any fine hair roots underneath. Slowly he brought the entire plant and root up to the surface. Some plants looked like potatoes and others like carrots.

The best for drinking were the potato variety. With a small knife, Size cut off one side of the potato, as if he had 'removed the left flank' but preserved the vertical stem and other half of the root. Then he put the entire plant back, gently reversing the process he had used to excavate the 'well'. The hole he had dug was backfilled with the same sandy soil. Finally, the leaf was sitting on the surface just as the plant was when he began. He said everything would grow again and find a way of repairing the part he had removed. He was like a magician, except that I had missed the drinking part. That was his next trick. He cut up the half potato and squeezed tightly in his hands to drink. There was a lot more juice than the plums I had brought.

I marvelled at his delicate respect for nature, that he could drink and then restore to the ground enough of the plant to leave a 'well' for others. A Bushman would see a plant leaf which had been recently 'tapped' by the evidence on the ground. I regretted my culture's lack of relationship with nature. The thought was painful.

Size taught me how to make string from the aloe plant, but this was more familiar. The way the fibres were rolled on our skin was just the same way the Gilbertese made their string from coconut fibre in the Central Pacific. But the string's use was quite different. Size made a snare with the assistance of a springy sapling, a rabbit's favourite berries and a string noose. The idea was that a rabbit would eat the berries, dislodge some twigs and set off the noose which would tighten around him. Mine went off too quickly and almost snared Size. He roared with laughter.

In the afternoon, Size stopped me and held my arm. "See that print, that's a hyena." I smiled and hugged him. "You know." I said, "There is something about you which is so safe and reassuring. I am so grateful to be walking with you; your spear; bow and arrow, instead of relying on a wretched vehicle." He knew what I meant.

Size was the highlight of my trip to Botswana.

After the day's walk with nature, we spent a last night in the lodge before setting off for Gaborone the following morning. I wanted to share the driving. At first Tich protested, but I persuaded him that the drive was long and tiring; also that I was no stranger to driving in Africa.

I had my hands on the wheel as we approached Gaborone in the late afternoon. I had to wake Tich to find the way to my hotel. After unwrapping the laptop packaging, we shook the cloth to remove all traces of sand before refolding the beautiful design carefully. I looked forward to meeting Tich at breakfast the next day. We were going to visit the highlights around Gaborone, and take a trip out of town to see David Livingstone's mission at Kumakwane.

But, the following morning, Tich didn't come. Mr Rowlands arrived instead. This surprised me, and I wondered why I had not been warned. Rowlands didn't look comfortable as we spoke over breakfast. "Is this about the tyre?" I asked. Rowlands shifted his weight rather uncomfortably. I continued, "Tich is a fabulous driver. I have had an excellent trip with him. We have enjoyed great conversations, and there is nothing he could have done about that nail in the rocky ground."

Rowlands said, "But he wrecked the entire tyre."

"No; the nail wrecked the tyre. You must know the section of ground just after the end of the tarmac road. You are very lucky indeed to have Tich on your staff. Let me be blunt with you. If I have the slightest idea that Tich will suffer consequences for this, I will regret having come to

Botswana." Just in case he was going to resist, I added, "And really, you could take some responsibility for the hour and a half in the sun we had to wait to remove the lock-nut. That has nothing to do with Tich."

"Do you want Tich to drive you today then?" Rowlands asked.

"Well, why don't we three all go together? I know you are free as you have just offered, and I know Tich is free." I had already learned during the previous days that Rowlands' travel agency consisted of himself, the vehicle and Tich. There was nobody else, but there was no need to share this information.

Rowlands could not disagree and seemed content with that. He telephoned Tich and asked him to come over. We hadn't finished breakfast, so Tich joined us. Before we left the table, and speaking in front of both of them, I said to Rowlands, "I had a really good adventure. We had some challenging moments but Tich handled them brilliantly. I am going to give your agency a tip. I am going to pay for that tyre myself. That will be the end of it."

All was well as we toured the villages around Gaborone together, and while having a lovely picnic under the tree where David Livingstone taught I suddenly remembered my laptop protection. "How was the cloth, Tich?"

His eyes lit up. "Better than my wedding night."

The Right Leadership

To obtain a good answer, we have to ask the right questions. There are so many publications on leadership; apparently four new books on the subject come out every day. Either we have been asking too many questions, or are still looking for the right question.

One answer which came to me after my first consultancy career in the '70s was the realisation of different leadership styles at Company Boards. Typically, it was more important for a German Board to complete all the items on the agenda; for the French to argue about at least one item on the agenda at length so everybody had been heard; for the Americans that everybody did what they agreed at the board; for the British it did not matter as they were not going to follow what was agreed at the board anyway. Looking back now, the reflection is: So what? What was the question? And the answer would be that there wasn't one. This was just an observation.

My objective in this book was primarily to understand the three guiding questions in the preface in terms of nations. My hope was that my readers could use my observations to re-examine their own culture. Perhaps a new reflection might come from the etymology of language. Or a different way of thinking might provoke fresh feelings of some effects of our culture's experiences.

With the benefit of hindsight, my observations taught me that the context of leadership exists within a culture. There is no definitive answer concerning leadership as the question is forever changing. The memes of a culture change and the needs for leadership change. Winston Churchill was absolutely the right leader for Britain's challenges against Hitler. But, less than two months after victory, the 1945 General Election decided he was not the right leader for the peace. The British memes demanded a different kind of protection against ill health and poverty. There is a lovely story that Churchill's butler was terrified of having to tell his boss, in the bath, that he had just lost the election. But the reply was "that was what winning the war was about; having this choice." Leaders can create memes, and memes can make or break leaders.

Meredith has spent his career studying the traits which make leaders and leadership teams successful. He has designed a number of 'instruments' to measure and determine the likely results. As he often said to me, the most important point was selection; who we choose for a particular appointment is critical as their nature will prevail.

My experience was based on keen observations of leaders and cultures, on the good fortune to have had so many wonderful mentors, and the luck to have had the chance to learn from my own mistakes in a number of leadership positions.

The subject on which Meredith and I agreed most was the difference between consensual and warrior leadership. Not only that, but we agreed how the consensual, the 'civic', needed a strong coalition with the primordial and service genotypes. Over time we hoped the tribal genotypes might lose their 'nationalist edge' and join us. We would then triumph over the warrior genotypes and finally put the Vikings to bed.

During one Saturday morning's conversation on the United States we returned to the subject of leadership.

Meredith: *You have much more experience of the USA and I wonder what you made of this book Synchronicity by Joseph Jaworski, particularly the points he makes on American leadership.*

Mark: *First of all, it is a lovely book. He makes such wonderful points. What did you have in mind? I hope he does not mind us using his critical points as signposts.*

Meredith: *He says, "The trouble with American leaders is their lack of self-knowledge".*

Mark: *This is true, but you could say that anywhere. In my experience there is not more self-knowledge in Europe than in the US. To find high degrees of self-knowledge you have to go to particular cultures. But I agree absolutely with his point that more self-knowledge is essential in successful leadership. Honesty requires self-knowledge, doesn't it?*

Meredith: *Yes, it does. And self-knowledge entails not only what you think about yourself but also how others see you too.*

Mark: *Absolutely. How else could we learn about ourselves without listening to what others see in us? You cannot be honest without openness to self-knowledge given by others. The views of others 'create honesty'. Honesty means straightforwardness. Without honesty, you can't have trust or true empowerment. For an organisation to grow, the leadership has to be willing to grow.*

Meredith: *Next he says, "The trouble with American leaders is their lack of appreciation for the nature of leadership itself."*

Mark: *I don't think there is anything especially American about this. Finding leaders who really understand the nature of leadership is rare. You can also find good teaching on the subject especially in ancient Chinese philosophical writings since much of Confucian thought was about leadership coaching. Primordial cultures understand the nature of leadership far more than others. In general, most Western companies are now over managed and under led. The point Jaworski is making is a very good one, but sadly this also applies everywhere and not just in America.*

Meredith: *It does. Then he says, "The trouble with American leaders is their focus on concepts that separate, such as communities, nations, disciplines, fields, methods, rather than concepts that express our interconnectedness."*

Mark: *Now, this one I would agree with quite a lot. But, I would suggest that this is an Indo-European 'disease' which the settlers took with them to the Americas. There is a fabulous book called 'The Puritan Gift' by Kenneth and William Hopper. They make clear how the first Puritan settlers thought quite differently and how the culture of meritocracy was born in the Massachusetts Bay Company. They also had a sense of morality and belief in their purpose which Confucius would have felt at ease with. The outstanding points in 'The Puritan Gift' show how the USA lost her way in Company leadership around the time of the Vietnam War. To use your terminology, the 'civic' leadership was overtaken by 'warrior' and Viking leadership looking for quick financial gains. 'The Puritan Gift' illustrates how many great American companies were initially led by former artisans, or those who had faith in artisans from having been promoted up though the levels of an organisation. After the Vietnam War many companies became led by financial engineers who sought to manipulate profits but did not understand the product at all. But, perhaps what Jaworski has picked up is the increase in American warrior leadership tendencies since the time of the Vietnam War. As you have often said, warriors are always looking for an enemy, like a hammer looking for a nail, so they would be focused on items which separate.*

Meredith: *Yes, this is the opposite of China. The next point Jaworski makes is, "The trouble with American leaders is their ignorance of the world and of US interdependence – their lack of world mindedness".*

Mark: *Let's look at this in a different way. America became the world's greatest power on the strength of her own economy. China was similar except over several thousand years. This is definitely something these two nations share.*

Meredith: *I think it's a fair statement to say nobody's done it apart from America or China, I think that's true.*

Mark: *Neither America nor China has needed to understand the rest of the world in order to be successful. Americans have also had a unique luxury of being able to borrow from overseas in their own currency. Nobody has done that before. They didn't even need to understand other currencies. Therefore it is not a surprise about their being less knowledgeable of the inter-connectedness of the world than other powers which grew through empire or trade. I sometimes tease Americans by saying: "You know, when we have a World Series we invite other nations." But, more seriously, the important difference between Americans and Chinese in this area is something else. The Americans, following on from the British, are keen to meddle all over the world and so this lack of understanding is serious. The Chinese are not so prone to meddle outside their part of the world and they have patience on a much longer timescale so the understanding is less critical.*

Meredith: *I agree, this lack of understanding of others also applies to China. They have been isolationist, usually because the West did not treat them well. They are now going into Africa but don't quite know how to handle the cultural situation. Then he says, "The trouble with American leaders is their inattention to values – forgetting to ask "Why" and "What for?"*

Mark: *I feel this is a little unfair compared to the rest of the world. Jaworski is right except that some American companies might be truer to their values than European ones. Perhaps their sense of their awareness of the subject makes them more aware of the gaps. The French have much less respect for their employees in a factory than an American company would, for example. There is a much stronger "power distance" between the French leadership and the people than there is in America. Perhaps this is a case of greater American awareness of the issue as the power distance is so much less. To cite the contrast with France, when I lived in Paris in the late '70s, the Presidents of my French clients were more remote from their factories than any other European nation. They did not like getting their hands dirty. By contrast, a President of an American company is proud of getting his hands dirty. When one arrives in an American factory the manager often wears jeans like everyone* else. He looks like one of them. This aspect also goes back to the early settlers where the successful leaders were 'one of the group' and not apart. By contrast the French boss will probably still wear a tie, to set himself apart. What Jaworski might be putting his finger on is my fear of an increase in Viking warrior leadership in Global companies. In this respect Jaworski's observation of an inattention to values is absolutely right.

Meredith: *The trouble with some American leaders is that they are less aware of social nuances and of how to analyse social architecture.*

Mark: *There are two points here. On the social nuances, I agree. But, on the other hand, I don't know a country which adapts quicker to a problem, they find a way around it.*

Meredith: *Yes, they're very empirical, aren't they?*

Mark: *They're very fast at putting together a group of people to solve a problem. American leaders know how to make changes. We need to concentrate more on the second aspect of analysing social architecture. This applies everywhere and is a foundation of change management and leadership. This is about understanding both the mind and the passions of others. I like an idea from Pythagoras. He was not really a mathematician but more a philosophy teacher, who went to Egypt as a young man. That was where he learned about the right angle triangle. The Egyptians had used this to build the pyramids over a thousand years before him. But, he got credit for the triangle when he set up a school on the south coast of Italy in 530 BCE. Maurice Nicoll suggested that the word 'upright' in the Testament is the same Greek word that was used to describe a central tent pole equally pulled from both sides. There was only one Testament in 535 BCE. Pythagoras suggests that the two equal pulls are the mind and the passions. So a man who could balance his mind and his passions would be upright. I like that. He would be 'isosceles'. This word comes from 'iso' which means equal, and 'skelos' which means a leg. Such a man has equal legs.*

Sadly too many of our managers rely on the mind, and do not have the leadership skills to understand the passions of others. We could apply this to an inability to 'analyse social architecture'. But this applies to all of us. Only primordial cultures truly understand all the nuances. As you have said to me before, one issue with China is that they do not speak up. They think the questions but do not articulate them. On the other hand, as you rightly say, the Chinese leadership is able to discern the wishes of the community and become more consensual. So the Chinese culture finds her way differently as a result of much earlier guidance and coaching from early philosophers.

Meredith: *Jaworski adds; one shortcoming with many American leaders is an insufficient appreciation of the relevance of stakeholders; of the implications of pluralism; and of the fact that no one person can be wholly in charge, and therefore each leader is only partly in charge of the situation as a whole.*

Mark: *I would love to have a conversation with Jaworski himself to see what he means by all these points. He may have understood something which we are missing. My experience suggests that the Americans are better at this than Europeans, particularly the last sentence. From their earliest settlement beginnings they have valued other craftsmen and their views. They have always had a more collegial leadership than the European hierarchies of power and nobility that they escaped from. Perhaps once again they value this more than Europeans do which is why Jaworski sees the issue more clearly.*

Meredith: *I would rephrase 'the relevance of stakeholders' with 'the culture'. One can change or take control of a culture – but the US is good at facing practical challenges. I thought I'd draw your attention to some of these points about America. I was interested to know what you thought. Much of it could also apply in any society. It is not necessarily an American phenomenon. I didn't show you to endorse it. I thought it would interest you. I think what we are saying about America and China is important for management today. We need a consensual style of leadership. But once we have consensus, we need a clear structure to put things into operation. Consensual leadership is the key to the future. We are moving more and more to that sort of situation with the Internet. I think the struggle in organisations is going to be between warrior leaders and consensual leaders. That's what the outcome of the future is going to depend on. Warrior leaders can be successful in the short term but consensual leaders are needed for the longer term.*

Following the conversation on America and China, perhaps the 20th century taught us that both Capitalism and Communism have their failings. 'The Puritan Gift' describes extremely well what happened to many American businesses around the time of the Vietnam War. We know how easy it is to get lost or to take the wrong path. There were two factors at work; greed in a culture, and greed among some business leaders. Ethics disappeared. Perhaps it is not a coincidence that the error began in the middle of the Vietnam War.

Meredith's analogy of the struggle between consensual or warrior leadership is helpful. We cannot hope for mental health in society without taming the Vikings at the helm of our organisations. Let us concentrate on our own issues before trying to change other cultures.

RETURNING TO THE PACIFIC BY LIFOU

I had wanted to return to the Gilbert Islands, Kiribati, ever since 1977. But, every time a plan was launched, the logistics were either too much of an obstacle or the fates wanted me to wait. At the beginning of my career, a week was necessary just to fly from London to Tarawa. Not much had changed. She was still on the International Date Line, as far from the Greenwich Meridian as possible. The flight from Fiji was still only once per week. Whenever my travels took me closer, somewhere on the Pacific Rim, a detour could not be fitted in. Besides, there was no point in going that far just for a few days in Kiribati. A proper visit needed several weeks.

I decided to go east, through Australia. Having time on my hands enabled some additional treats. An absolute must was a stopover in New Caledonia. This island had always intrigued me; she must somehow have the same relationship to Australia as Madagascar has to Africa. That is to say, apart from being a very large and long island to the east, probably not very much. Millions of years had let these pairs of neighbours develop different species and plants. Recent human migrations had come in different epochs and by different paths.

New Caledonia would be more aptly named 'very old Caledonia'. She has preserved plant lineages from the Mesozoic Age. That's the time about 252 to 66 million years ago, when dolphins, whales and porpoises were still walking on earth, and had not yet decided to return to their old ocean habitat from another hundred million years previously.

Another aspect of New Caledonia intrigued me. This island hosts the most intelligent bird species on earth, the New Caledonian Crow. She is smarter than the great apes. These crows don't just use twigs to forage; they have a complete toolkit in reserve. Just like my local plumber, with a white van filled with precise tools, the New Caledonian Crow has plenty to choose from and knows just what she needs for the upcoming task. But she has to make hers from plants. The distinctive way in which the tools are made, and the differences of style from one part of the island to another, distinguish the village whence each crow was raised as clearly as the branded livery on the side of my plumber's van.

I contacted the tourism office in New Caledonia. "If you want to know about birds, ask Isabelle at Caledoniabirds," they replied. Isabelle was delighted to guide me around her island. I was even happier when she told me she also knew about plants. There are so many trees that only grow on New Caledonia. And ferns; she has the world's tallest fern, all of forty metres tall. That's a fern growing seven storeys high, hovering over the forest like a natural helicopter. Isabelle also organised for me to stay with the indigenous Kanak tribe.

Then, I decided to visit Lifou, one of the smaller Loyalty Islands, a forty minute flight away.

New Caledonian ferns, 40 metres tall, tower over the forest...

...and look magnificent from underneath.

I found a guide who was an expert on the natural habitat of Lifou. He suggested I hire a car at the airport and drive to meet him in front of the Luecila village church. The directions given to me were rather specific, and odd; including a precise intersection of latitude and longitude. This seemed like a spy assignation. Not finding a church on Google maps, I tried the guide's grid reference to see what came up. The answer was a bend in the village road. Feeling adventurous, I reported to Google there must be an error in their map. Google did not offer an option to report a missing church, but I could report a missing museum or temple. I chose 'missing temple'. A few days later, Google emailed to thank me and to confirm my local report. A temple in Luecila was duly inserted on Google maps. I felt rather proud of myself for a first online map correction. On the evening before my arrival, I tried to call the mobile of my Lifou guide to confirm, but he did not answer - perhaps he was on a trip.

The idea that all of this planning was out of sync with my true objective to visit nature did not occur to me. On arrival in Lifou, picking up my small reserved rental car was easy enough. The first snag was that I had no Internet signal, so my clever insertion of the temple on Google maps was to no avail. I had printed the detail on paper though, so was able to find the spot. There was a church there, but no guide. I checked across the street. Two men were building a boat. They had no idea. A few yards up the road, a family was building a house. They knew the guide's name and suggested I wait. I watched their roof thatching for a while. When they suggested that maybe something had happened and he couldn't come, I agreed.

From my experience of many wanderings, these plan failures are usually a sign that I was supposed to be doing something else. With a small car, I would just drive around and explore this island of twenty miles wide and thirty miles tall. My rental car's glove-box contained a one page map of Lifou, which I examined closely. My attention was immediately caught by a picture of a 'sacred house' in the north where the King or Chief met. The map specified that permission to visit was required as well as respecting all the traditional customs. Tourists could not park nearby, according to the map. Unusually, all the words on the map tried to dissuade a visit.

That sounded at once much more interesting than my plans with a missing guide. I decided to drive slowly towards this village and find out more. My energy changed. Everything around me took on greater significance, details were seen which I had missed in the previous hour. Approaching the edge of the village, I noticed a couple having a conversation across the road. The lady was on the left and the gentleman on the right. Their conversation seemed to affect the air between them, like a giant spider's web faintly across the road. Driving through would have broken the web. I stopped the car and waited. Once they finished their conversation, and walked away, I inched forward. An older man was on my right. I paused to ask permission to ask him a question. He accepted. I then asked him gently if there was any possibility of approaching the sacred house.

He said, "Of course. The King is my brother and my father was the last King. Let me come with you." I opened the passenger door and he jumped in.

We followed the ritual customs before entering the meeting house. Once inside, we sat together for a long conversation. I spoke of the maneaba, the sacred houses in Kiribati and how much I loved them, that I was on my way back to visit islands I had missed for over forty years. He replied that I was meant to be with him today. Obviously the spirits had waylaid my original guide. He remembered the way I stopped the car for the couple to finish their conversation. He had noticed my asking his permission to ask him a question before asking a question. He said that he was the only person I could have asked in order to visit the sacred house as his brother, the chief, was away. Tears welled in his old eyes. We wept together.

One of his cousins came to tend the log fire, and enjoyed the summary of our auspicious meeting. As he left, he gave me a sacred regal feather.

The chief's brother invited me to drink cava at his home, but while saying how much I would enjoy that, there was something I would enjoy

The sacred meeting house.

His brother's residence.

more. He looked curious. "Since I have found the guide I was meant to find, would he be willing to come with me and to show me where to go?" His eyes lit up. "Yes, and we will visit my relatives."

As we toured the island, everywhere we went he was warmly greeted. The islanders were all family. After their first words of greeting, I chipped in that he now had a car and a proper English chauffeur. Everybody laughed.

Pauses in those places which still sustain the sacredness of life are such a pleasure. In the 'third layer' one sees differently, like the cobweb of a conversation across the road'.

The east coast of Lifou.

THE POOL OF BETHESDA

After an absence of the length of my entire career, my tears flowed as Kiribati appeared again through the clouds a few weeks ago. On landing, there was a message from my old friend Ieremia Tabai, their first President, who was waiting to see me. We picked up the conversation as if we had been talking the day before. Not having been able to contact him in advance of my arrival, I had already booked a flight to his home island Nonouti in the hope of finding him there. But the grapevine had alerted him to my return, hence the message. Wishing, as always, to see for myself how their culture had evolved during the intervening years, we decided to resume our conversation after my visit to the more remote island of his birth. He reminded me that he was still the Member of Parliament for Nonouti and said he would be interested in my observations. Air Kiribati took me south to Nonouti, passing over Abemama Island.

The Island Mayor was on the same flight and offered transport to my guest house. The following morning, a motorcycle was available for rent at $10 per day but my planned guide did not arrive. However, setting off towards the south, in the first village I bumped into a young Protestant Lady Minister. We started a rich conversation and she offered to be my guide. Just like Lifou, she was clearly the guide I was meant to have. Before we set off, she recommended a *unimane*, an elder of the island, should come with us as he could share the indigenous sacred spaces. He was likewise thrilled to come and brought out his motorcycle to transport the Lady Minister. Following behind them, this felt rather like 'belt and braces' guiding support.

As we stopped at the first indigenous sacred site, she was so open to both ancient and Christian traditions, a joy to behold. Following along

Abemama Island

Astride a motorbike on Nonouti Island

behind them again, I wondered why the early Christian Church could not have been like that. Could this be because they hadn't always appreciated feminine teachers? An opportunity to share my love of indigenous traditions seemed destined. The next time we stopped at a sacred site, I offered the thought that these ancient traditions can be found in some of Christ's parables, as well in many other religions. Her eyes lit up, and the *unimane* smiled. Sitting under the coconut trees, in a gentle breeze, I knew this was the place for my story to be told.

I started by sharing how the I-Kiribati culture I experienced at the beginning of my career was like *The Garden of Eden*. I was in heaven. I enjoyed the wholesome smiles of the children, the way their smiles were not just a twitch of the mouth like my culture, but their whole body and spirit smiled together. I loved the laughter and chuckling of the adults and their freedom of sexuality. When I left these islands in 1977, I had such a strong feeling of having experienced something which I couldn't explain.

Since that time, I have had the good fortune to be with many other cultures and a few which also had the fulsome spirit of the I-Kiribati.

I learned an expression from Michael Meade; *If the First Layer of human interaction is the common ground of manners, kind speech, polite greeting, and working agreements; if the Third Layer is the area of deeply shared humanity, the universal brotherhood and sisterhood of all people, of the underlying, fundamental oneness of human love, justice, and peaceful coexistence; then the Second Layer is the territory of anger, hatred, wrath, rage, outrage, jealousy, envy, contempt, disgust, and acrimony. And, the Second Layer always exists between the First Layer and the Third.*

At once, I recognised that the I-Kiribati were able to live in the 'Third Layer' whereas my culture, and other cultures guilty of colonisation, lived primarily in the 'First Layer'. I added that I have discovered how the cultures of the 'Third Layer' don't seek revenge. They shared an expression like the I-Kiribati that, *the sun and the ancestors will do what they will to your ill-wishers.*

My culture has great difficulty with many emotions of the 'second layer' and therefore finds great difficulty in finding the 'third layer'. The I-Kiribati can express themselves freely so they can be *emotional, friendly to strangers, and can be the best of friends and the worst of enemies.* My culture neither understands the virtue, nor what is meant by *the worst of enemies.* That sometimes the spirit calls us to stand up.

I had also wondered whether this might be a meaning of: *Enter by the strait gate: for wide is the gate, and broad is the way, that leadeth to destruction, and many there be which go in there. Because strait is the gate, and narrow is the way, which leadeth unto life, and few there be that find it.* The Lady Minister reminded me this was from Matthew 7:13. My curiosity wondered whether the gate from the first to the second layer might be the wide gate which leads to destruction, and the straight narrow gate might be from the second to the third which few cultures find. I shared, from my many wanderings, how there are sadly few cultures which know and enjoy the gateway to life of the third layer.

The epiphany had come to me on a visit to Greenland a few years earlier. A Danish anthropologist told me of the annual Inuit rituals. They always told the same stories, and cracked the same jokes year after year. Yet, they still fell about themselves laughing even more. My immediate response was not thought out, emerging from my mouth spontaneously: "But of course they would; that's how connectedness works."

I remembered then that all the cultures where I had experienced the 'third layer' had stories which they loved and laughed with, unable to contain their glee and rocking. The legends and sacred traditions were brought to life at a certain season and healed everyone with fresh spirit. I had also been lucky enough to have heard the same culture's indigenous story more than once. This made me feel even more connected internally. Somehow my mind allowed the more spontaneous part of me to live as there was less need to be on guard against something unknown – less need to concentrate on the words of the story to understand what was being said.

Suddenly something else came to mind, remembering my daughter Alika's desire for the same bedtime story night after night. There seemed to be a connection. A colleague had suggested perhaps she had wanted to 'master the story', but this is clearly insufficient to explain the joy in listening to her favourite bed-time story. The joy was too full and alive to be a simple tick for mastering something. The 'mastering of the story' had to have another benefit. The idea which came was, once every page and picture had been captured in her memory, she could allow her spontaneity to change a word for fun, or to be pronounced with a different feeling and laugh. The story thus became a safe container for the dancing spirit. Perhaps this was the link to the valuable lessons of legends and primordial rituals.

I started to think of the story of Cain and Abel differently; that this was not about jealousy or fratricide, but about a culture where the spirit or spontaneity has to be buried underground. If you remember, Abel offered up 'first born animals' which could represent animal spontaneity, and Cain offered the 'cultivation of the land' which could refer to culture. Abel's offerings were preferred, which is natural as spirits are also spontaneous. But Cain was protected, despite burying Abel underground, because Cain's role is essential in culture. All cultures arising in the Middle East suffered brutal enslavement, as did the first Indo-European cultures. If our ancestors had expressed their spirit during the enslavement, they would have been killed. So we needed to learn this lesson that a part of us, the Abel or spiritually spontaneous part, must be buried or entombed. We need to rescue him. Perhaps this gives another meaning to the parable of the Prodigal Son; *It was meet that we should make merry, and be glad: for this thy brother was dead, and is alive again; and was lost, and is found.* I thanked the Lady Minister for reminding me this was from Luke 15:32 and added that I wondered if one meaning of the Prodigal Son was about Abel's return. That once Cain had 'got through his jealousy', the two brothers could dwell together in unity. When, in a culture of the 'third layer', an indigenous ritual was about to begin, Cain would go and 'fetch' Abel. In English the word 'fetch' has a

Icebergs in Greenland

249

second meaning. The word also means 'to arouse the feelings of' which we use for a 'child who is fetching'.

I had to show them, on my phone, a picture from Greenland. Showing the clear blue waters but with floating ice. They gasped. They did not shiver or shudder as they had no experience of the chill of an iceberg.

After my visit to Greenland, the memories of reading bedtime stories to my daughter make sense in a different way. She wanted to hear the same story over, and over, and over again. In so doing, her nature was alive. Our looks, laughter and spontaneity in those stories are the connection, and the story is not the point at all. Once our children know the story, the active thinking part of the mind is able to relax, and a child can fully enjoy the interaction with the storyteller. A child that knows, and loves the story-teller, can feel so connected and full of delight, so happy and whole. They can invent and enjoy a spontaneous variant as even more delightful.

The sadder part is that, by encouraging a child to leave their favourite story for a new one before they are ready, we may extinguish the flame of their spirit before they have the strength to let their flame reignite. Or we let them know that, in our culture, a new story would be better. Hence we devalue connectedness. We show them how we prefer the 'consumptive' part of our culture. In so doing, we domesticate their spirit just as easily as if we had smothered them with a pillow in the night. We don't even see ourselves doing it.

By following our culture's need for more 'consumptive entertainment' we write off what the older stories and legends have given us. Each culture has her own ancient stories which bring forth the healing balm for traumas and disconnections. Just as in many parts of the world one can find plants which cure many of the local diseases, so the ancient stories are the healing plants. Thus, we must treasure all religions as they each have stories which may help their culture to become whole. And who are we to criticise another religion when their plants may be different because their culture has undergone different afflictions.

When I mentioned that I had found a parable which seems to link Christ's teaching with the indigenous traditions, both the Unimane and Lady Minister sat up. They asked me more. I suggested the parable at the Pool of Bethesda. Since this parable was such a crucial part of my explorations in *Mannership*, I remembered the words by heart, but so did the Lady Minister. We spoke the words together.

The Pool of Bethesda

1. *After this there was a feast of the Jews; and Jesus went up to Jerusalem.*

2. *Now there is at Jerusalem by the sheep market a pool, which is called in Hebrew Bethesda, having five porches.*

3. *In these lay a great multitude of impotent folk, of blind, halt, withered, waiting for the moving of the water.*

4. *For an angel went down at a certain season into the pool, and troubled the water: whosoever then first after the troubling of the water stepped in was made whole of whatsoever affliction he had.*

5. *And a certain man was there, which had an infirmity thirty and eight years.*

6. *When Jesus saw him lie, and knew that he had been now a long time in that case, he saith unto him, Wilt thou be made whole.*

7. *The impotent man answered him, Sir, I have no man, when the water is troubled, to put me into the pool: but while I am coming, another steppeth down before me.*

8. *Jesus saith unto him, Rise, take up thy bed, and walk.*

9. *And immediately the man was made whole, and took up his bed, and walked: and on the same day was the sabbath.*

10. *The Jews therefore said unto him that was cured, It is the sabbath day: it is not lawful for thee to carry thy bed.*

11. *He answered them, He that made me whole, the same said unto me, Take up thy bed, and walk.*

12. *Then asked they him, What man is that which said unto thee, Take up thy bed, and walk.*

Their eyes were wide wondering where I was coming from next. I had learned from Maurice Nicoll's teaching that this story suggests two paths; one to the sheep market and the other to the pool with five porches. As if living by the manners of culture would be following a sheep to market. The pool is 'by' or 'adjacent' but very different. The part of us we need to find to become 'whole' or cured of 'whatsoever affliction we have' is not a sheep of habit or culture. The First layer is a culture of habit, but the third layer is health. The first and third layers are close *by* and next to each other, even though for some of us the journey to connect them is long.

Maurice Nicoll suggests that the five porches may relate to the five senses. In ancient times there were five orders of architecture, drawn like porches with each representing one of the senses.[91] Perhaps we had to go 'through the five senses' or through the 'Second Layer' to find the third.[92] Perhaps this is the significance of the 'five husbands' in the parable immediately before the Pool of Bethesda. The woman from the Samaritan town of Sychar, who came to draw water from a well, was said to have five husbands. If this was meant literally, this would be quite a story. But the husbands, like the porches, are not mentioned again. Maybe the five husbands also represent the five senses. Cain, or the culture, would take the path to market, but Abel would be in the pool through the five senses.

Nicoll suggests, in the language of parables, that the blind, halt and withered refer to states of self-awareness; whether we are aware of Abel's entombment. The word 'impotent' is also significant and might refer to potency of spirit or of allowing another spontaneous force to rise up and lift us. As if Abel needs to rise and 'stand up' from within his tomb.

Perhaps the role of the angel is to draw our attention to something beyond our self; we should not follow the sheep part. Christ's question is significant: *Do you want your health restored?* If the man had been literally blind or lame, then it would not be necessary to ask if he wanted to be made *whole*. The point of Christ's question seems to highlight the importance of *standing up*; that the man must first decide he wants to become whole. One cannot have the desire to escape Abel's entombment unless one has obtained sufficient self-awareness, or metanoia, of our condition. There is a further clue in the angel descending 'in a certain season', or from 'time to time' which is how this phrase is sometimes translated. This reminds us that the parable is not a 'miracle' since the story happens from time to time, whenever the angel troubles the water.

---

[91] Tuscan represents smell, Doric for sight, Ionic for hearing, Corinthian for taste and Composite which unites them all like the skin and touch.

[92] A more complete exploration of this parable is described in *Mannership*.

I had wondered if, in I-Kiribati, the words *aomata* and *Katei ni Kiribati* could be interpreted as 'standing up' in the sense of the Pool of Bethesda.

The first person whosoever steps in could also be referring to the part of us which is spontaneous. To be made whole, the spontaneous part of us must stand up and step out. Maybe the sentence, *I have no man, when the water is troubled, to put me into the pool: but while I am coming, another steppeth down before me* could suggest that the ailing man thinks he needs 'a helper' to help him to be spontaneous, which is not the case. *Another steppeth down* could refer to a part of his own mind which frustrates him from being spontaneous.

After the metaphors in verses two to seven, there is different mystery in verses eight to twelve. *Take up thy bed and walk* appears five times; like a repeated chorus. For a sacred story to include a phrase five times suggests a particular significance or relevance. Perhaps the *five times* was to underline the sacred importance of this phrase instead of a literal interpretation of the sentences in which the same phrase appears.

Lifting the 'bed' did not initially make sense to me in the story. When I discovered that other Biblical versions translated this word as 'mat', a different understanding came to me. I remembered that, in many indigenous cultures, their initiations included a phase in which the initiate was lying on the ground and covered with a hide, or some other material. In the Mayan tradition this could be an animal hide and in a West African tradition could be 'armour' for example. The idea of animal hide made my heart jump as the double meaning is obvious; wearing an animal hide also implies 'hiding the animal within'; or hiding Abel within. In a number of native initiations the initiate is instructed to name the armour so as to walk freely beside him or to throw off the animal hide; to jump up and live again. They do not use the term 'rebirth' but 'walk freely' or 'live again' is rather similar.

I wondered whether the original word which Christ spoke might have been closer to a pun like an 'animal hide'. Last year, having found an Aramaic version of the Gospel of John from Syria, I looked immediately for this word in Aramaic. I shed a tear of joy, discovering the Aramaic word is a *quilt*. A quilt is both a bed and a covering. But my first image of a quilt is of a series of multi-coloured pieces of fabric patched together by my grandmother. An image of the covering of my spontaneity which had been handed down and woven together by a

253

patchwork of ancestral culture filled me. Both sides of the coin are in this word. We have both an idea of warmth and support as well as something which hides and smothers us so that we are no longer visible.

The parable could be teaching us to lift up our ancestral quilt or protection and become true to ourselves again. The *another* who steps ahead of us might be a part of our quilt; our ancestral inheritance of suppression which needs to be 'cast aside' for us to 'stand up' and walk. The quilt may thus represent our resistance to spontaneity; the image reminds me of those nightmares when trying to run but my legs get all tangled up in the bed clothes.

Looking back now, remembering my time with the I-Kiribati, the children all lived spontaneously. They were themselves. They did not need the tuition of this parable. So, my learning from the forty something years since I was last in Kiribati, and my experience of many different cultures is that you should beware of some missionaries. They have come from 'First Layer' cultures and are in desperate need of the lessons of the Pool of Bethesda. Their desire to teach comes from their need to learn this. I am also in the same position because of my culture. So, some priests are living vicariously through others. They think they are being successful because of your joy, when in reality they are sucking up your joy and song for themselves. Please be careful not to fall into the trap of giving up your indigenous traditions in the hope of finding 'something better' when Christ might be suggesting that your culture already has that which the parable implies. Don't forget, Christ was teaching a people who suffered brutal enslavement and repression from other cultures. Had Christ been with the Inuit, the Choctaws or the I-Kiribati he might have said something else.

Our conversations lasted all day. It is not my place to write what the others said. At the end of my visit, the Lady Minister gave me a beautifully made pandanus fan which I treasure.

The time had come to leave Nonouti. On my return to Tarawa, back with Ieremia, he was delighted by my account. He knew both guides very well and remarked on my good fortune to have journeyed with such a pair of souls.

Ieremia is three years older than me. I was just twenty-one when appointed District Officer Tarawa, and Ieremia was twenty-four when elected the Member of Parliament for Nonouti. He became the Leader of the Opposition in Parliament and we were good friends. Ieremia liked all the changes I was making on Tarawa in consultation with the elders of the villages. For example, we decided that each village should have a 'sweeper' to encourage clearing and cleaning. Each village chose the person who was best suited for the task, and who needed a little extra financial support. Our island funds were recycled wisely following decisions in the *maneaba*. When the I-Kiribati voted for their first President, the choice was between a much older man who believed in Westernisation, Central Government and the islands' first defence budget, or a young Ieremia who was in tune with the needs of the islanders, who listened and communicated well, did not want to waste money on guns, and believed in their ancient traditions. He embodied the Chinese ancestry of the word 'win' rather than the weaponised English etymology of 'win'

Ieremia and I were kindred spirits. Just over forty years later, we continued with our frank conversations:

Mark: *Back in 1977, I felt there were four major pollutions in the Pacific: Christianity, Traders, Colonialism and Plastic. We are all struggling with plastic and need to manage this mess. I am naturally very happy you have been liberated from Colonialism. But, for me, the biggest tragedy is the way that the Churches have taken over. Before independence, we had the Church on a leash but now they have grown like bindweed strangling the indigenous plants.*

Ieremia: *It is much worse than that. We have become enslaved by Christianity. We are spending half our time fund-raising for the Church.*

Mark: *Maybe you should pass a law demanding complete transparency - what money is collected and how it is spent.*

Ieremia: *They think they are above the law and only report to God. They think this should excuse them from taxes.*

Mark: *How absurd. What has struck me, coming back to the Pacific after such a long time, is the extent of the repression of spiritual sexuality by the Church. The I-Kiribati culture had many indigenous traditions which operated as safety valves against any form of domestic violence. Suppressing these may have an effect of increasing the risk of domestic violence, which is escalating throughout the Pacific. Roman Church elders are not supposed to know anything about sexuality. Why on earth are we allowing them to make pronouncements on the matter?*

Ieremia: *We have television screens in Parliament House now. I have been following these stories of abuse of children by the Church in the West.*

Mark: *It is a scandal that they continue to get away with a few apologies here and there. We mustn't allow a fear that they might be 'specially connected' to interfere with our duty to eradicate misguided behaviours. I think this is your biggest challenge in Kiribati now, to get a grip on the Church. I have since learned how the corruption began in the Roman Church and others with a disregard for feminine spirituality, the loss of admiration of Mother Nature and ignorance of indigenous traditions.*

So many global religions are trying to teach the same salvation. Just as the Gospel of John begins with "in the beginning was the word;" so many Chinese sages would agree, "in the beginning was the Tao." Buddha seems to suggest a similar line with re-adoption of Dravidian primordial values. But, once we lose access to our indigenous nature, we become so hungry that we create havoc by looking. I suggested to the Lady Minister that the Churches are asking the I-Kiribati to 'look for' something which the spontaneous I-Kiribati children already have. She liked that. Aomata and Katei ni Kiribati are the Holy Grail. While I was with your Lady Minister on Nonouti, I implored her to safeguard the indigenous traditions which had made your islands my first truly safe spiritual home. Maybe I should not have worried, considering the way she asked a Unimane to come with us as a guide.

The main island road on Efate, Vanuatu. At first glance the scenery is so green until one suddenly realises that bindweed has completely enveloped most of the indigenous plants.

Having observed the changes over the last forty years, I can now see the cultural history of Kiribati over the last 150 years quite differently. Let me share what I have learned.

Back in May 1892 when Captain Davis arrived on HMS Royalist to declare a British Protectorate, this was in the nick of time for some. Captain Davis arrived on Abemama Island in the middle of a murderous spell of Chief Tem Binoka; thus lives were immediately saved and vile practices stopped. Likewise the rumbling civil war on Tarawa came to an immediate end. But the Christian missionaries had been there for two generations and had already made many island laws. In the early years of the British Protectorate we only had two administrators without a boat, so the Church continued to make many more island laws. Except, the I-Kiribati assumed these laws had British blessing because we were 'notionally in charge'. By the 1920's under Grimble, the British managed to restrict the power of the Church. We did not interfere very much with local traditions. As you know, Grimble was able to overrule the Church's wish to ban Kiribati dancing because it was too sexual.

What I had not expected, when the British lowered their flag forty years ago, was that this would be an opportunity for the Church to step in and subtly assume control in a way the British never attempted. This is terribly sad. It would be truer to say that Kiribati culture was not colonised by the British, but was colonised by a missionary version of Christianity quite different from some of Christ's teachings.

My greatest joy is to see the indigenous spirit of the I-Kiribati again. Their smiles have not diminished and fill me with life.

Ieremia smiled. We continued talking a while and were on the same wavelength as we had been in the years before he became President.

Perhaps a conclusion of this chapter is to remind us how hard it is for a child in a 'first layer' culture to know themselves, and be known, if the culture contains so much repression that the culture does not remember either. Many 'first layer' cultures have picked apart and tossed aside their legends and sacred stories. The 'fairy stories' with their healing balm are loved by our children who understand something which we have forgotten. If the past is remembered, a culture naturally provides the womb of stories whereby children can be spiritually nourished.[93] Elders who are reluctant or who do not 'want to know' their past become one of the greatest 'headwinds' for our children.

---

[93] The etymology of remember implies 'put back together again' in Latin.

A Greater Understanding and Spontaneity

After my short visit to the calm egalitarian consensual primordial civic island of Ieremia's birth, returning to Tarawa by the island hopping Air Kiribati, we were met at the airport and taken directly to Tobaraoi Travel in the village of Bikenibeu. The foremost travel agency in the Central Pacific, in addition to having organised my trip, offers for sale a few books on Kiribati, some local handicrafts and contains a fine restaurant. The room was full with those waiting for their lunch while my attention was caught by delicate and beautiful models of I-Kiribati sailing canoes sporting small pandanus leaf sails.

Suddenly the manager, Toka, stood up and announced to the whole restaurant, *"We have the former District Commissioner Mark here today. Let's ask him to tell us about his experience of the islands."*

Normally there is more than a nanosecond to prepare such a response. In an instant, surveying my audience, brought recognition that many of them were Australian teenage girls coming to the end of a visit during which they had volunteered to help in different primary schools on the island of Tarawa. They had been staying in the same George Hotel on Betio which had welcomed me before the journey to Nonouti. Having spoken to some of them over breakfast a few days before had given me insight to their experiences. Apart from a couple of tourists, the remainder of my audience was I-Kiribati.

The lessons of my Irish public speaking coach in Trafalgar Square guided me. Needing to find my feet quickly and being somewhat unprepared, a story which connected with my audience was necessary. That was easy. Beginning with my teenage years as a voyager and my trans-Saharan crossing, I remembered being only a couple of years older than most of my audience when first arriving on these islands. Having told them the tale of my interview and posting to the Gilbert and Ellice Islands led me naturally to extol the beauty of the islanders and the heavenly greetings. The I-Kiribati audience beamed and gave me confidence to find my way instinctively.

Continuing with my memories of being enveloped by the aliveness of warm open-hearted and spontaneous primary school children, there was no need to ask my audience a question. They all screamed out "Yes". I took a risk. "When Christ speaks of 'being like little children' I think these are the children he means, not the reserved children of my childhood." There was silence among the I-Matang (I-Kiribati word for foreigners) but a wise smile from the I-Kiribati.

"When you leave Tarawa and return to Australia in a few days, perhaps you can also tell others of this beauty among children which is hard to find any more in our Western Culture. These children are not associated with a Facebook profile. They are themselves." Reaching out for a copy of *Kiribati, Aspects of History*, on the bookshelf next to me enabled a reading of the delicious words on *Katei ni Kiribati*, 'the Gilbertese identity'. That *children should be taught to know themselves; they should learn their genealogies, skills and knowledge. A person who has pride in himself, and what he is, would be less likely to get into trouble. He would be hard working and able to face hardship in times of drought and at sea. He or she is emotional, friendly to strangers, and can be the best of friends and the worst of enemies. A man is a real person when he practises and believes in te katei ni Kiribati.*

My suggestion was that my audience should remember these words, and the task of being ourselves again. Quickly, one young woman asked whether this was still possible for us. I thought it was. She asked, "How?" My reply was, "I think there are two parts to the answer. Firstly, to come to know yourself and to understand yourself better. There is no prescription here. Choose whatever you can to help you to find and learn more about yourself, to know more of who you are. Never forget that your Facebook profile is not who you are. Secondly, spend time with someone who is truly spontaneous and let them infect you." Recognising the young Tobaraoi Travel guide sitting next to my questioner, and having instantly noticed the interaction between the two of them while coming into the room earlier, I continued, "There is one sitting next to you. I saw how spontaneous she was when I arrived for lunch. More time together like that might also help you to learn about yourself."

We opened up the restaurant to a 'large group conversation'. There were a few teenage I-Kiribati boys who we asked to step up and share their childhood memories. We had a wonderful conversation all together.

Much later in the afternoon, sitting alone while digesting the Tobaraoi group conversation, reminded me of another young British District officer, Wilfred Thesiger. He had served in East Africa, particularly in Sudan and Abyssinia contemporaneously with Arthur Grimble's time in the Pacific. Thesiger's writing had also touched me deeply with his descriptions of loneliness while crossing deserts such as The Empty Quarter. My Saharan crossing had felt similar; only a love of indigenous peoples could fill the deep hole which Thesiger and Grimble also felt. The contrast between an I-Kiribati upbringing and that of a British colonial officer could not have been starker.

Thesiger writes of his time in preparatory school as a young boy; *St Aubyn's had a good reputation when my father decided to send us there.*[94] *Unfortunately, just before we arrived, a new headmaster R.C.V Lang took over. He was a sadist. He beat me on a number of occasions, often for some trivial offence. Sent up early to the dormitory, I had to kneel naked by the side of my bed. I remember crying out the first time, 'it hurts' and Lang saying grimly, 'It's meant to'.*

For two or three days after each beating, I was called to his study so that he could see I was healing properly. Though I had never been hurt like this before, strangely enough I bore him no resentment for those beatings, accepting them as the penalty for what I had done. It never occurred to me how disproportionate was the punishment to the offence.[95]

Caning may have begun five millennia ago in Uruk, but we are not yet free. As I found in *Mannership*, a sudden withdrawal of affection, a sudden leap from the third to the first layer and bypassing the second layer has a very similar effect on an infant mind as violence does. Stopping the caning is a good step but this does not halt the incidence of the repression or the 'stiff upper lip'.

Maybe the inability to see the disproportionate nature of the punishment to the crime is one of the keys to the 'stiff upper lip'. Unlike a Sri Lankan elephant who remembers every time his mahout used the wrong 'nila' and caused great pain while domesticating him, our shame was too great to digest the experience and remember it correctly. The

---

[94] He is speaking of himself and his brother Brian.

[95] Wilfred Thesiger, *The Life of My Choice.*

rage and aggression becomes buried. Instead a door opens to loneliness. Thesiger writes of withdrawal into himself, treating overtures of friendship with mistrust and being easily provoked as a small boy. As a consequence, he adds; '*Strangely, I have found this comradeship most easily among races other than my own. Perhaps this trait could be traced back to the hurtful rejection I suffered from my contemporaries at preparatory school when I was a small boy freshly arrived from Abyssinia in an alien English world.*'

All three of us, Grimble, Thesiger and myself, had ignored the Colonial advice 'that for Government prestige, British officials should keep aloof and not involve themselves socially with those they administered.' Instead, we served with the love we felt for these 'native' peoples. We received by giving what we had missed.

Perhaps the British stiff upper lip was simply a 'lid on our spontaneity'. Arthur Grimble speaks of 'a benign paternalism' towards these islanders. This made me wonder if the 'benign paternalism', which I also felt, was a technique to avoid the shame in my silent years.

At the conclusion of Arthur Grimble's wonderful book *A Pattern of Islands,* describing his experiences in the Gilbert Islands, he offers a delicious paragraph. Perhaps Wilfred Thesiger would also nod quietly, sharing the wisdom in Grimble's words:

It began to dawn on me then that, beyond the teeming romance that lies in the differences between men – the diversity of their homes, the multitude of their ways of life, the dividing strangeness of their faces and tongues, the thousand-fold mysteries of their origins – there lies the still profounder romance of their kinship with each other, a kinship that springs from the immutable constancy of man's need to share laughter and friendship, poetry and love in common. A man may travel a long road, and suffer much loneliness, before he makes that discovery.

And then I realised, we still need to become free to chuckle like Choctaws.

ANSWERS TO THE YAMASHINA TEST

The key to Yamashina's puzzle is to follow directions. Firstly link the As and then the Bs as in the left picture below. The solution on the right is then obvious. Because Japanese schoolchildren 'trust the process', they start as directed and see the answer instantly. The Western hunter mind, by contrast, needs to 'see the answer before beginning' and immediately sees an obstacle which does not exist.

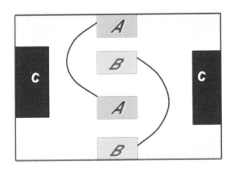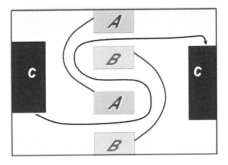

I enjoyed teasing the French by referring to their long history with cave art from primordial hunters. For this ancestral hunter, seeing obstacles is an advantage. After all, you can use the obstacle to hide behind as you approach, or to rest your arm while aiming, or to hide from a predator running after you. You still do the same in organisations. When a manager asks why you have not done something, you rely on this or that obstacle which prevented you. Obstacles are your friends in this case.

In my question, the first things which a hunter thinks of are the themes 1 and 2 below.

1. To know where you are going.
2. To know how to sail (like if a tack might be necessary, to attain the destination).

Hunters come up with many other answers which are, in reality, parts of 1 or 2.

3. The third thing which you have to know is 'what to avoid'.

After all, we don't want another Titanic. The farming mind often thinks of the obstacles first. But despite the reliance on obstacles in primordial hunting, this is not immediately brought to the mind in a question of sailing.

The hunting mind is conditioned to think of an obstacle in Yamashina's test, but finds the idea of an obstacle difficult to see when we are no longer 'on land'.

BV - #0209 - 250324 - C278 - 234/156/16 - PB - 6640522164917 - Gloss Lamination